Law, War and Crime

Law, War and Crime

War Crimes Trials and the Reinvention of International Law

GERRY SIMPSON

polity

First published in 2007 by Polity Press

Polity Press
65 Bridge Street
Cambridge CB2 1UR, UK

Polity Press
350 Main Street
Malden, MA 02148, USA

ISBN-10: 0-7456-3022-7
ISBN-13: 978-07456-3022-9
ISBN-10: 0-7456-3023-5 (pb)
ISBN-13: 978-07456-3023-6 (pb)

A catalogue record for this book is available from the British Library.

Typeset in 11.25 on 13 pt Dante
by SNP Best-set Typesetter Ltd, Hong Kong
Printed and bound in India by Replika Press

The publisher has used its best endeavours to ensure that the URLs for external websites referred to in this book are correct and active at the time of going to press. However, the publisher has no responsibility for the websites and can make no guarantee that a site will remain live or that the content is or will remain appropriate.

Every effort has been made to trace all copyright holders, but if any have been inadvertently overlooked the publishers will be pleased to include any necessary credits in any subsequent reprint or edition.

For further information on Polity, visit our website: www.polity.co.uk

This book is dedicated to my mother, Mary Simpson, and to the memory of my father, Gordon Simpson.

Contents

Acknowledgements

This book would have remained unfinished but for the generosity of the LSE Law Department, and, in particular, Chris Greenwood, Hugh Collins and Rob Reiner, the Department's Convenors during the period when I wrote the bulk of it. In the final stages of writing, Melbourne Law School, at very short notice, and again, gave me the space and support to help me work. Thanks to Jenny Morgan, Tim McCormack and Michael Crommelin.

Deborah Cass, Alejandro Chehtman, Rob Cryer, Sarah Finnan, Jessica Gavron, Tim McCormack, Alexandra Milenov, Bruce Oswald, Vladimir Petrovic, Declan Roche, Philippe Sands, Ruti Teitel, Raynor Thwaites and Jon Turner read extracts from the book and offered wise counsel. Two anonymous reviewers took their jobs very seriously. An American reviewer sent pages of (alarmingly) pertinent insights. I hope he considers this time well spent.

My parents-in-law, Moss and Shirley Cass, housed and fed me for six months in Melbourne at the beginning of 2006. This book, the writing of which had been endlessly deferred, was completed during those months. My wife, Deborah, gave me the time to complete this book at a time when I had no right to ask for it.

My LSE graduate classes have been a joy to teach. The International Criminal Law students from 2000–6 know who they are and will recognize their role in shaping these ideas.

Louise Knight combined patience and persistence as Commissioning Editor. Her assistant, Emma Hutchinson, prepared the ground for submission of the manuscript. Belle Mundy's assiduous copy editing improved greatly the published version of this book.

A fragment of chapter 1 began its life as 'Concepts of the Political', a chapter in *The Permanent International Criminal Court: Legal and Policy Issues*, eds Dominic McGoldrick, Peter Rowe and Eric Donnelly (Hart Publishing, 2004). The final chapter appears in various truncated forms: as 'Piracy and the Origins of Enmity' in *Time, History and International Law*, eds Matthew

Craven, Malgosia Fitzmaurice and Maria Vogiatzi (Nijhoff Publishers, 2006), and as 'Enemies of Mankind' in *Ethics, Law and Society Volume II*, eds J. Gunning and S. Holm (Ashgate, 2006).

This is a book about war. It seems appropriate to note, then, that my grandfather, William 'Blake' Simpson, whom I never met, served in the Gordon Highlanders during the Great War. My Dad, Gordon Simpson, was in Singapore, with the RAF, at the end of the Second World War. He died, just before I finished writing this book, in November, 2005.

Preface

In the first half of the twentieth century the law of war crimes began to effect a reinvention of international law, and a transformation of argument and discourse around war. This book is about these changes, and, in particular, their intensification at the beginning of the twenty-first century. In the book, I consider the meaning and implications of this development through an examination of the relationship between law, war and crime. The book traces the origins and trajectory of the war crimes field from the outlawing of piracy through to the now common recourse to war crimes trials, and situates these practices in the context of broader social and political forces. The argument is that international law produces a form of displaced politics or conducts politics in a different key. I call this juridified diplomacy (chapter 6): the phenomenon by which conflict about the purpose and shape of international political life (as well as specific disputes in this realm) is translated into legal doctrine or resolved in legal institutions. War crimes trials are one of the institutional manifestations of this phenomenon. More specifically, I argue that the field of war crimes is constituted by a set of relationships – between politics and law; between local justice and cosmopolitan reckoning; between collective guilt and individual responsibility; between making history and performing justice; between legitimating dominant political forces and permitting the expression of dissident views; between the idea of impartial and honourable justice, and the spectre of the war crimes trial as a show trial; between the instinct that war, at worst, is an error, and the conviction that war is a crime; and between projects dedicated to the elimination of 'enemies of mankind' through political action and regimes intended to provide for the prosecution and trial of adversaries. These relationships *are* the law of war crimes (or, international criminal law). Understanding this field requires an understanding of these relationships.

To put this less abstractly, the book is a collection of eight essays on what I take to be the symptomatic aspects of international criminal law, i.e. political trials, hybridity, individual responsibility, history and dissent, show trials (or 'victor's justice'), aggression and piracy. These, in turn, each raise a number of questions: What does it mean to talk about war in the language of the criminal law? What are the consequences of seeking to criminalize the conduct of one's enemies? How did this relatively new convention of trying perpetrators of mass atrocity and defeated enemies come into existence?

The book's central preoccupation concerns war crimes trials, and the area of study or sphere of practice sometimes known, loosely, as the law of war crimes or international criminal law. It represents a conceptual approach to the area rather than an analysis of its rules (Cassese, 2003a; Kitichaiseree, 2001; Bassiouni, 1986), procedures (Jones and Powles, 2003) or institutional history (Bass, 2000). In the book, I treat the law of war crimes as a discursive field and, perhaps ambitiously, make an argument about the whole field: its suppositions, deformities, proclivities and patterns of thought. This, primarily, is a lawyer's view of that discursive field (I am concerned with doctrine, text, principles, crime and rule-making in the international system) not, say, a sociology (Cohen, 2000; Fein, 1993; Hirsh, 2003) or a philosophy (Bauman, 1989). Having said that, I take a lawyer's task to be one of understanding how the law operates and what its effects (political, cultural, historical, social) might be (Shklar, 1964; Arendt, 1994; Osiel, 1997; Mégret, 2002).

Much of this book could be read as a rejoinder to the moral enthusiasms embedded, instrumentalized and institutionalized in the project of international criminal law. This legal order has been indicted as imperial (opening space for the export of liberal or Western norms to other places (Mutua, 1997)) and partial (working against particular groups on the basis of race (e.g. the treatment of Japanese defendants at the Tokyo War Crimes Trials (Prevost, 1992)), ethnicity (the perceived emphasis on Serb defendants at The Hague) or outlaw status (Security Council Resolution 1593 referring Sudan to the International Criminal Court) and gendered (insufficiently attentive to the problem of rape or careless about the kind of collateral damage suffered disproportionately by women (Gardam, 1994).[1] There is some of this critique in the book. But, this work is largely directed at identifying structural tendencies in the field, for example the way in which morally culpable behaviour often is understood as psychological or individualized rather than collective or social, or the teleology of war crimes law as an expression of the international over the national, or the field's self-projections as law against politics or as legalism opposed to show trials. Nothing is closed off by these critiques. The book is not *against* international criminal law (at its most critical it involves a reading designed to unseat some of that field's chief complacencies).

I wrote the book in the wake of an extraordinary period in the life of the law. The invasion of Iraq, in March 2003, by a US-led 'Coalition of the Willing' convulsed the international community and destabilized political regimes in Madrid, London, Riyadh and elsewhere. Mass opinion was mobilized for and against the war. In anti-war marches in London, banners were held aloft: some declaiming the war as immoral and illegal, others calling for George Bush and Tony Blair to be arraigned as war criminals. International lawyers released legal opinions characterizing the war as unlawful, letters to the newspapers warned the government against embarking on illegal wars, and cases were brought before the courts in which the legality of the war was questioned (Singh and MacDonald, 2002; *CND v. Prime Minister*, 2002; *R v. Jones*, 2006). Meanwhile, the Western powers themselves published legal briefs outlining the lawfulness of the war, and insisted that the existing structure of international law permitted invasion (Goldsmith, 2003). After the war various enquiries were held into the quality and use of intelligence on Iraq's alleged weapons programmes (the Butler Inquiry in the UK), into the media's sensitivity in reporting the Government's role in presenting the material (the Hutton Inquiry in the UK) and into corruption and bribery at the heart of the UN's Oil for Food Programme (the Volker Inquiry at the UN, and the Cole Inquiry in Australia (into kick-backs associated with wheat sales to Iraq)). And, in Iraq itself, the role of law became a central issue in discussions concerning the legitimacy of the post-war occupation, the extent of human rights protections in occupied areas (*Al Skeini*, 2005) and, most notoriously, the treatment of Iraqi prisoners and detainees at Abu Ghraib. Finally, there was Saddam Hussein. His capture set in train the establishment of a war crimes tribunal under Iraqi jurisdiction that tried the former Iraqi leader for crimes against humanity.[2]

One of the more remarkable features of this period in some jurisdictions, is the centrality of legal debates and manoeuvrings during it. In anti-war protests at the beginning of, say, the Great War, it is inconceivable that protesters would have referred to the legality of the war. War crimes tribunals were unheard of. Tony Blair has embarked on five wars since becoming the British Prime Minister. In all five cases, trials were regarded as an indispensable part of the post-war peace.[3] Something happened, then, to political consciousness in the twentieth century to make law seem more suited to the resolution of international disputes (law) (e.g. Kellogg-Briand, the Hague Conventions of 1899 and 1907) and more attractive as a tool of political retribution (crime) (e.g. Tokyo and Nuremberg) after war. This book is about the consequences of this shift. But the argument is not simply that law has become a natural way of thinking about war and post-war retribution but that this way of thinking has adjusted the relationship between law, crime and politics in international relations.

I develop and elaborate a schema for understanding this rapidly enlarging field, by showing that international criminal law (broadly understood) is constituted by, and properly understood through, a set of dilemmas and relationships. It is neither one thing (e.g. 'international') nor the other (e.g. 'domestic'). The search for single models or unified theories of war crimes law is a fruitless one. Instead, to paraphrase Martin Wight, war crimes law is a field of repetition and recurrence. What repeats and recurs are unresolved arguments about the shape and fate of retributive justice in the international order. Each of the chapters is organized around one of these dilemmas or arguments.

In chapter 1, 'Law's Politics', I consider what people mean when they describe war crimes trials as 'political trials' or ascribe political motives to this or that institutional development in the area. This chapter traces a dialectic between the languages and premises of activities designated as 'legal' and those characterized as 'political'. It is about the ways in which certain activities are removed to or aligned with the political and others are shaped and understood through the juridical. Or, to put it differently, I ask how the relationship between law and politics is managed, understood and oriented both in the context of the project to build a permanent international criminal law order and in our retrospectives of the trials that have become the pre-history of this project. The language of politics and law (a language grounded in a sometimes under-theorized split between law and politics) is probably indispensable to the ways in which we, as international criminal lawyers, imagine our field and the place of our own work in it. This chapter, then, describes some of the linguistic tics and rhetorical repetitions that accompany these self-understandings before disentangling what is meant by or what space is occupied by 'the political' and 'the legal' in the work we do. I look, first, at four standard approaches to the relationship between law and politics. I call these deformed legalism, transcendent legalism, utopian politics and legalistic politics. These patterns of thinking dominate the terrain on which argument within the larger field occurs. Following this, I consider the relationship between law and politics in the context of a recent bout of international institution-building in the criminal field: the establishment of an International Criminal Court. In particular, I consider the concepts of the political that informed this process from the inside.

One of the abiding arguments that constitutes the field of war crimes law concerns where justice ought to be pronounced and how it ought to be performed. In chapter 2, I consider the place of place in the discipline and, in particular, the interminable debates between localists (preferring national trials or domestic proceedings) and internationalists (preferring treaty-based trial mechanisms or Security Council authorized ad hoc tribunals). This is linked, too, to the question of humanity and what it means to act in the name of humanity as opposed to some more particular politics (Teitel, 2002; Simpson, 2004a). I conclude that the system of international criminal law is a hybrid. It is neither truly or exclusively 'international' nor entirely derivative of national models of justice. It is rather a particular way of doing law, informed both by cosmopolitan and nationalist inclinations, for which the hybrid tribunal (in Sierra Leone or East Timor) represents a microcosm if not a model. Law's place, then, is both here and there (Knop, 2000).

Those who argue in favour of internationalist approaches to justice often do so because the scale of the crimes appears to defy a local approach. When the state is criminal, how can it also be the judge of that criminality? One long-standing project in international criminal law is focused on the criminalization of the state. Not everyone, though, concedes that states can be criminal. For many writers, statesmen, and practitioners, states cannot commit crimes. For them, crime is personal and the law of war crimes is a law of individual responsibility (Kelsen, 1973). The state is implicated only inasmuch as it is captured by a 'gang' of criminals (to use Churchill's terms for the Nazis). The history and practice of international criminal law, then, is structured around a dialectic that follows what I take to be our intuitions about accountability, i.e. that it is both social and individual. The subject of chapter 3, 'Law's Subjects', is this dialectic, and the way it plays out in the doctrinal embellishments of war crimes law, its institutional history and its moral and psychological underpinnings.

War crimes trials are a work of memory as well as law. Youk Chhang, director of the documentation centre in Phnom Penh, welcomed the prospect of a Cambodian trial, saying: 'It will give a lesson to the people of Cambodia: the truth has to be proved in the court-room' (Gittings, 2001). Law's promise, then, is that it will deliver both justice and a form of truth. In chapter 4, I discuss the didactic function of war crimes trials (Simpson, 1999; Douglas, 2001), i.e. their capacity to tell a compelling story of human suffering. I set this function against what are often thought of as the limits of the law. These are associated with the problems of propor-tion (do war crimes explode these limits?), compatibility (are justice and history in harmony during such trials?) and legitimation (are the truths produced by war crimes trials ideologically innocent?) (Farer, 2000; Osiel, 2000). The chapter ends with a brief delineation of themes around the problem of forgetting, and the role of war crimes trials in facilitating the erasure of memory.

A large part of the chapter is dedicated to the question of dissident histories (Simpson, 1997). When Rudolf Hess (whose sanity was questioned throughout the Nuremberg Trials) compared the trial to the Moscow show trials, or when Okawa Shumei (who was declared clinically insane and unfit to stand trial in Tokyo at the International Military Tribunal for the Far East (IMTFE) compared the use of military force by the Japanese in the Co-Prosperity Zone to colonial doctrines of pre-emption, each was engaging, unwittingly, in a form of dissent from the dominant messages of each trial. Here I consider the potential of the judicial form to act as a vehicle for a politics of resistance or dissent. Could it be that war crimes trials, as well as functioning as legitimating mechanisms for dominant ideologies, are unusually suited to the disclosure of alternative histories (e.g. Milosevic's narrative of Serbian abasement, Speer's references to Nazi-Soviet collaboration), the assertion of potentially embarrassing political truths (e.g. Saddam Hussein's intended strategy of revealing the collusion of Western powers in his rule) and the inauguration of new counter-hegemonic legal stories (Justice Pal's anti-colonial dissenting opinion at Tokyo)? After all, there is a commitment in trial proceedings to an 'equality of arms'.[4] In the optimal cases, prosecution and defence are afforded equivalent legal expertise and allocated equal time for their respective arguments and histories. War crimes trials, then, may be show trials but they are shows for the defence, too (Koskenniemi, 2002). They offer the potential for a politics of dissent expressible through the form of adversarial law.

The erasure of memory reminds us of Stalin's penchant for re-ordering history through show trials. Advocates and cheer-leaders for war crimes law like to point out that, even if war crimes trials are political trials, they, at least, are not show trials. Defendants and their lawyers, on the other hand, find the show trials defamation irresistible when challenging the legitimacy or constitutionality of a tribunal. In Philip Roth's *Operation Shylock*, his novel about the Demjanjuk trial, the author has his Palestinian character, George Ziad, criticize the trial on these grounds: 'And this explains why there is the show trial of this stupid Ukrainian – to reinforce the cornerstone of Israeli power politics by bolstering the ideology of the victim' (p. 133). In this passage, Roth has captured something of the tendency, when decrying war crimes trials, to compare them with show trials. Saddam Hussein has described his trial as 'theatre', Slobodan Milosevic opened his defence by comparing the indictments to political pamphlets, and Pinochet's supporters in London sought to undermine the extradition process by characterizing it as something akin to a show trial.

Both sides are referring back, for differing purposes, to the Moscow show trials – regarded by most liberals as the apogee of illiberal judicial politics. Chapter 5, 'Law's Anxieties', is about show trials. Here, I ask whether the assumption by supporters that war crimes trials are the antithesis of show trials is just as complacent as the conflation of the two made by some critics (and defendants at trial). I argue that while the differences are visible and well-rehearsed, the parallels between show trials and war crimes trials are less prominently advertised. I identify some resemblances in procedure, in the ad hoc nature of the tribunals, in the choice of doctrine (in particular charges related to conspiracy or criminal enterprise) and in the selection of defendants. I conclude by giving some attention to Merleau-Ponty's notion of objective guilt and subjective innocence (Merleau-Ponty, 1969). This pair of concepts seems tailored to horrify the liberal legal conscience but I argue they can illuminate something about the nature of war crimes trials (particularly those associated with defeat in armed struggle). The purpose of the chapter is to demonstrate, first, the repressed affinities between show trials and war crimes trials, and second, that bright-line demarcations between liberal legalism (committed to equality, transparency, and accountability) and illiberal 'show justice' (marked by selectivity, secretiveness, and corruption), whatever important work they do at the level of ideology, are analytically unhelpful (Mégret, 2003).

A larger question looms over this whole discussion. Why law? What happens when war takes place through law or under law? Can international politics be conducted in the courtroom? Is this dispute resolution? Blindness? Utopianism? Chapter 6, 'Law's Hegemony', investigates the custom by which political controversy about international affairs is (un)settled through law. In mass protests conducted against the oncoming Great War in Europe in 1914, the protesters spoke of the immorality of the war, its undesirability, and the potentially disastrous impact of the war on working people, on civilization, on culture and on the economy. Politicians, too, railed against their potential adversaries, employing the language of ethics, of brinkmanship, of strategy and of prudence. War was a political or, occasionally, moral phenomenon. In 2003, protesters took to the streets of London with banners proclaiming the war's immorality, its potential to bring about global catastrophe and its links to rapacious global capitalism ('a war for oil'). But these protesters were using another language, too. And this language, as I have already indicated, would have been largely unfamiliar to their counterparts in 1914. On banners unfurled at that time, there were slogans declaring the Iraq war illegal and describing Prime Minister Blair and President Bush as war criminals. And these politicians, too, were mounting arguments on the terrain of law and crime. The debate about the legality of the war occupied centre stage for much of the run-up to the war, and there were promises from the Americans and British that Saddam Hussein and his coterie would stand trial for crimes committed in Iraq during his time in power. There was general acceptance on almost all sides that war must be justified in legal terms and that serious violations of war law could result in criminal retribution. The idea of using law for the prevention of, justification for, criminalization of, or in argument about, war, is, in some respects, rather curious and novel. Chapter 6 is about this apparent shift, in war talk, from politics to law and crime. Of course, as I have argued, this is politics in a different style or place. This chapter subjects this displaced politics to a critical examination.

If chapter 6 is about the way political events are given juridical form, then chapter 7 ('Law's Origins') can be viewed as an inversion of this relationship because it concerns the way international law segues into apparently extralegal politics in the form of straightforward retribution, revenge, Great Power prerogative and the establishment of outlawry or pariah status (an under-appreciated aspect of war crimes 'law'). These 'alternatives' to law are continually pressing against law, shaping and misshaping it. In this book, the paradigm instance of extra-legalism is piracy. But while law cannot escape politics but merely reconstitutes it during trial and inquiry, so too, politics re-forms itself into law in the juridical construction of extra-legal space and outlaw identity. Piracy, in a sense, is an amalgamation of the many themes outlined in the book. Piracy is a category around which law and politics coalesce. Pirates are, after all, the original war criminals but they also were the figures who exploded the territorial limits of the law. The repression of piracy involved both an extension of 'national' jurisdiction of piracy and, at the same time, the inauguration of 'international' criminal law.

Piracy was the first crime in international law to give rise to individual punishment. The Nuremberg war criminals were the descendants of the pirate tradition of *hostis humani generis*. But piracy or, at least, the figure of the pirate state, provides a way of understanding collective responsibility, too. Germany, following the Great War, provided a paradigmatic instance of piracy in the international order. That state's removal from the order, and the calamitous and radical punishment inflicted on Germany by that system at Versailles, operate as a precursor for the treatment of other outlaw states later in the century. Law, war and crime recombine through the image of the pirate state and the pirate. At the beginning of the twenty-first century, such enemies of mankind have become symbols of our age.

The topics taken up in these chapters, then, seem to me to be the most important, perhaps defining, relationships that make up the problem of war crimes law. Of course, there are several other matters that I might have usefully taken up. Two, in particular, come to mind. The first concerns the relationship between tort-based responses to mass atrocity, and criminal law remedies. This is a growing issue and one that deserves a more assiduous treatment than I could have afforded it here (Scott, 2001). Second, I have said relatively little about the relationship between law and alternative methods of doing justice or resolving disputes (e.g. truth commissions or interventionary wars (Wheeler, 2000)). There is a compendious literature on transitional justice, of course (Teitel, 2000; Boraine, 2000; Hayner, 2002) but not so much on the specific relationship between the two fields of war crimes trials and truth commissions (Roche, 2005). I regret that this book was unable to develop some of the ideas in this sort of work.

In Sloan Wilson's *Man in the Grey Flannel Suit*, Judge Bernstein looks back over his life in law:

> How violent Schultz had sounded over the phone. '*I want justice*' he had said. I wonder how many murders have been committed, and how many wars have been fought with that as its slogan . . . Justice is a thing that is better to give than to receive, but I am sick of giving it . . . I think it should be a prerogative of the gods. (Wilson, 2005)

In the end, this book, while concerning itself largely with the elaboration of arguments around war crimes trials, also is a book about justice and evil. I have elaborated very little on that evil in the text itself. There are no descriptions of machete attacks or hell ships. The world is awash with such images. There is an obsession with the Nazis, with genocide and with crimes against humanity in popular culture (on television, in the newspapers). It seems to me to be often unhealthy and prurient. I have no wish to add to it but I do want to say something about 'evil men' and what we ought to do with them. It is important to do so because one typical retort to work in this vein is that it over-intellectualizes a simple proposition: evil must not go unpunished. Ralph Lemkin, the Polish jurist who coined the term genocide, is reported to have said: 'retribution has to be legalised' (Power, 2002). War crimes law, it is claimed, signals 'the end of impunity' for oppressive dictators, abusive functionaries, and murderous soldiers (Roht-Arriaza, 1995).

It seems unarguable that justice ought to be done, and that war crimes law has done much to achieve that end. This book does not seek to prove these propositions wrong but it does foreground some other concerns about the nature of justice and the juridified repression of evil: concerns that, perhaps, ought to figure in the thinking of practitioners and scholars in this field (I include myself among these individuals). First, I place a question mark against a particular sensibility that equates justice with forms or places. It seems morally disfiguring, for example, to believe that justice is a matter of place rather than practice or outcome, or that trial must always trump negotiation or that the collective is guilty but the individual not. Second, I ask whether punishing evil may be a way of advancing damaging political projects (e.g. projects that seek to individualize evils that are structural, or projects that emphasize the role of human agency in war but deny its role in famine or child poverty or deaths due to lack of clean water). Third, I suggest (though this is not a question pursued overtly in the text) that we might ask what is *not* done when we are busy spending moral capital or political energy on using law to punish evil (e.g. a negotiated peace agreement (Anonymous, 1996) or an $800 million project to provide clean water in Bangladesh).[5] Fourth, I confront the problem of equality or generality. Do powerful interests within the international system (interests necessary to advance the war crimes agenda) have any intention of permitting the application of international criminal law to their own citizens or military personnel? If they do not, can the system be more than simply the expression of these interests? Fifth and finally, but not exhaustively, there is the identity of justice and evil. Should reference to such concepts trump the needs of legality or the everyday struggle of political contestation? What happens when we introduce these categories into international political life? Can we be sure we know who the 'worst of the worst' are? Can we be certain that the majesty of law can help us with this knowledge? Justice is one of the great virtues, and evil abounds in the world. Yet this book, in recognizing this, also struggles against 'the certainties of people who claim always to know where good and evil are found' (Todorov, 2003).

War crimes trials and the law of war crimes are increasingly pervasive features of the aftermath of conflict. This book, then, is an argument about what it might mean to talk about war in the language of law and crime, about the conceptual problems associated with responding to evil through law, and about the compatibility of categories such as crime and individual responsibility with the structure of international society.

1

Law's Politics
War Crimes Trials and Political Trials

> This is a criminal trial. It is unfortunate that the accused has attempted to use his appearances before this Chamber to make interventions of a political nature.
>
> Carla Del Ponte, *Milosevic* (Transcripts)

> I never heard of indictments that resemble political pamphlets with poor, bad intentions.
>
> Slobodan Milosevic, *Milosevic* (Transcripts)[1]

1 Concepts of the political[2]

The star defendant and the Chief Prosecutor in the Milosevic case may have disagreed about the nature of the indictment or the conduct of the defence but they shared a conception of the political as something that did not belong in a war crimes trial. 'Politics' for Milosevic, Del Ponte and many others in the war crimes field is an abnormality or defect (Bassiouni, 1997). Ideally, the trial is a place liberated from politics and the contamination politics threatens. In the present chapter, I challenge this orthodoxy by arguing that war crimes trials are political trials. They are political not because they lack a foundation in law or because they are the crude product of political forces but because war crimes law is saturated with conversations about what it means to engage in politics or law, as well as a series of projects that seek to employ these terms in the service of various ideological preferences. War crimes trials are political trials because concepts of the political remain perpetually in play. What follows then is a discussion and dissection of the implications, associations and meaning of this insight.

The idea here is to show that war crimes law is neither simply the expression of Great Power preferences nor an assembly of institutional and doctrinal tools working against those preferences. Nor is it a practice that transcends politics altogether (and, in relation to which, politics is an external spectre threatening to undo its good works).[3] Instead, I argue that war crimes law is a distinctive, sometimes legitimating, sometimes dissenting, often ambiguous, presence in international political life. The rest of the book seeks to demonstrate this through an unravelling of law's place, subjects, promise, anxieties, hegemony and origins in the midst of trials conducted in relation to breaches of war's fundamental norms (chapters 2–5) and at the fulcrum of justifications for war and arguments against war (chapter 6). In the end, war crimes law is a place where politics happens. This politics is constituted through the set of dialectical relationships that form the subject matter of the book.

But these relationships, too, can be understood through the prism of a meta-dialectic. Often, the sponsors of war crimes trials concede that the field of war crimes law is political but that this is a particularly *liberal* form of politics (Bass, 2000). I argue, in this chapter, that the politics of war crimes trials is a politics of compromise between a liberal cosmopolitanism with its roots in procedural justice, equality before the law and individualism, and an illiberal particularism (anti-formal, violent, sometimes chauvinistic, exceptional and collective).

I begin this chapter, then, by discussing (with a view to complicating our understanding of) some conceptions and misconceptions about the relationship between law and politics in the international sphere. This is in essence a description of some instincts circulating in the field about 'the political'. All of this then congeals into four concepts of the political (and legal) that I take to be pervasive in the work done by international criminal lawyers and others. Here I discuss the ways in which these concepts manifest themselves in institutional innovation and at trial, and in related commentary. With a view to illustrating some of these points, the chapter ends with a brief analysis of a recent case at the International Criminal Tribunal for the Former Yugoslavia (ICTY) involving the Kosovan leader, Ramush Haradinaj, and an excursus on the negotiations at the Rome Conference to establish an International Criminal Court (ICC).

War crimes trials are political trials but they are not political in the sense imagined by many commentators and participants (e.g. Milosevic and Del Ponte) when they describe such trials as 'political'. For them, the use of the epithet 'political' is meant to suggest that such trials are events or projects pre-destined to perform certain political functions, for example victor's justice. The Moscow show trials are regarded as political trials in this sense, they are politics unconstrained by trial or judicial process. Here the phrase 'political trials' loses its second word to become all politics, no trial. Besotted with disclosing the political in law, critics often dismiss the presence of the legal, the procedural and the formal elements of trials. There is certainly an excitement about umasking law's Olympian pretensions to detachment but this unmasking often masks the law that is left in trial after politics has its say.

There are a number of respects in which war crimes trials are political trials in a more interesting sense (I do not discuss all of these in detail in the book). They can be, for example, trials of the 'political' or, at least, indictments of the political. In the course of a war crimes trial, one of its (sometimes) unspoken purposes is to expose the grubby world of politics to the disinterested grandeur of the law. The trial is a way of conveying the message that mass criminality is what happens when politics is allowed to run riot. The very idea of lawlessness, then, is put on trial. The trial of the major war criminals at Nuremberg, for example, was a rebuke to the absence of law during the Third Reich, and this lack of law was directly on trial in 'The Justice Case' at Nuremberg.[4]

As well as politics in general, particular forms of politics are on trial. Most obviously, the trial is an investigation of, and accusation directed against, the political project of the accused. Accordingly, at Nuremberg, fascism (from the Soviet perspective) and Nazism (from the Anglo-American perspective) were on trial. In The Hague, during the Milosevic trial in particular, nationalism was in the dock, and in Arusha at the International Criminal Tribunal for Rwanda (ICTR), the consequences of racism were central to the process of judicial reckoning. Put more agnostically, war crimes trials can be understood as the proceduralized clash of competing ideologies. The Nuremberg War Crimes Trials, for example, are often described as the final moments of a struggle between liberal decency and Nazi evil (Clay, 1950: 250; Overy, 2003: 27). The trial, as chapter 4 demonstrates, also can be a trial of the accusers and their political projects. This was a feature of the 'Barbie' trial (where the French state was subject to an agony of self-reflection) and it loomed large again during the trial of Saddam Hussein. On the other hand, the clichéd reference to 'victor's justice' conveys the idea that these are political trials in the sense that the prosecuting party will pursue a certain type of politics throughout the case in order to vindicate its behaviour in a recent armed conflict. Finally, a war crimes trial, as an event, can be viewed as a trial of politics in the sense of a series of tribulations or tests to be undergone before a new politics can emerge untainted by the old.

So, the phrase 'political trials', though it carries with it a degree of power, is laden with ambiguity and instability. The politics of political trials are plural and contested, and the legalism of such trials is variegated.

The 'legalism' pursued at The Hague in the cases before the ICTY is to be distinguished from the more attenuated and martial forms of law found at Nuremberg. Equally, the 'politics' pursued in the *Eichmann* case are distinct from those found in, say, the *Akayesu* judgment at the ICTR.[5] This book is an exploration of the many different forms this politics might take from, for example, the production of knowledge about the state of international or national life (teaching history), to the dissemination of alternative histories and politics (dissidence).

When we treat our enemies as criminals, when world-historical evils are proceduralized or vengeance legalized, we end up with political trials. Of course, there is a sense in which the trial and conviction of a mobile phone thief is political (in its response to public outrage or as an expression of law's fixation with property crime). Every trial from the prosecution of a road-rage killer to a summary hearing on shoplifting is to some extent political, involving questions of social power, prosecutorial discretion and legislative choice. Meanwhile, show trials such as those held in Moscow in the 1930s, also are political (perhaps solely political or merely theatrical – they operate within an edifice of legal procedure but are not constrained by that procedure). A war crimes trial is different from both these types (though the continuities with show trials are explored in chapter 5). War criminals are not just 'plain, ordinary murderers'.[6] The typical war crimes trial is political in the sense that it can involve the performance of political contestation within the confines of a somewhat constraining legal procedure.[7]

What I want to do in the remainder of this chapter is to disentangle a little more the discourse around politics and law in the war crimes field. I begin by sketching some concepts of the political found in the field as a whole. I label these: deformed legalism (bad law), transcendent legalism (good law), utopian (or delusionary) politics (bad politics) and legalistic politics (good politics). It is not my intention, in doing this, to referee the disputes between the four. I do conclude, however, that war crimes trials are best understood as a form of legalistic politics, a law in the midst of politics and not detached from them (Shklar, 1964).

1.1   Deformed legalism

The most ubiquitous criticism made of war crimes trials is that they are political and *therefore* illegitimate. Slobodan Milosevic began his Defence at The Hague by characterizing the trial as a sham: 'I wish to say that the entire world knows that this is a political process. So we are not here speaking about legal procedures that evolve into political ones. This is a political process to begin with, and as far as what I would prefer, I would prefer the truth.'[8]

Saddam Hussein concentrated his fire on this aspect of the trial, too. On 1 July 2004, in his first appearance before the court, he portrayed the judges as American lackeys and the trial as 'Bush's theatre'. These comments recall the efforts of the Nuremberg defendants to cast their trial as a piece of political theatre on the part of the Allies (chapter 5). In Tokyo, Hideki Tojo, the former Japanese Prime Minister, said of his trial before the IMTFE: 'In the last analysis this trial was a political trial. It was only victor's justice' (Minear, 1971: 3). Even some of the judges characterized the trial as political. Justice Röling conceded that the Japanese were being tried for 'political crimes' (Minear, 1971: 53) while Justice Pal agreed with Georg Schwarzenberger that the distinction between aggressive and defensive wars was of purely 'propagandist relevance' (Pal, 1955: 264).

A subtler version of this image is found in the various constitutional challenges to the authority or jurisdiction of tribunals in general. The legitimacy challenge dates back to Charles I who, at his trial, protested '. . . at the illegality and unconstitutionality of the court while avoiding the fact that the evidence showed him to be guilty as charged' (Robertson and Devereux, 2006). This challenge to the legitimacy of the proceedings is a staple of war crimes trials. The Defense Counsel Appeal to General MacArthur described the verdict in the Tokyo War Crimes Trials as an 'atrocity against the law and justice' (21 November 1948). In the Tadic case, the defence argued that the ICTY had been improperly established, that the Security Council had no power vested in it by the UN Charter to create criminal tribunals and that the creation of such bodies had no nexus to the questions of peace and security over which the Council did have authority.[9]

Lawyers, in particular, from James Brown Scott in the 1920s to Justices Harlan Fiske Stone, Pal and Rutledge in the 1940s to Dr Servatius in Jerusalem in 1960 and onwards, have, to varying degrees, objected to the application of legal procedures to fallen enemies on the basis that this would politicize law. The legalist criticisms have been numerous but they can be divided into three broad categories. First, it is argued, international politics simply does not lend itself to the application of criminal sanction of the sort contemplated in war crimes trials. The international system is decentralized and horizontally ordered. It is, in Hedley Bull's famous phrase, an 'anarchical society', i.e. one in which there is no single unifying sovereign authority with a governmental and judicial apparatus. Criminal law depends on the existence of precisely this sort of sovereign with the capacity to emit the legislative orders from which criminal sanction acquires its legitimacy. Furthermore, criminal law is the juridical re-enactment of the moral life of a society. It is a prerequisite of the criminal law that there be at least a minimal level of moral consensus. This, too, according to these critics, is lacking in international society. What (ersatz) criminal law there is must be based on E. H. Carr's 'harmony of interests', a harmony imposed by, and representing the particular interests of, a small coalition of Great Powers or 'self-regarding units' (Zimmern, 1936: 94–8) within the system.

The result, then, and this is the second line of legalist criticism, is that war crimes trials can be partial and selective. They are a form of selective justice (McCormack and Simpson, 1997; Cryer, 2005). As Dr Servatius said at Nuremberg: 'To fail is abominable crime, to succeed is sanctified action'. 'Victor's justice' is a not hugely enlightening cliché of critical commentary around war crimes trials but it may be useful shorthand for the concerns of legalists.[10] On 8 August 1945, the Allies signed the London Charter establishing an international tribunal to try the major German war criminals. This was to presage a new era in which the requirements of justice and the concerns of universal human rights were to guide the conduct of international relations. Acts of criminality during war were declared intolerable and the wholesale destruction of civilian populations was condemned as a crime against humanity. On the same day in 1945, the United States dropped its second atomic bomb on Japan devastating the city of Nagasaki and immediately killing at least 70,000 of its largely civilian inhabitants. The history of war crimes is a history suffused with irony but the conjunction of these two acts – one, a manifesto declaring the subordination of force to law; the other, an act of violence contrary to a basic requirement of the laws of war – is perhaps the most ironic of all. For some observers, Nagasaki is a symbol of the death of an idea at its birth: the idea of universal application of international criminal law to all offenders regardless of affiliation, status or nationality (McCormack and Simpson, 1997).

It might be possible to take a more optimist view and argue that Nuremberg and Tokyo are imperfect precursors to a more consistently enforced, and jurisdictionally complete, legal order such as that found in, say, much of Western Europe today. Whatever the asymmetrical mechanisms present at Nuremberg and Tokyo, the argument goes, the victor's justice criticism carries less weight in relation to the ICTY and the ICTR where the concept of victors and losers lacks purchase. When the trials in The Hague began, defendants were largely drawn from the Serbian factions who had themselves *gained* a great deal of territory from the internal war in Bosnia (gains largely ratified by the international community). In any event, the Court has turned its attention to Bosnian Muslims and Croats (*Delalic*), and the current trial focusing on the Srebrenica massacre in 1996 involves the leader of the Bosnian Muslims in that area (*Oric*).[11] The ICC, of course, is to have a form of general jurisdiction applicable to alleged violators wherever or whoever they happen to be.

However, even the current round of international tribunals has not been impervious to accusations of victor's justice. Carla del Ponte, the ICTY Prosecutor, has complained of political pressure from Rwanda designed to prevent her investigating military abuses carried out by the Rwandan Patriotic Front (RPF). She was encouraged to prosecute those who committed the genocide (the Hutu Interahamwe) but not war crimes carried out by soldiers (on both sides). Eventually, she claimed, this led to her being removed from her post as Chief Prosecutor at the ICTR (Osiel, 2005).[12]

The spectre of victor's justice, then, will not disappear. The Rwanda Trials (and to an extent those in Sierra Leone and the proposed trials in Cambodia) are directed towards the prosecution of the defeated enemy. The Review Committee established by the Prosecutor at the ICTY to assess whether indictments should be issued against NATO personnel following the Kosovo war decided, in a report criticized by commentators, that there was no prima facie case to answer (Benvenuti, 2001; Bothe, 2001). And, now, the ICC has begun investigations into four situations, all of them in African states: namely, Sudan, the DRC, the Central African Republic and Uganda. The choice of potential defendants raises suspicions that the Court has been vested with the task of applying international justice to international society's outsiders.[13] International criminal law, from the perspective of the industrialized North, appears to be what other states breach. This concern is given added weight when one considers the various methods by which some Western states have sought to evade the application of international justice. The United Kingdom (as part of the International Security Assistance Force), for example, has a Status of Forces Agreement with the Afghan Government that prevents the latter from surrendering British personnel to the ICC. Meanwhile, the United States has sought to protect its personnel through a variety of mechanisms ranging from Article 98 agreements (providing immunity for US personnel on the territory of state parties) and Article 16 arrangements (whereby the Security Council can pass resolutions preventing the ICC from investigating abuses carried out by UN-authorized peacekeepers from non-state parties) through to provisions included in Security Council referrals to the

Court (as with Darfur) excluding certain categories of individual from the Court's jurisdiction.

The victor's justice imputation is crude and incomplete as an analysis of how war crimes trials operate but it continues to have a great deal of resonance in the contemporary world. Perhaps, today, though, and in light of the preceding discussion, war crimes law may be better understood as embodying the provisional immunity of the hegemons rather than the justice of the victors. In Shakespeare's *Henry V*, the French are condemned, by one soldier, for their massacre of the English boys at the base camp (''tis expressly against the law of arms') but in the same exchange the soldier's comrade reminds us that King Henry himself, 'most worthily, hath caused every soldier to cut his [French] prisoner's throat. O, 'tis a gallant king!' (IV. vii). The law of war crimes remains caught between its universalizing impulses (''tis expressly against the law of arms') and the structure of international political intercourse (''tis a gallant [and immune] king [and always ungallant enemy]').

The selectivity found in war crimes law is not confined to victor's justice or the immunity of the hegemons, though. It has been present in the failure, until recently, to accord gender a central role in vindicating the victims of international crime (Dixon, 2002). This has been particularly true of the question of rape in warfare, originally subsumed under other categories or treated as a breach of honour rather than a violation of physical and emotional identity. War crimes trials have been criticized too for the way in which race has played a role in determining the question of responsibility. The Tokyo War Crimes Trials have been chastised as both victor's justice and Western justice (Pal, 1955). It might be said, also, that until the 1990s, the whole field was skewed by its obsession with the Nazi era. As genocides and crimes against humanity were exposed with increased frequency (in Bangladesh, Cambodia, Guatemala, and the Soviet Union), categories of criminality continued to be associated, in the legal and public mind, with National Socialism in Germany. The configuration of forces in the Cold War meant that no action was possible in relation to contemporary war crimes. The Nazis, enemies of both protagonists, could safely be assigned the role of war criminals *par excellence*. In 1988, the Australian Parliament enacted the War Crimes (Amendment) Act and soon after the British introduced their own War Crimes Act 1991. In both cases, a full half-century and more after the Second World War, the legislation applied only to events taking place in Europe between 1939 and 1945.[14]

For strict legalists, there is a third problem. The structure of the system and selective forms of justice thereby produced has its consequences, they argue, in the deformed nature of the procedures applied in war crimes trials. In war crimes trials, proper legal procedures have been absent and rule of law principles compromised. At Nuremberg, Roosevelt had insisted on a trial procedure that incorporated a looser, non-technical version of the Western mean (chapter 5). In the Eichmann trial, much was made of the illegality of Eichmann's abduction from Jerusalem and the questionable jurisdiction asserted by the Israelis. In The Hague, too, there were transfers of dubious legality, a lack of access to intelligence supplied by Western intelligence agencies and the spectacle of a judge dying and being replaced half way through trial (*Milosevic*).[15]

Charges of ex post factoism, of course, have been standard in relation to war crimes trials. This was the import of the legalist objection to trying the Kaiser in 1918. The American delegation at Versailles could find no pre-existing legal framework that would have permitted a trial of the Kaiser. Neither the 'crime' of aggression nor crimes against humanity were thought to be part of international law prior to the Great War. These non-retroactivity objections became more strident at Nuremberg and Tokyo (Pal, 1953: 53–68). Lord Hankey believed that each of these trials offended the principle of non-retroactivity, and the principles newly enunciated in the 1948 Universal Declaration of Human Rights (especially, Articles 11 and 12). For him: '. . . the value of the Nuremberg and Tokyo trials for the establishment of the Rule of Law appears negligible' (Hankey, 1950: 132). The *ex post facto* problem raised its head again at the ICTY (established after the Balkan Wars had begun and applying new norms to conduct during these wars) and in discussions of the Australian and UK legislation referred to above. The UK Hetherington Report, for example, noted that '. . . while the moral justification for trying crimes against humanity is understandable, the legal justification is less clear'.[16]

1.2 Transcendent legalism

For every legalist concerned about the deformation of law, there is another with an overwhelming sense of mission (and confidence). Chief Prosecutor, Carla Del Ponte, began the Milosevic Trial with a stirring rhetorical statement: 'Today as never before we will see international justice in action'. War crimes trials, it is clear, represent a higher order of business in the international system (Meron, 1999). Geoffrey Robertson, one of the most eloquent of advocates of war crimes trial, has claimed that, '. . . the trials of Milosevic and Saddam, for all their faults, demonstrate that the immunity problem has been solved, and usher in a period when international justice will have its own momentum' (Robertson, 2006). Even the conviction of small fry like Tadic is, for Robertson, '. . . a deeply symbolic moment: the first sign of a seismic shift, from diplomacy to legality, in the conduct of world affairs' (Robertson, 1999). Cherif Bassiouni bemoaned the fact that the 'dream' of a permanent international criminal court had been '. . . eroded by the tension of ideological and political conflict' (Bassiouni, 1987: 11) and he has devoted much of his life trying to overcome these (political) tensions. In *For Humanity* (a title that reveals something of this tendency), an autobiographical account of his time as Chief Prosecutor at the ICTY, Richard Goldstone, one of Del Ponte's predecessors, describes those who are hostile or indifferent to reconciliation or war crimes trials. There is the occasional recalcitrant (former British Prime Minister, Ted Heath, describes the prosecution of war crimes as 'a ridiculous job'), and the media will not always understand the intricacies of criminal prosecution. There are the enemies of those who do good in the international sphere (war criminals such as Karadzic and Mladic, 'right-wing elements', petty bureaucrats (usually at the UN) and, of course, 'politics'). The reader does not get a sense of the many genuine concerns of those who disapprove of war crimes trials, or of the mixed motives of those who want them. The lure of legalism is all-consuming. War criminals must be prosecuted; it is as simple as that.[17] Gary Bass quotes Goldstone as saying, 'I've got no function other than to expose the causes of violence' (Bass, 2000).

A standard position emerges from all this that seeks to implicate something called 'politics' in the ruination or compromise of something called 'law'. A just and meaningful international criminal order could only then be created by cleansing that system of political influence (Bassiouni, 1997). When politics interferes with judging, then politics must be swept aside. The Tokyo and Nuremberg war crimes judges were wedded, too, to this transcendent legalism. Some of the judges at Tokyo were bitterly disappointed at the failure to indict the Emperor of Japan. Justices Bernard and Webb, for example, felt that the decision compromised the trial. Richard Minear believed 'the decision to exclude the emperor was a political decision, not a decision based on the merits of the case' (Minear, 1971). For these war crimes enthusiasts, there is only prosecution and trial on one hand, and the failures of politics on the other. Only the merits of the case matter.

1.3   Utopian politics

The merits of the case are not all that matter, though, to two sets of critics for whom war crimes institutions represent a form of utopian politics.

Lord Hankey writes in *Politics, Trials, Errors*:

> The first aim in war is to win, the second to avoid defeat, the third to shorten it, and the fourth and the most important, which must never be lost sight of, is to make a just and durable peace. Emotionalism of all kinds, hate, revenge, punishment and anything that handicaps the nation in achieving these four aims are out of place. (Hankey, 1950)

Henry Kissinger's book on *Diplomacy* (a fairly standard account and well-received in many quarters), meanwhile, is notable for managing to avoid any mention of war crimes trials or the law of aggression in its 1,104 pages (Kissinger, 1994). For 'realists' like Hankey and Kissinger, war crimes trials are bad politics. Generally, such pragmatists are hostile to the idea of applying principles of justice at the international level. The justice of action is to be evaluated by statesmen and women acting on behalf of, and in the interests of, the people they represent. There is no over-arching and trumping justice in the international system that would override these concerns. In post-war settlements, the key virtue is restoration not retribution. The certainties of the criminal law must give way to the subtleties of diplomacy. Buttressing this dislike of legalism is the belief that war crimes trials create martyrs of the accused, or retard the rehabilitation of outlaw states, or paralyse those governments (such as the Weimar Republic) that succeed criminal or aggressive governments and then become prey to revisionist nationalism (Hitler and Göring met at a rally to protest the post-First World War trials of German war criminals). Winston Churchill began as a legalist, calling for the trial of the Kaiser, but by the end of the Second World War he had renounced legalism, chastened by the humiliating failure to try either the Kaiser or the perpetrators of the Armenian massacre (Bass, 2000). For such realists, the sort of sensible, instinctive politics to be opposed to this delusionary legal purism is found in the decision, in 1946, to exonerate the Emperor and allow a degree of continuity in the life of the Japanese nation, and in the pragmatism that saw Shigemitsu, the former Ambassador to China, released from prison after two years (he became Japanese Foreign Minister in 1954).

For other anti-legalists, war crimes trials are utopian because they are insufficiently vengeful.[18] There is a belief not only that statesmen and soldiers do commit crimes against humanity but also that these crimes are so horrible that summary execution is the only appropriate punishment (though castration, too, was considered favourably by both Roosevelt and Churchill). Henry Morgenthau, Roosevelt's Treasury Secretary, worried that trials might end in acquittals or endless procedural debates. For him, the punishment for sin was death, not indictment. In 1815, Lord Liverpool, frustrated by Castlereagh's bloodless shuttle diplomacy and Wellington's chivalric distaste for extra-judicial killings, said: 'One can never feel that the King [Louis XVIII] is secure upon his throne till he has dared to spill traitor's [the Bonapartists'] blood' (Bass, 2000). Blücher, the Prussian leader, agreed. It was his intention to have Napoleon executed on the spot as revenge for the war crimes committed against Prussian troops by the French during the Napoleonic Wars. In the end, of course, Napoleon was disposed of in a manner that pleased neither legalists (calling for trial and conviction) nor those who craved something more punitive than trial or exile.

Critics, whether of a realist or punitive inclination, are indifferent to the question as to whether a war crimes trial represents good or bad law. Trials are usually dangerous, utopian and misdirected political forms (Rabkin, 2006). All the criticisms that were made of the interwar institutionalists are redoubled and magnified in the case of international criminal law (Simpson, 1999). The idea of applying legal standards to decisions about war and peace was regarded by the likes of E. H. Carr and George Kennan as a foolish illusion. Kennan warned that '. . . the legalistic approach to international affairs ignores in general the international significance of political problems' (Kennan, 1951). With international crime we are in the territory of full-blown fantasy. The role of international law, for these commentators, is to secure a basis for the minimal forms of cooperation possible in international politics. A modest international law is there to enable politics – not to stifle it. The principle of sovereign immunity, and the protective veil it has cast over Heads of States and high-level officials, are essential for the continued viability of international relations. Organizations like the ICC become the enemy of politics – calling for punishment instead of negotiation, individual guilt and blame in the face of collective responsibility, and trial instead of immunity. The war crimes field circumscribes and defaces politics with a highly partial, ad hoc and gestural legalism. It leaves too little to Caesar.

Domestic courts have long accepted this distinction, of course, between legal questions (susceptible to resolution in domestic courts) and political questions (reserved to the executive branch in its international relations). In the United States this was made explicit in a recent case involving allegations of war crimes arising out of the Second World War. In *Hwang Geum Joo et al. v. Japan* (2005), the US Court of Appeals held that the claims of a group of women alleging sexual slavery and torture by Japanese forces during the Second World War were non-justiciable because such claims had been settled at the interstate level by the executive branch under the

terms of the 1951 Peace Treaty between Japan and the Allied Powers (3
U.S.T. 3169), a treaty in which 'all claims of the Allied Powers and their
nationals' had been waived. Matters of war and peace (even those encompassing possible breaches of fundamental human rights guarantees) were
left to the realm of politics.[19]

The UK Courts have made the same point in relation to detainees in
Guantanamo Bay and the legality of the Iraq War (*Abbasi v. Secretary of
State, CND v. Prime Minister*). Even the International Court of Justice has
deferred to the political in some of its decision-making. In the Arrest
Warrant case, for example, it chastised Belgium for its over-zealous pursuit
of 'international justice'. In that case, involving a Belgian warrant requesting the arrest of the Democratic Republic of Congo's Foreign Minister,
Ndombasi Yerodia, the Court found that the proposed trial and punishment of high-ranking officials suspected of committing acts of genocide
and crimes against humanity in foreign domestic courts had to give way
to the larger imperatives of political intercourse. As the Court put it:
'. . . the mere risk that, by traveling to or transiting another State a Minister
of Foreign Affairs might be exposing himself or herself to legal proceedings
could deter the Minister from traveling internationally when required to
do so for the purposes of his or her official functions' (para. 80).

The realist critique of international justice, in other words, is not outside
law but forms part of its structure and doctrine. The relationship between
the political and the legal is under constant negotiation within the courts,
among commentators and in the realm of executive decision-making. As
international criminal justice expands its range and scope, the resistance
from interests who view it as a form of utopian politics is unlikely to dramatically recede.[20]

1.4   Legalistic politics

The previous models of politics and law reflect different approaches to
international criminal justice with each exerting some influence over the
field. One retort to all of them would be that, of course, there is no evading
politics at one, perhaps trivial, level. Treaty-making is political – it seeks
to secure political ends, it is 'an architecture of compromise', and it involves
a pooling of political aspirations. As Hans Kelsen described it, law is 'a
specific social technique for the achievement of ends prescribed by politics'
(Kelsen, 1957). Indeed, law could have no meaning in the absence of politics. Law is politics transformed. In this sense, law can neither be reduced
to politics nor can it be incubated against politics. Ultimately, war crimes

trials pursue political ends through jurisprudential means. They are a form of legalistic politics. But what sort of politics?

For Gary Bass, these politics are liberal politics. He views war crimes trials as expressions of liberal international statesmanship (Bass, 2000). They represent the relocation of domestic judicial procedures found in liberal political systems onto the international scene. Put bluntly, only liberal states will support international war crimes trials because only liberals within those states will have any moral investment in the idea of legality, an understanding of the virtues of fair trial and legal resolution, and a population capable of agitating in favour of such techniques. This is not to say that liberals always decide on trials and that non-liberal states never do. Non-liberal states do hold trials; but these tend to be Soviet-style show trials where legalism is entirely absent. There are also numerous occasions on which the pull of liberalism was insufficient to outweigh the many factors operating to discourage liberal elites from establishing war crimes trials, for example hostage-taking by criminal states (Serbia in 1994, Turkey in 1920) or a sudden awareness of the dangers of war crimes trials to reconciliation (Germany in 1919). Bass's argument is a more limited one. Liberal states support war crimes trials but only when circumstances are propitious (victory in war, territorial dominance or no risk of further loss of life in apprehending or trying the accused). Nuremberg had few costs in this respect, whereas the tribunal in The Hague for the former Yugoslavia is hampered by the reluctance of NATO to risk its soldiers in policing operations against suspected war criminals. Bass's argument is appealing in that it recognizes that war crimes law instrumentalizes rather than transcends politics. This book shares that view but rejects the notion that this politics is 'liberal'.[21] Instead, I argue that war crimes law negotiates between a liberal cosmopolitanism (emphasizing individual responsibility, the rule of law, internationalism, tolerance of one's adversaries) and an illiberal or romantic nationalism (emphasizing collective guilt, national prerogatives, procedural anti-formalism, and exemplary justice for outlaws, see e.g. chapters 2 and 7).

This is not to deny that it can be functional, perhaps even necessary, for lawyers and judges to regard themselves as aloof from politics (Goldstone, Del Ponte). Indeed, this whole notion is central to judicial self-representations. The distinctive power of legalism depends on the appearance of insularity (Shklar, 1964). There is no need, though, for commentators to accept this representation. Nor is it necessary to accept that liberal states produce either liberal politics or liberal law. For Judith Shklar, perhaps the most compelling writer on this subject, law is implicated in politics not apart from it. For her, war crimes trials are a choice not an imperative or an irretrievable act of folly. Legalism is simply one technique for social control and reform to be 'projected into the greater political environment of multiple and competing ideologies' (p. viii). What she calls 'tribunality' (a recourse to rules and judicial institutions) ought to be judged in comparison to other methods of doing politics, for example fairness, justice, compromise, power, religious truth, military values, friendship, charity or Marxism (p. ix). Is judicialization to be preferred to the politics of expediency and negotiation? For her, legalism would be much more attractive if it gave up on the pieties and principles (solemnly intoned at every opportunity) and instead understood itself as 'creative policy' (p. 112). As I have said, there may be reasons why practitioners might want to deny or underplay the existence of this creative element in the war crimes field (funding, Great Power support, public credibility) but these need not bind critics and academics studying the field, one of whose tasks it is, '. . . to account for the difficulties which the morality of justice faces in a morally pluralistic world and to help it recognise its real place in it – not above the political world but in its very midst' (p. 123).

2   The politics of 'politics' and 'law'

The politics of war crimes trials and international criminal law, at least partly, involve the expression of tensions arising out of the various concepts of the political identified and adumbrated above. To take one recent example, in the case of Ramush Haradinaj, the ICTY became embroiled in a dispute about the limits of the law and the boundaries of the political. Haradinaj was a guerrilla leader in the Kosovo Liberation Army (KLA), and had been chosen to be Kosovo's first Prime Minister. The ICTY indicted him on 4 March 2005, accusing him of crimes against humanity and serious violations of the laws of war. Realists, including those at the UN Mission for Kosovo, criticized the initial indictment and the Trial Chamber decision for lacking sensitivity to the delicate political situation in Kosovo (one that might require the political intuitions and experience of someone like Haradinaj) ('Utopian Politics'). As one diplomat put it, '[he could] play a useful role in terms of telling hardliners he knows to stay calm' (Judah, 2005). Trial Chamber II, on 12 October 2005, in a 'reassessment' decision on a motion for provisional release, and partially modifying an earlier Decision on Provisional Release,[22] had released the Kosovar leader (facing charges of war crimes and crimes against humanity), permitting him to engage in a limited number of political activities while remaining head of his party, stating: '. . . the Accused may appear in public and engage in public political activities to the extent UNMIK (the United Nations Mission in Kosovo) finds would be important for a positive development of the political and security situation in Kosovo, subject to the prior approval by UNMIK of a request by the Accused regarding each individual activity concerned . . .'. This was a controversial move. Legalists were appalled by the decision to allow an indicted war criminal to remain as the head of a political party (this would simply confirm the lack of fit between law and politics at the international level for some ('Utopian Politics'), while for others it was viewed as a failure of nerve on the part of the Tribunal ('Deformed Legalism')). The Appeals Chamber confirmed this decision on 10 March 2006 and added further conditions to his release.[23] The result of all this was that Haradinaj's activities were to be overseen, jointly, by both UNMIK (a political body) and the ICTY (a judicial organ). This form of rather delicate decision-making could be viewed, though, as simply politics by other means or legalistic politics: the court applying legal standards as honestly as it could while, at the same time, remaining aware of the political effect of its judgment (but allowing neither to entirely trump the other).

   Haradinaj is one recent example of the play of the legal and the political. The politics of politics, though, have been most visible perhaps in the negotiations at the conference in Rome at which the ICC Treaty was finalized. Organizationally, there was an unstated split between the diplomats and the lawyers, partially reflected in the division of responsibilities between the two bureaux: the Working Groups (technical, legalistic, detailed) and the Committee of the Whole (debating the wider procedural, jurisdictional and political matters). And this split was reflected in the professional division between the diplomats (seeking agreement) and the lawyers (seeking agreement and committed to the idea of legality (fair trial, *nullum crimen sine lege*)). Legal advisers were representing their state's interests but also the ideal of a legal order (and, at times, the interests of as yet unnamed accused). On the other hand, the diplomats and lawyers saw themselves also as building a workable legal structure in the face of unwarranted political intrusion from the outside (represented sometimes by the harsh nationalisms of the likes of Jesse Helms, sometimes by the utopian politics of the NGO community). Indeed, I suspect many of the delegates found themselves occupying both sides of the politics/law divide simultaneously. The Australian delegation, of which I was part, viewed itself, variously, as representing political common sense working against the legalist idealism of the NGOs, legal purism opposed to the *realpolitik* of the

Americans, moral universalism to the cultural atavism of the 'Arab bloc', and so on. At a more mundane level, law and politics were split along conventional lines. In the Drafting Committee, lawyers beavered away on juridical formulations that would reflect the 'consensus' while outside the conference hall the diplomatic elites met in private to bargain, cajole and threaten. In the middle were the 'informal formals' searching for a position that would bring law and politics together under one roof.

The struggle over the political took place primarily, though, in relation to three matters. These concerned the role of state consent or state sovereignty in the final structure of the Court, the autonomy and authority of the Prosecutor, and the privileges and powers of the Security Council.

In the case of state consent, a number of delegations wanted the new Court to possess a form of universal or inherent jurisdiction over the core crimes. The German delegation (and it was supported here by a small group of other states and a larger number of the NGOs and activist groups) advocated a mechanism that would have permitted the Court to assert jurisdiction over events, individuals and situations in the absence of any specific requirement that states cede jurisdiction or the Security Council defer competence to the Court. This move was criticized by states who believed it would create a court insensitive to the realities of international politics (the central role of states, the power of the Security Council) and who viewed it as a form of utopian politics. But the German position was defended by legalists who wanted a Court with the prerogatives to apply law in any cases where there had been large-scale crimes, regardless of the political ramifications of such decisions.

In the end, the German proposal was rejected either because, as some saw it, the proposal failed to tether law closely enough to politics or, as others viewed the proposal, it threatened to politicize the Prosecutor's Office by bestowing too much autonomy on the Prosecutor. The autonomy of the Office of the Prosecutor was deemed essential by those legalists anticipating another bout of deformed legalism with the attendant concerns about selectivity, politicization and bias. 'Politics' in this case was defined as state control itself. On the other hand, there were those who were concerned about the opposite: a Prosecutor so fiercely maverick that she would engage in a form of rebellious politics, employing the Prosecutor's Office to engage in activities against the interests of the Great Powers (thereby discouraging their efforts in the fields of peacekeeping, peace enforcement and state building). A major criticism of the idea of the independent prosecutor came from the Americans, who believed that an unfettered prosecutor would politicize the judicial and prosecutorial process. 'Politics', here, was defined as something beyond state control – partiality or lack of restraint – that might disadvantage the Great Powers.

Finally, there was a debate about the Security Council and its role. Would it be excluded from the process altogether in the name of depoliticizing the Court and ensuring it was free from Great Power interference (transcendent legalism)? Would it be given the job of anchoring the Court to existing collective security arrangements in the UN Charter that reflected the difficulties in securing peace and security without executive action (thereby avoiding the utopian politics feared by critics of international criminal justice)? Would it become so fused to the Court's operation that the ICC could no longer function as a judicial body (was, for example, the prospect of a Council finding of aggression becoming necessary before any indictment for the crime of aggression, an intolerable intermingling of political imperative and legal purity (corrupted legalism))? Each side claimed an institutional high ground by characterizing the other as 'political'. These were struggles over the future of the ICC but they were also conflicts about the meaning and resonance of 'the political', and debates between transcendent legalists, legal purists (worried about deformation), and realists. These were debates about the proper role of law or politics but they were also disagreements about what constitutes politics or law in the first place.

In this chapter I have considered the forms taken by the 'political' in arguments about war crimes trials or institutions. I argue here that the 'political' is best understood through four (composite) images circulating in the field. I call these: *deformed legalism* (the idea that war crimes trials represent a form of flawed or deformed legal practice); *transcendent legalism* (the idea that war crimes law promises the application of uncontaminated legal categories to the problem of war and mass atrocity); *utopian politics* (the idea that war crimes trials are a form of bad or imprudent or insufficiently retributive politics); and *legalistic politics* (the idea that war crimes trials can achieve defensible or indefensible results depending on the political arrangements that define them).

These images have very often framed or distorted the discourse around war crimes trials but they tell us a great deal about how the discipline is structured and how institutional programmes in the field are mapped. The rest of this book lays out an alternative way of thinking about law and politics in the field of war crimes law. It does so by arguing that the politics of war crimes trials can be thought of as a set of relationships: between the cosmopolitan and the local (chapter 2); between the collective and the individual (chapter 3); between the didactic and the juridical (chapter 4); between show trials and legitimate proceedings (chapter 5); between law in war and law of war (chapter 6); and between legal sanction and extralegal action (chapter 7). These relationships *are* international criminal law.

2

Law's Place
Internationalism and Localism

... only international courts can take adequate and appropriate judicial action when a case involves very complex crimes.

Antonio Cassese, *International Criminal Law*

1 The Hague or Baghdad: trying Saddam

Where should justice be done in cases where crimes against humanity are alleged to have been committed? This question of place has hovered over the war crimes field since its inception. It is a question complicated and enlivened by the existence of two conflicting assumptions about international criminal law. One assumption is that international criminal law is, if it is anything, *international*. For some, it is inevitable that international war crimes trials must take place at the international level before multilateral institutions applying cosmopolitan justice. Such institutions, they aver, are best placed to deliver impartial, majestic justice on behalf of the international community (Cassese, 2003b). This internationalizing impulse, though, finds itself in tension with a key assumption of criminal law, i.e. that justice is best served at the local level where the crime has taken place, where the evidence is located, and where the witnesses live (Alvarez, 1999).

In this chapter, I explore the history and contemporary incidences of international criminal justice in order to show that the question of space or location is always in play (even when apparently resolved in favour of the international or local sphere). This is true of both the choice of place (domestic and international) and the choice of style (provincial and cosmopolitan). This chapter, then, is about the *place* of international criminal law. I argue here that one of the constituting relationships of the field of war crimes trials and international criminal law is that between two spaces: domestic and international, and between two modes of prosecution and defence: sovereigntist (or metropolitan) and cosmopolitan.

This double movement between the international and the domestic, and between cosmopolitan and provincial styles of justice again was brought into sharp relief from the moment Saddam Hussein emerged from his hideout in Tikrit. The lines were drawn early on the question of whether the former President should be tried by an international or domestic tribunal. The idea of a domestic tribunal gained favour among those who were concerned not to interfere with Iraq's sovereignty by imposing a structure from the outside or who worried about the colonial overtones of an international tribunal (Greenwood, 2003). Meanwhile, internationalists attacked the domestic trial model because they believed the judges would be biased or because of a lack of 'international legitimacy' (Byers, 2004: 16). Curiously, many of those who had been supporters of the war, with its attendant, largely negative, effects on Iraqi sovereignty, were now highly attuned to concerns about domestic jurisdiction and sovereign prerogatives while opponents of the war, many of whom had worried about Iraqi sovereignty, now turned back to the international sphere in search of a just trial.

Harking back to the debate over, say, Klaus Barbie's destiny, these groups divided, too, on the question of the death penalty. For internationalists, the application of the death penalty was the logical conclusion of a coalition war tainted with illegitimacy from the beginning. On the other side are localists, who were content for the Iraqis to make the decision to kill Saddam because they approve of capital punishment (George Bush called for 'ultimate justice' for Saddam) (Byers, 2004) or because they have cast the whole invasion as a way of restoring Iraqi sovereignty even if this has some unsavoury side-effects.[1] Meanwhile, the former Iraqi President called for an international trial declaring the domestic process to be corrupt and biased.[2]

The result was a trial process that was nominally 'domestic'. Saddam and his associates were tried before Iraqi judges in a Special Tribunal established as part of the Iraqi court structure. The Tribunal was a creation of Iraq's interim Governing Council, and the lawyers involved were largely Iraqis. The law applied, too, included distinctively Iraqi national offences such as 'attempting to manipulate the judiciary', the wastage of natural resources and threatening war against another Arab country (Article 14, IST Statute). But this was a trial that was also 'international'. During a very lengthy pre-trial period, the defendant was in the physical custody of a foreign occupying power (the United States). This power undertook most of the interrogations, the Statute was drafted largely by experts from the United States Crimes Liaison Unit, and the Coalition Provisional Authority played a large role in permitting the creation of the Tribunal (Bhuta, 2005; Alvarez, 2004). Much of the law applied was recognizably international

law with its references to crimes against humanity, war crimes and genocide, and the definition of these crimes was drawn from the existing Rome
Statute for the International Criminal Court.

In Cambodia, too, the proposed trials of the Khmer Rouge became
bogged down in a controversy about international involvement in the
trials. Here, the 'nationalists', if this is the right word to describe those
placed in power by foreign intervention, had, for some time, obstructed
United Nations efforts to influence the formation of war crimes courts.[3]
Hun Sen's regime was keen to maintain control over the trials for the
obvious reason that the Prime Minister himself and many of his associates
were once members of Pol Pot's party. Indeed, the UN, exasperated at
Cambodian intransigence, withdrew from negotiations altogether in 2002.
As of January 2006, however, the shape of the tribunal structure was in
place with indictments issued against two defendants, including Ta Mok,
who subsequently died, and UN representatives arriving in Cambodia to
begin work on the Court. As with the Iraqi Tribunal, the Extraordinary
Chambers in Cambodia is a hybrid of domestic and international elements.
The composition of the judiciary will reflect this balance, with Cambodian
judges forming a slim majority.[4] The Prosecution team, too, will be part
international, part Cambodian. The law to be applied reflects this balance
with the Court having jurisdiction over classic international war crimes
(e.g. crimes against humanity) as well as violations of the Cambodian penal
code. In resisting a full international war crimes tribunal of the sort recommended by the UN's Commission of Experts who visited Cambodia in
1999, the Hun Sen Government has simply acknowledged a truth about
war crimes trials, namely that even a commitment to retributive justice
and truth-telling leaves open a number of questions (e.g. who delivers
justice and records history, and where do they do this?).

But this debate is not only about place but about the way in which
international criminal law is to be performed. For many, the creation of a
cosmopolitan legal order is an implicit rejection of the regressive nationalist impulses underlying the commission of so many war crimes and crimes
against humanity. As the *Guardian* put it on the first day of the Milosevic
trial: 'His [Slobodan Milosevic's] prosecution also constitutes a watershed
event for a fledgling system of pro-active international justice that, if it can
ever be perfected, will mark a crucial step in the necessary ascent of
mankind beyond the quasi-barbaric constraints of ethnicity, race, tribal-
ism, nationalism and the accidents of geography' (Leader Comment,
12 February 2002).

On this view, Milosevic speaks for an atavistic Serb chauvinism
while the Prosecution at the ICTY in The Hague advances the cause of

international justice and world order. This relationship, too, recalls the international community's initial attempt to reconfigure the Balkans. The Badinter Commission sought to apply the standards of international law both to the break-up of the Yugoslav state and the subsequent recognition of the new nation-states established as a consequence of this disintegration (Rich, 1993). But Badinter confirmed also the centrality of nationhood in international society. The procedure may have been cosmopolitan (arbitrators drawn from a number of different states impartially enacting international mores and norms) but the substance of the law was mired in statism (which of the Balkan peoples were to become recognized states?).

Finally, there is the whole notion of 'universality' or 'humanity' or 'community'. From the perspective of cosmopolitan justice, some crimes are assaults on humanity's self-conceptions; they 'shock the conscience of humankind'. It is an article of faith among some lawyers, then, that such acts must be tried by humanity in humanity's courts and in humanity's style. But, often, humanity's creed turns out to be that of the state acting (putatively) on its behalf (Teitel, 2004: 381) or is constrained by territorial nexus or subject to sovereign decree (see section 3).

This equivocation is surely the story of international tribunals in an anarchic order. The history of war crimes law can be comprehended as a series of undulations between recourse to the administration of local justice and grand gestures towards the international rule of law. An oversimplified and highly schematic version of this history would trace international criminal law back to the early efforts of the Romans to internationalize justice through the *ius gentium* before following this process through to the international tribunal convened to try Peter von Hagenbach in 1472 (a favourite opening for historians of the law of war crimes). The field's history continues with a series of ad hoc, largely domestic initiatives (military law, domestic trials) before the inclusion in the Treaty of Versailles (Article 227) of proposals to try the Kaiser and his associates before an international tribunal. This internationalism, though, gives way to a return to localism at Leipzig where the German Supreme Court is given the task of trying alleged German war criminals under German domestic law. This return to the domestic sphere signals a temporary suspension of efforts to internationalize justice. During the interwar years, developments in the field are largely confined to military manuals, courts-martial and ineffectual League of Nations resolutions before Nuremberg and Tokyo burst on the scene to establish the grounds for an international criminal order with the *International* Military Tribunal (IMT) applying international justice to the Nazis.

This was to mark the rebirth of international criminal law but while Nuremberg's progeny were many and influential (including the various prohibitions on the use of force, as well as the human rights movement), they did not include a permanent international criminal law machinery. The Nuremberg legal order lasts only about half a decade before the Control Council Trials are wound up giving way to a lengthy period in which the international criminal law field goes into recess. This recess endures for another half-century until the creation of the International Criminal Tribunals in The Hague (ICTY) and Arusha (ICTR) for the former Yugoslavia and Rwanda respectively. In the interim, there is a lengthy reversion to the domestic sphere where international criminal law is played out in trials like those of Adolf Eichmann and Klaus Barbie.

For some international lawyers, these are not arbitrary historical tensions but rather a working through of the cosmopolitan trajectory. Domestic trials, courts-martial, amnesties, or political settlements are viewed, quite often, as 'setbacks' for international justice. The Leipzig Trials, for example, are usually regarded as a failure or sham: a hiatus before international criminal law reasserted itself at Nuremberg. The trials of Klaus Barbie and Adolf Eichmann are offered as examples of hard cases making bad law. The future is said to lie with international criminal courts and the supercession of the provincialism of domestic courts. The ICC itself, then, is not simply a high point of international criminal law but something of an end-point, too (the domestic finally ceding to the international).

This narrative is not wholly misconceived but it misses an important aspect of international criminal law, i.e. the way in which each of the moments in this history are themselves constituted by the relationship between the local and the international. In this next section, I examine some episodes of international criminal justice in order to bring out this relationship.

In its aspirational mode, international criminal law involves working towards a comprehensive global social order. We shall discover in later chapters that this manifests itself as a tendency to convene trials that seek to demonstrate the inevitability of global normativity (chapter 5), but it also generates opposition from particularist nationalisms (the Bush Administration in the context of the ICC, Milosevic in the context of the ICTY) and from dissenting political projects (chapter 4). For the time being, I juxtapose this commitment to cosmopolitanism against concerns arising from sovereignty and nationalism. I begin with the International Criminal Court negotiations in 1998 and work backwards in order to show how the field of international criminal law is constituted, not by some inexorable surge towards 'global' justice but by this opposition or movement between the domestic and the international. The international rule of law struggles against its local variants at every turn.

2   International space/local place

The International Criminal Court is regarded by many observers as the brightest star in the cosmopolitan firmament. The Court regularly is enlisted in aid of arguments for the existence of globalized justice or deepening multilateralism or, even, globalization itself (Glasius, 2004). The Global Policy Forum, a respected NGO, claims, for example, that '. . . the new Court offers progress towards the long-held ideal of global justice'. For an institution that has only just detained its first accused, it has already accomplished a great deal at the symbolic level. Here at last, it is argued, is the international criminal law machinery promised at Nuremberg and Tokyo but deferred repeatedly through a sixty-year hiatus in which Great Power bickering and middle-power fecklessness had failed the international legal order. The ICC is imagined as a way of removing from the field the local peculiarities and prejudices of national criminal justice systems, and putting in their place a unified system of transnational justice. The Preamble of the Rome Statute itself reaffirms this internationalism with its clichéd references to 'common bonds', 'shared heritage' and 'delicate mosaics'. What we might expect from all of this is a highly robust piece of international justice machinery, reaching its tentacles into states and prising war criminals away to The Hague to face exemplary international justice, alongside an absolute commitment to the international over the parochial.

There is no doubt that the negotiations at Rome in 1998 and the resulting court structure do manifest some of these internationalist tendencies. Procedurally, the Rome Conference can be regarded as a cosmopolitan performance. After all, 160 of the world's states came together to establish a mechanism for trying those responsible for grave atrocities. There were conversations across cultures, languages and national inclinations. There was an effort to subvert sovereignty through law. Indeed, lawyers on the various delegations sometimes felt themselves to be serving two masters: their government and the ideal of an international rule of law. And the realization of this ideal itself was designed to transcend its local incarnations. Most notably, from the Western tradition, civil lawyers and common lawyers came together to construct a criminal law that would bring out the best of both systems. In the end, not everyone signed on to the project, but on 17 July 1998, 120 states voted in favour of adopting the Bureau Draft, and the Rome Statute was opened for signature. Subsequently, and as of January 2007, 104 states have now ratified the Statute (in many cases having enacted domestic legislation giving effect to the Statute in their own territories).

According to some commentators, the ICC negotiations, then, were not simply multilateral (bringing states together), they were cosmopolitan (bringing humanity together) (Hayden, 2004). State delegates were working for a conception of international justice, and, keeping them honest were representatives from 135 NGOs. This was a civil society triumph (Glasius, 2004). Never before had non-state actors played such a prominent role in bringing a treaty into existence. NGOs such as Amnesty International, No Peace Without Justice and Human Rights Watch were highly influential – providing expertise and advice, drafting and circulating proposals and cajoling delegates. Not only that, but the NGOs themselves put aside many of their own differences to establish clearing houses and coalitions. The Coalition for an International Criminal Court became one of the most powerful players at the conference and, especially subsequently, when it became a key mover behind the various preparatory committees designed to clarify some difficult organizational and jurisdictional matters.

In substance, too, the Court reflected a universalist orientation. The Court's jurisdiction extended over crimes of 'international' concern (I discuss this in greater detail later). A contentious debate over the appropriate role of the prosecutor, also, was largely resolved in favour of this orientation. The prosecutor was given authority to initiate investigations, subject to approval by the judges (an authority missing in the original drafts of the Statute by the International Law Commission). This suggested that the Court had an identity distinct from that of the Great Powers or from sovereign states generally. If the Security Council represented hegemonic ambition and the states parties sovereign constraint, then the prosecutors (and judges) could be viewed as an instantiation of global justice.

But the International Criminal Court does not quite embody universalism to the extent one might expect from commentary (whether laudatory or dismissive) about the Court. Indeed, a perfectly functioning ICC would be one that did not function at all: all cases would be heard at the national level. What the Statute envisages as its idealized global legal order is a matrix of increasing active and resolute domestic courts ending the impunity afforded suspected war criminals. But, of course, sovereign states are imperfect and national courts will, at times, fail. The result of this insight is a typical, if sometimes imaginative, compromise between cosmopolitan desire and nationalist or statist pride. This is typified by the manner in which crimes were defined, and the way in which the jurisdiction of the Court was provided for.

The internationalists' centralizing push was made by the Germans and Japanese, understandably keen to make universally applicable the principles elaborated at Nuremberg and Tokyo. The largely unconstrained jurisdiction acquired by the Allies in the Moscow Declaration 1943 (and applied at Nuremberg) was to be their preferred model for the ICC. The Moscow Declaration after all began the law of war crimes on an explicitly non-territorial footing, speaking of the need to 'punish by joint decision' those high-level Nazi war criminals whose crimes lacked a territorial nexus. Nuremberg had its cosmopolitan credentials further enhanced by acquiring the support of twenty-three nations who signed the accompanying treaty, and the General Assembly shortly after confirmed that the principles of Nuremberg were part of international law (Taylor, 1970: 14). At Rome, then, the belief was that these were international crimes and they were to be tried in international courts. As Alain Finkielkraut put it, in relation to the Klaus Barbie trial, crimes against humanity ought to be prosecuted in the courts of humanity (Finkielkraut, 1992). Some delegates clearly wanted the court to exercise unfettered global authority over heinous crimes. The Germans, for example, proposed that the Court have automatic universal jurisdiction over crimes against humanity and genocide, i.e. jurisdiction independent of any consent granted by states themselves. The ILC, in its initial draft of the Statute, had adopted a variant of this approach in its proposal that the crime of genocide should give rise to 'inherent' jurisdiction.

Some of this universalism survived the negotiation (chapters 1 and 6) but the Rome Statute resembles Nuremberg in its deference to sovereignty and hegemony, too. At Nuremberg, the four victorious Allies, arguably, were exercising territorial jurisdiction in lieu of the non-existent German Government. In other words, international criminal law begins on an expressly territorial footing. In one sense, this is not universal jurisdiction or, even, an international court. Instead, we have the Allies exercising a form of temporary sovereignty over Germany. Note, too, that the Nuremberg Trials were convened by only *four* Allies (and dominated by one of these). The Nuremberg Trials towered over later trials in the public imagination but these later trials were more numerous and represented a shift from the cooperative (albeit, limited) internationalism of the IMT to the local administration of justice found, for example, in Frankfurt during the

Auschwitz-Prozess between 1963 and 1965. General MacArthur's Proclamation of 19 June 1946, meanwhile, having decreed the creation of the IMTFE, recognized that: '. . . nothing in this order shall prejudice the jurisdiction of any other international, national or occupation court' (Article 3).

The ICC's cosmopolitanism is similarly qualified in its subservience to sovereignty and hegemony. Article 1 of the Rome Statute acknowledges that the Court shall be 'complementary to national criminal jurisdictions'. The Preamble reassures states that their rights to territorial integrity and political sovereignty will be unconstrained. The Court creates no right of intervention to enforce cosmopolitan norms. Most pointedly, though, (at least) two key provisions of the Court's Statute defer quite explicitly to sovereign power and domestic jurisdiction respectively. Article 12 makes it clear that the former is to prevail over cosmopolitan justice where there is a clash. Except when acting at the behest of the Security Council, the Court may only exercise jurisdiction over alleged crimes if either the state of perpetrator nationality or state on whose territory the acts in question are alleged to have occurred have given their consent or accepted the jurisdiction of the Court. State consent, in other words, remains key. Article 17, meanwhile, provides for complementarity between national and international legal systems. Potential jurisdictional tension is resolved on functional grounds with the domestic institutions given a degree of primacy or presumptive jurisdiction. The Court is obliged to declare a case inadmissible in situations where 'the case is being investigated or prosecuted by a State which has jurisdiction over it.'[5] Jurisdiction falls to the ICC only in the *exceptional* instance where 'the State is unwilling or unable genuinely to carry out the investigation' (Article 17). Examples of this might include the collapse of the national legal order, unjustifiable delay or absence of intent to prosecute. So, it is only in cases of national paralysis that the International Criminal Court fills the jurisdictional lacuna. This system can be compared to the one operating in the ICTY where the Tribunal has clear primacy over national laws in the Balkans. Complementarity operates in a quite different manner preferring fully functioning sovereign entities over international institutionalism. It is only dysfunctional or aberrant sovereignties that forfeit their claim to primacy over the Court. In this way, international criminal law is the exception, the place where law goes when it is annihilated or undermined by local politics.

Elsewhere, the Statute defers to sovereignty in its provisions on national security (Article 72), on questions of cooperation (Part 9) and on the crime of aggression (still undefined). And, in the end, much of the enforcement of the Rome Statute must take place at the national level, facilitated by pieces of domestic legislation such as the UK's International Criminal Court Act 2001 (allowing for the surrender of suspects to the Court and enacting some provisions of the Rome Statute into UK law). Ultimately the ambiguity found in Nuremberg between the territorial 'displacement of German sovereignty' and the international 'epoch of universal justice' is reiterated at the ICC.

Rome recalls Nuremberg, too, in its arrangements of the relationship between the needs of the Great Powers and international criminal justice. In the case of jurisdiction acquired through the Security Council's Chapter VII powers, it had been argued throughout the negotiating process that the Security Council, because of its special peace-enforcing role in the Charter, ought to retain a referral power built into the Court's Statute. This makes sense when seen in the light of the Charter system but may appear questionable to those immersed in legal traditions that find intolerable the overt involvement of political organs in decisions of a judicial nature. More controversial still, were the various proposals to give the Security Council a veto over proceedings at the ICC. These proposals took two forms and were embodied in the ILC's original Draft Statute for an International Criminal Court. Under Article 23(2) the ICC was to have no jurisdiction over the crime of aggression unless the Council had determined that an act of aggression had already taken place. This was problematic on a number of grounds partly because it seemed to prejudice the rights of the accused and partly because the Council has never found there to be an act of aggression (this whole issue is now moot because of the failure to reach agreement on a definition of aggression). Article 23(3) of the ILC Draft included a provision which barred the ICC from commencing proceedings arising from a situation which the Security Council was dealing with under its Chapter VII powers. This provision has been retained albeit in a modified form. Under Article 16 of the Rome Statute, the Council has to pass a resolution, renewable every twelve months, maintaining exclusive jurisdiction over the relevant situation.[6]

The relationship between sovereignty and the international is ambiguous in the case of Security Council-initiated prosecutions because, while the consent of the Council members represents a fetter on judicial institutionalism, it is also the expression of a particular form of realist internationalism dictating *against* state consent mechanisms. Another way to put this is to say that the consent of some states (Council members, the Permanent Five) is elevated in importance while the consent of other states is reduced. In the Statute, the Council then occupies a position poised between hegemony and cosmopolis. The Darfur Resolution, the Council's first referral under the Article 13 mechanism, has been understood in precisely this way: another Great Power intervention in Africa or a moment of assertive humanitarianism.

This relationship between the national and the international during each moment of institutional reform marks the whole history of the field. One need only think back to its various pre-Nuremberg 'founding' moments to see this. This is, after all, a field that finds its most regular expression in domestic war crimes trials and courts-martial; these constitute the hidden history of international criminal law.

It is a body of law that begins as a field manual drafted by a survivor of the Napoleonic wars, Francis Leiber, in 1863, prohibiting Union forces in the US Civil War from engaging in murder, rape and pillage. But its earliest incarnation as *criminal* law comes at the beginning of the Great War. Standing among the remembered masters of British imperialism, across the road from the National Portrait Gallery in London and facing Whitehall from Trafalgar Square, is a statue of Edith Cavell, the English nurse who was shot by the Germans in October 1915 for helping Allied prisoners escape from Belgium. Her death, one might argue, catalysed a whole field of law.[7] The level of outrage in Britain after her murder meant it became necessary that some sort of punishment be promised for the defeated Germans. Fed a diet of news about German atrocities in Belgium and elsewhere, neither the French nor the British public were in a forgiving mood. But as the Great War drew to a shabby and, in some respects, inconclusive, close (the German Army returned to Berlin to receive a heroes' welcome from the citizenry), the Allies were faced with a problem. International criminal law was in a state of infancy. The sorts of crimes the Germans were alleged to have committed (aggression, crimes against humanity) simply did not exist under international law. Those that did exist (war crimes) had historically been dealt with by the states or armies to whom individual perpetrators owed allegiance.[8] Breaches of the law of war crimes were a matter for national courts and military courts-martial. Undaunted, the Allies included (in the face of German objections) provisions in the Treaty of Versailles promising a trial for the Kaiser as well as German soldiers and officials suspected of having committed war crimes.

These, then, were to be the first international war crimes trials, piercing the veil of sovereignty, and making world leaders and statesmen personally liable for commencing illegal wars. But, as I have indicated above, the trials either did not take place at all (in the case of the Kaiser who fled to the Netherlands where the Dutch Government declined to surrender him for trial) or were reconvened at the domestic level (the unsatisfactory proceedings in Lepizig where 900 were initially under investigation but only a handful convicted (to serve minute terms) (Bass, 2000; Taylor, 1970: 24; Mullins, 1921; Willis, 1982)). This reassertion of sovereignty at the expense of internationalist ambition is anticipated in discussions at the Commission on the Authorship of War, a group of high-level representatives from the victorious powers brought together to decide on the details of the proposed international war crimes trials. Fascinatingly, the objections of the American delegation led by Scott Brown and Lansing at Versailles mirrored in essence the reservations felt by the United States eighty years later in Rome during the negotiations for the Rome Statute. For Americans, aggression was not a matter for courts, it was a matter for other sovereigns. The dissenting Americans in the Commission on Authorship were ultimately as anxious in 1918 about displacing history and morality with an over-ambitious legal order as their fellow nationals were to be eighty years later.

As I have shown, the question of place was present at both Nuremberg and Tokyo, but it was at the Eichmann trial fifteen years later that the agonized relationship between the universal and the particular was enacted by the judiciary at both the procedural and the substantive level. Procedurally, the Jerusalem District Court partly relied on an exercise of universal jurisdiction. On one hand, Eichmann's crimes were so heinous that international law permitted any state to claim jurisdiction. He was a latter-day pirate, and his crimes were crimes against all states; they were crimes against the international community, its interests and its moral presuppositions. The Jerusalem District Court, then, was acting as a conduit for the application of international justice; it was an agent of the international community (Allott, 2002). Israel was, for the purposes of the trial, 'Everystate'. But this anonymous dispenser of international justice, acting as any other state could have done, is rarely the story of international jurisdiction. Just as pirates were the enemies of empire or particular states rather than humanity (chapter 7), so too has jurisdiction over war crimes and crimes against humanity been exercised by those with specific national interests. Israel's interest in Eichmann was not an incidental consequence of universal disgust with Eichmann's crimes (Stone, 1961). Indeed, in many respects, the trial was specifically not about universality or crimes against humanity. The imperatives of sovereignty dominated the trial. Jurisdictionally, the prosecution and court relied on two other bases of jurisdiction alongside universality (Silving, 1961). These were passive personality and the protective principle, and each firmly re-establishes the link to sovereignty, though, typically for the Eichmann trial, these bases of jurisdiction could not be applied in a straightforward manner (Schwarzenberger, 1962). Under international law, states, in the exercise of their sovereignty, may have jurisdiction over crimes committed against nationals. By relying on this basis of jurisdiction the Israeli state was in effect casting the Jewish people as the relevant victim. The court was acting not as an agent for the international community but for six million murdered Jews (Gideon Hausner, the Prosecutor, had begun his opening statement by referring to his six million fellow accusers).

The third basis for exercising jurisdiction was the protective principle. But this again was an explicit nod to the particularities of the circumstance. States are permitted to take jurisdiction over circumstances that threaten their own security or future. But these grounds for trial meant that Eichmann's acts had to be recast as an effort to prevent the Jewish state from coming into existence rather than as a crime against humanity (the substantive crimes on which the Court focused were crimes against the Jewish people and not crimes against humanity). Eichmann thus became one more enemy who tried to destroy the Israeli state to be placed alongside its contemporary enemies. The Eichmann trial represented not deference to sovereignty in the midst of international sensibility, but an act of reasserting sovereignty in the face of an international failure to save the Jewish people, global indifference to the capture of fugitive Nazis and regional enmity. Ultimately, the Eichmann trial was about cosmopolitan justice *and* national reinvigoration.

The way in which international justice is tempered by sovereign prerogative is palpable in recent exercises of universal jurisdiction, too. The pattern of cosmopolitan enthusiasm followed by sovereign deference is repeated in both Spain's and Belgium's war crimes legislation. In 1993 and 1999, Belgium enacted two war crimes statutes giving Belgian courts unfettered jurisdiction over war crimes, crimes against humanity and genocide wherever these are carried out and regardless of the nationalities of either perpetrators or victims (Smis and Van der Borght, 1999). This expansive internationalism led to several indictments (and a complaint against US General, Tommy Franks), subpoenas and arrest warrants, including the one issued against the Democratic Republic of Congo's Foreign Minister (see *DRC v. Belgium*). The trial of the Butari nuns and their accomplices was the most notable example of this extensive jurisdictional reach (and there was a great deal of support both for this prosecution and for the extension of jurisdiction) (Simons, 2001). But this extra-territorialism was curtailed in a number of different ways. The legislation was gutted after interventions by US officials and those of other states worried about the propensity of

Belgian magistrates to issue indictments against high-ranking officials. These may be understood as sovereign institutions (states, domestic courts) carefully preserving or limiting their power, but this need to hold the international and the domestic in perpetual balance was fully elaborated in the 'Arrest Warrant' case (*DRC v. Belgium*), where the International Court of Justice itself decided that Belgian's exercise of universal jurisdiction over Ndombasi Yerodia, the Congolese Foreign Minister, violated the DRC's right to sovereign equality and Yerodia's claims to sovereign immunity (derived from the DRC's sovereign prerogatives).[9]

In the Spanish cases, the Courts themselves often pulled back from exercising the very jurisdiction conferred on them by the legislature. In the Guatemala Genocide case, for example, the Spanish Audiencia Nacional acknowledged the extraterritorial reach of the Spanish Genocide Law (its impulse to universalism) but made it equally clear that it would defer to any local court able and willing to take jurisdiction over the matter (its deference to sovereignty).[10] In many anti-terrorist treaties there is the same delicate negotiation between national prerogatives and global action. The 2005 Council of Europe Convention on Prevention of Terrorism is typical in this regard.

The logical conclusion of all this hybridity is, of course, the hybrid tribunal itself (Romano et al., 2004). In Sierra Leone, in Cambodia, in Kosovo and in East Timor, mixed tribunals of different types (there is hybridity within hybridity) have become the norm. These courts are either the self-standing result of a treaty arrangement between the United Nations Secretary-General (acting at the behest of the Security Council) and the national government (the Special Court for Sierra Leone), or are established as part of the domestic law but brought into a relationship with the UN by an accompanying side agreement between the UN and the state concerned (the Cambodian Extraordinary Chambers) or are the creatures of fiat by a transitional administration acting under the authority of the UN Security Council but embedded in the local legal order (the Kosovo 'Regulation 64' Courts, the Special Panel at the Dili District Court). Typically, these courts combine a mixed subject-matter jurisdiction (including domestic law and international law) with a prosecutors' office and judges' chambers composed of both international and national personnel.

In Sierra Leone, for example, the Court (made up of international judges and Sierra Leonean judges) possesses jurisdiction over war crimes and crimes against humanity as well as indigenous crimes such as arson and sexual offences against minors.[11] This is not simply a relationship between 'international' elements and 'domestic' elements. Sometimes, even these elements themselves are subject to the movement between the international and the domestic. One of the Sierra Leonean-appointed 'national' judges, for example, is an English barrister, Geoffrey Robertson. The war crimes over which the Sierra Leone Special Court (self-characterized in the Charles Taylor case as an 'international' court) will have jurisdiction are only those committed in *internal* armed conflict.[12] In other words, the apparent polarities within hybrid courts are themselves subject to qualification. This should come as no surprise. In the field of international criminal law, place is always in play.

3   Cosmopolitan law?

In this section, I want to turn more explicitly to international criminal law's cosmopolitan or internationalist credentials. Is international war crimes law humanity's justice? Can the category 'humanity' carry this weight? What makes some crimes, crimes against *humanity*? I will argue that in the same way that the question of place is constantly subject to negotiation, the styles of justice deployed represent a perpetual accommodation of the hopes for cosmopolitan justice and the requirements of sovereignty and particularity. Humanity's law (Teitel, 2002), it turns out, is the law of the cosmopolis, the law of the sovereign and the law of the hegemon all at once. Sovereignty and hegemony condition cosmopolitan enthusiasm in two broad ways. First, the construction of the international criminal order remains subject to the inclinations of the Great Powers. The field is built on a wish to reconcile an apparent contradiction between calling on elite states to enforce criminal law in the name of humanity, and demanding that justice be applied universally, or explicitly against Great Power excess. This is linked to a second problem for the idea of cosmopolitan law. States (and their citizens) tend to approach the violation of fundamental human rights and humanitarian law norms by foreign nationals as a matter of international justice but are much less comfortable when asked to view the felonies of fellow nationals in the same light.[13] Cosmopolitan law is for other people.

But, first, why *international* criminal law at all? When Dusko Tadic kicked and beat Hase Icic, a Bosnian Muslim detainee, during the Balkan conflict, why was this act an international crime? Was it any different from the dozens of beatings (in the street, in the home) occurring every day in, say, the United Kingdom or Australia? There are three answers offered for why certain crimes are 'internationalized'. The first is that there is something intrinsically 'international' about certain situations. In the case of

Tadic, the offences took place in the context of an ongoing armed conflict with an international dimension.[14] It is certainly true that serious violations of the laws of war in international armed conflicts have, since 1945 at least, been subject to criminal repression (e.g. Articles 146 and 147, Geneva Convention III (1949)). On the face of it, an interstate armed conflict is clearly international. It was this international element that allowed the International Military Tribunal (IMT) at Nuremberg to assert jurisdiction over crimes against humanity committed in Germany against German citizens, for example. The United States Chief Prosecutor, Robert Jackson, made it clear that had the Germans not embarked on a war of aggression, the Court would have had no competence to examine such offences. The Holocaust, in other words, was internationalized by the invasions of Poland and Czechoslovakia. Aggression is, by definition, international; it involves the *act* of crossing borders. The international community has extended international criminal law to cover analogous acts such as hostage-taking, offences against civil aviation and nuclear terrorism.[15] Indeed, the original impetus for a permanent international criminal court came in 1989 from a Trinidad and Tobago worried about the inability of Caribbean states' judicial systems to deal with transnational drug trafficking.

But the category international crimes encompasses more than simply those acts with transborder consequences. The second reason for internationalizing certain crimes, then, is their perceived threat to the international legal and political order. Crimes against internationally protected personnel (currently the subject of jurisdiction in Cambodia) and the criminalization of apartheid owe something to the need to protect the international community and/or regional stability from acts which, while largely confined to a single state, nevertheless threaten the functioning of international diplomacy or promise to spill over into other states.

Third, though, there are those international crimes that possess no transnational elements and provide no obvious challenge to the functioning of the international order. The ICTR in Arusha has criminal jurisdiction over crimes committed in internal armed conflict. Such conflicts have been deemed a threat to international peace and security by the world of states (acting though the Security Council). Similarly, acts of torture (criminalized under the 1984 Torture Convention and the subject of the *Pinochet* proceedings) and crimes against humanity (or, even, genocide) committed in a single state have been internationalized. In these cases, international criminal law is galvanized by the idea of humanity as a category to be protected (Teitel, 2004: 381). 'Crimes against humanity' captures the idea that torture, for example, or certain acts of persecution, are offences against the whole of humanity or, indeed, the very idea of humanity. They shock 'the conscience of mankind', regardless of their location or the identity of the victims. This ground of international criminal law is also linked to the idea of a cosmopolitan law with crimes against humanity at its heart.

Recent writing has suggested that war crimes trials are cosmopolitan trials. One recent book, for example, includes in the category 'cosmopolitan trials' not just classic war crimes trials in the Nuremberg mode (e.g. the ICTY hearings in The Hague) but also domestic trials (*Sawoniuk* in the UK under the War Crimes Act 1991) and civil cases (the defamation proceedings brought by David Irving against Deborah Lipstadt and Penguin Books) (Hirsh, 2003).[16] These trials are cosmopolitan, so the argument goes, because they form part of the transformation of international law, the decentring of the state and the inception of a potentially universalizable justice. War crimes law is, along with the doctrine of humanitarian intervention, in the vanguard of a new project dedicated to establishing the conditions for a cosmopolitan legal order. Part of the excitement attending this cosmopolitan law is that it can no longer be confined to the projections of liberal visionaries but is now part of an observable social reality (Pinochet was subject to extradition proceedings, Milosevic was tried in The Hague, NATO did intervene in Kosovo).

A paradox, though, of this cosmopolitanism is that it represents an attempt to transcend sovereignty while remaining largely reliant on particular instantiations of it. 'People-based' strategies and global institutions often depend on sovereigns to enforce the norms they ardently support. It was the Great Powers who established the ICTY and ICTR, while the trial of Sawoniuk and the defamation action brought by Irving were heard in the courts of one of the Great Powers, the United Kingdom. This raises the prospect that cosmopolitan values may simply be a projection of Great Power primacy or pseudo-colonial interference or liberal hegemony. Do war crimes trials advance the ends of highly particularized political projects (chapter 5)? Are they about friends and enemies rather than dispensing justice? Or is it possible that cosmopolitan law may begin as legitimation but end with a degree of relative autonomy?

Advocates of cosmopolitanism argue that war crimes courts can bite the hand that shapes them. Crimes against humanity are the exemplary case: brought into existence by the Great Powers but now subjecting those same Great Powers to its jurisdiction. Thus, the concept of crimes against humanity generally is said to mark a 'recognition that there is no sovereign right to commit such crimes and that the claim made by cosmopolitan law, that it has jurisdiction within all sovereign states in relation to such crimes is legitimate' (Hirsh, 2003: 152).

Can cosmopolitan justice bear the weight of these claims?[17] Most of the cases heard so far under this rubric, for example a civil case involving defamation in the UK (brought by one British national against a British company), a criminal case involving a UK resident, and a handful of trials held in The Hague under a form of highly selective jurisdiction, suggest that if this is cosmopolitan law, it is in a state of highly uneven development. It is true that international tribunals exist and that they are '. . . competent to prosecute crimes against humanity' (Hirsh, 2003: 152) but these tribunals surely are swallows failing to make a summer. The ICTY has limited temporal and territorial jurisdiction (and is partly beholden to the Great Powers for funding). It may be that its failure to fully investigate the NATO attack on Serbia was necessary to its survival (notwithstanding the Review Committee's recommendations to this effect). Other ad hoc tribunals are similarly selective. Meanwhile, the ICC may have jurisdiction over crimes against humanity but this is certainly not universal jurisdiction (universal jurisdiction was specifically rejected by the delegates at Rome). Any US soldiers suspected of committing crimes against humanity in Afghanistan would not be subject to it, and Russian Special Forces accused of murdering civilians in Chechnya are not subject to it. Indeed, one might go further and say that after Resolution 1422 (and its successors), the Article 98 side agreements and the various Status of Force Agreements concluded between occupied states and Western powers, alleged war criminals in most places, most of the time, will not fall within the jurisdiction of the ICC.

According to David Hirsh, though, the difference between institutional domination under liberal conditions and those under totalitarianism is that liberal-bourgeois forms allow for disagreement, independence and dissent. Thus, he claims, judges working in institutions established by the Great Powers are able to act autonomously or semi-autonomously despite the origins of these institutions in *realpolitik*. Relative autonomy, though, does not penetrate the critical decisions about whether to establish these institutions in the first place or the permissible limits of jurisdiction enjoyed by these institutions. Hirsh argues that the ICTY indicted Milosevic, 'at a moment during the Kosovo conflict when it might have been inconvenient for NATO' (p. 156). When war crimes trials threaten to become too inconvenient, though, they simply do not happen. The Review Committee's recommendation to the ICTY Prosecutor that there was no basis for investigating alleged NATO breaches of the laws of war in 1999 illustrates the problem.

Hirsh has converted a plausible argument about professional ethics (international judges do act independently) into a project for cosmopolitan justice. One judge irritating the Great Powers in The Hague does not a system of autonomous universal justice make. Nor is it the case that the Pinochet judgment stands for 'the principle of universal jurisdiction over crimes against humanity' (Hirsh: xi). In fact, this principle is still highly controversial and a single judgment of a domestic court (no matter how tectonic) is not capable of transforming this picture. Most of the judges in the majority found against Pinochet on narrower grounds related to the jurisdiction established under the terms of the Torture Convention. This is why Pinochet could not stand trial for crimes such as hostage-taking, or torture committed pre-1988 (the date on which the UK ratified the Convention). Nor is it the case that Tokyo, Nuremberg or the ad hoc tribunals stand for universal jurisdiction. How could The Hague Tribunals do so when their territorial and temporal competence is so severely circumscribed by their own statutes? Nuremberg and Tokyo meanwhile established certain acts as crimes under international law but these tribunals neither specified the jurisdictional consequences of this nor were they, themselves, exercises of universal jurisdiction (indeed, there was something anti-cosmopolitan about Nuremberg (Luban, 1987: 779–829)).

The same goes for the Genocide Convention; it is lauded by cosmopolitans for providing universal jurisdiction over the crime of genocide but the Convention does no such thing. Arguments about customary international law notwithstanding, it provides for a form of territorial or international jurisdiction but not universal jurisdiction.

Even the cosmopolitan credentials of that most totemic of categories, crimes against humanity, are not secure. Crimes against humanity have been understood, in retrospect, to lie at the heart of the Nuremberg Trials. It is after all remembered as the trial of the Holocaust but the genocide (an aspect of crimes against humanity) was not the 'crime of crimes' at Nuremberg as it was in later trials such as that of Akayesu in Arusha at the ICTR. At Nuremberg, crimes against humanity were announced on the world stage accompanied by rhetorical commitments to their durability and universality, but the legal position was somewhat different. Instead of being applicable everywhere and at all times, crimes against humanity were to have application only at Nuremberg (and Tokyo), only in relation to the Nazis, and only to the extent that these crimes were yoked to a larger armed struggle. It was Hitler's attacks on Czechoslovakia, Poland

and Norway that gave the Court its jurisdiction over his crimes against German Jews. How did this happen?

Crimes against humanity were introduced at Nuremberg to remedy a serious gap in international criminal law. Crimes against peace found some, albeit insecure, basis in the prohibition on force found in the Kellogg-Briand Pact of Paris, and the limitations placed on discretionary violence in the League of Nations Covenant. War crimes, meanwhile, seemed a natural, if somewhat retroactive, attachment of criminal liability to breaches of war law already found in a body of legal regulation. The law of war crimes *stricto senso* was concerned with the treatment of protected persons (largely foreign military and civilian personnel). War was required to internationalize the prohibited acts. War crimes were acts committed by foreign sovereigns. As Malcolm Bull put it recently, states didn't mind their citizens dying, they just didn't want anyone else killing them (Bull, 2004).

Accordingly, to place the treatment of a state's own citizens by that state under public international law supervision was a radical step in 1945. The zone of sovereign power was being internationalized. The Allies were faced, though, with a dilemma. They could choose to apply a largely invented category of criminality to the Nazis, or they could convene a trial that covered all aspects of Nazi criminality *except* the destruction of Germany's Jewish, Gypsy, Slav and other national minorities. The latter, of course, was a moral and political impossibility, and so crimes against humanity entered the legal and moral lexicon of our time. Domestic space appeared to have been internationalized. But, there was a catch. Robert Jackson, in a statement preceding a trial, explained why this cosmopolitan impulse could not have global reach.

> We have some regrettable circumstances at times in our own country in which minorities are unfairly treated. We think it is justifiable that we interfere or attempt to bring retribution to individuals or states only because the concentration camps and the deportations were in pursuance of a common plan or enterprise of making an unjust or illegal war in which we became involved. (Marrus, 1997: 45)

International law had managed to constrain sovereign power but only that of two (already denuded) sovereigns: Germany and Japan. A jurisdictional nexus between crimes against peace and crimes against humanity was written into Article 6 of the IMT Charter in order to accomplish this. As Hannah Arendt put it, the category 'crimes against peace' (and not 'crimes against humanity') encapsulated for the tribunal 'the accumulated evil of the whole'. What this emphasis, and the wording of Article 6, meant was that crimes against humanity could be prosecuted only if they were linked to the wider crime of aggression (or, less commonly, linked to ordinary war crimes).

This led to a peculiar and misleading emphasis on the role of the Holocaust as an aspect of the crime of aggression. The decision to link crimes against peace and crimes against humanity was part of a more general deference to sovereignty at the height of judicial internationalism. Article 6, rather than announcing the inviolability of the human being or the universality of criminal justice, established sovereignty as an unbreachable barrier to the jurisdiction of the international criminal law machinery. The Nazis had forfeited their sovereignty by seeking to dominate Europe. This was not the case for most other states. For the vast majority of states in a system, the jurisdictional reach of crimes against humanity was to remain, for some time, highly attenuated.

The relationship between domestic sovereignty and international ambition played out differently in later trials. Control Council Law no. 10 breaks the explicit link between crimes against peace and crimes against humanity, and this detachment of crimes against humanity from crimes against peace continues in the Genocide Convention of 1948 and in the later trials of Eichmann, Barbie and Tadic. But this did not mean that the prosecution of crimes against humanity was untethered from sovereignty altogether. Crimes against humanity were yet to be tried in Alain Finkielkraut's 'courts of humanity'. The ICTY and ICTR are limited in their jurisdictional reach while the ICC is constructed around the idea that national courts will prosecute crimes against humanity under local law.

The prerogatives of the sovereign remain jealously guarded. Indeed, frequently the sovereign takes a risk in applying international justice to its own citizens. When the United Kingdom authorities announced that investigations into the alleged killing of Iraqis by UK personnel would proceed under the ICC Act (UK), there was an outcry in the press, much of which took the view that crimes against humanity and war crimes referred to acts akin to the Holocaust, and not one-off atrocities committed by UK soldiers. The latter, it was argued, ought to be dealt with in the United Kingdom, under UK domestic law, largely divorced from the norms of international criminal justice. As Tim Collins, a former officer in the British Armed Forces, put it, following the decision to open investigations under the ICC Act:

It is right that the cases should come to a military court. Military law takes account of the fact that extraordinary circumstances pertain when we deploy armies into the field, and that some norms of society are suspended. What would be a disaster and national embarrassment of epic proportions is if a single British serviceman or woman found themselves instead at the international court in The Hague (traditionally, the UK military delivers the suspects rather than being the defendants). (Collins, 2005)

Nuremberg, then, established a pattern of justice. Perpetrators and their circumstances were particularized. Crimes against humanity were understood as 'Nazi crimes against humanity in the context of aggressive war'. This particularization continues in more implicit forms today. The subject is not 'man's inhumanity to man' but the inhumanity of specific categories of men (Serbs in Bosnia but not Americans or Iraqis in Falluja, Hutus but rarely Tutsis, Sudanese or Ugandans but not the Northern Alliance or the Russians in Chechnya).

Paradoxically, though, when the IMT at Nuremberg universalized the *victims* of crimes against humanity, it elided the unique circumstances of particular classes of victim. To put the matter in the terms employed by Hirsh, the tribunal chose to see crimes against humanity as crimes against the cosmopolis rather than as crimes directed at the Jewish people. The concentration camp film shown at Nuremberg was construed as evidence of atrocities committed against POWs and individuals of various nationalities rather than as a cinematic representation of the Holocaust. 'The Holocaust', indeed, did not exist at Nuremberg.[18] The Shoah was submerged under the neutral category 'crimes against occupied populations'. The Eichmann trial redressed this feature of Nuremberg by focusing on 'crimes against the Jewish People' (as the legislation put it). The trial, more importantly, offered up a testimonial rendering of the murder of the European Jews. In a series of devastating narrative accounts, survivor-heroes told their stories about the terrible events of 1933–45. Some of these accounts were related only tangentially to Eichmann, and some of the history was hearsay, but the impact of these testimonies was profound. The Holocaust was established as the central fact of the war and, arguably, the twentieth century, and became an important element in the national re-orientation of the Israeli state. But the Eichmann trial, in substituting crimes against the Jewish people for crimes against humanity, reminded the world that 'man's inhumanity to man' was not a universal experience subject to universal laws but the experience of particular groups at the hands of other groups.

4   Negotiating the international

International tribunality and cosmopolitan justice are conditioned or qualified by the claims of local space, national self-assertion, group identity,
sovereign prerogative and hegemonic imperative. The Security Council's
first referral to the International Criminal Court came amidst reports of
genocide in Darfur. This referral, though, depended on the support or
acquiescence of the P5 in the Security Council, and was qualified by a
clause excluding from the jurisdiction of the Court peacekeepers affiliated
to states not party to the Rome Statute (including the United States).
Meanwhile, the Sudanese Government continued to assert their right to
deliver justice internally. Sometimes, this renegotiation worked the other
way. In July 2005, political manoeuvring around the Iraqi Special Tribunal
resulted in some disquiet among US officials working for the Regime
Crimes Liaison Office, who reportedly threatened the Tribunal that
Saddam and his associates would be transferred to The Hague to stand
trial before an international criminal court (Burns, 2005). This, in turn, was
reflected in the former Iraqi President's varying demands first that he be
tried before genuine Iraqi courts, then that he be subject to international
justice.

The hybrid nature of 'international' justice is exemplified, too, in the
mixed courts themselves, the dependence of national courts and international justice on their reflections and, now, the literal movement one sees
between national and international jurisdiction in relation to the transfer
cases in the Balkans. A recent instance of this took place at the end of 2005
when the ICTY Referral Bench agreed to authorize the transfer of two
relatively high-ranking Croatian indictees back to Croatia under the procedure known as Rule 11b *bis*. Rahim Ademi and Mirko Norac were
accused of having terrorized the population of the Medak area in Krajina
during the Balkan conflict. But this transfer back to the national space is
accompanied by provision for continuing international oversight. Any
tendencies in the direction of national particularity or ethnic bias have to
be supervised or eradicated before transfers take place (this includes, recalling Badinter, assurances that the death penalty will not be applied, along
with provisions requiring the judges to be satisfied that any national trial
will meet 'international standards' and afford 'appropriate justice').[19] Similarly, when the ICTY agreed to transfer Zeljko Mejakic (accused of committing violations of humanitarian law in the infamous Omarska Camp in
Bosnia) to the new War Crimes Court in Bosnia-Herzegovina, Mejakic
became a physical symbol of the whole field, oscillating between

international and domestic space, and between cosmopolitan and provincial justice. Mejakic, initially indicted by the ICTY operating under its apparently unqualified international jurisdiction (the Tribunal, after all, has primacy over domestic courts) is transferred to the Bosnian courts but on the understanding that the Bosnians are capable of delivering ersatz cosmopolitan justice (with the ICTY prosecutor requesting to file reports on the progress of the investigations and Court processes). How much is the Bosnian Court *like* the ICTY? Are its procedures overseen by international bodies (such as the OSCE)? Mejakic's transfer was endorsed by the ICTY but the Bosnian Court, it turns out, is composed of international and national judges, applying international and domestic law.[20] This, in turn, mirrors parallel reconfigurations of justice's place in the past (e.g. the transfer of jurisdiction in 1949 from the IMTFE at Tokyo to the local Japanese courts).

International criminal law's most recent innovation, then, is simply a physical rehearsal of a movement between the domestic and the international that constitutes the field itself. The modalities of international justice involve a perpetual negotiation between the claims of the cosmopolitan and the needs of the local, the former constantly threatening to collapse into hegemony, the latter into parochialism. As this chapter has argued, this negotiation is the very stuff of international criminal law.

3

Law's Subjects
Individual Responsibility and
Collective Guilt

> ... the latest and most formidable form of ... dominion: bureaucracy or
> the rule of an intricate system of bureaus in which no men, neither one
> nor the best, neither the few nor the many, can be held responsible ...
>
> Hannah Arendt, 'Reflections on Violence'

> The true culprits are those who mislead public opinion and take advantage
> of the people's ignorance to raise disquieting rumours and sound the alarm
> bell, inciting the country and, consequently, other countries into enmity.
> The real culprits are those who by interest or inclination, declaring con-
> stantly that war is inevitable, end by making it so, asserting that they are
> powerless to prevent it. The real culprits are those who sacrifice the
> general interest to their own personal interest.
>
> Baron d'Estournelles de Constant, Chairman, International
> Commission to Inquire into the Causes and Conduct of the Balkan Wars

1   Men not abstract entities

War crimes trials are understood and imbibed as dramas of individual
human reckoning. The popular image of the trial is that of the defendant
facing up to his responsibility, accountable for his crimes before the court
and the eyes of the world. In Jerusalem, there was Adolf Eichmann behind
his glass booth looking out at his '6 million accusers' (Hausner, 1966). At
Nuremberg, two rows of variously dazed, defiant, emotionally crippled,
high-ranking Nazis slowly absorbed a picture of the gross misdeeds contained in the accusations. In The Hague, there was Slobodan Milosevic,
apparently bullish, facing down his accusers, and in Baghdad, the personality of a remorseless Saddam Hussein came to dominate the process of
legalized retribution. One commentary on the Baghdad trial emphasizes
the perceived value of such proceedings: 'Trials that reach the hearts and
minds of Iraqis reinforce other important social and political messages. By
establishing individual rather than collective responsibility for these crimes,
they will place blame where it belongs: on the shoulders of Hussein and

his cabal, and not on the Sunnis collectively or any particular village or clan' (Ward and Hieman, 2005).

But if popular understandings of the war crimes field are dominated by notorious individuals, this reflects an inclination in the academic and professional world of international law to think of international criminal law as an expression of the growing role of the individual in international law generally. International criminal law, indeed, is often equated with the application of individual responsibility to international law. While most international legal norms subject states to certain behavioural constraints and hold states accountable for breaches of these constraints, international criminal law has been regarded as controversial and innovative precisely because it makes individuals liable for infractions of international law's most fundamental norms. At Nuremberg, the International Military Tribunal, in its final judgment, declared that the hideous crimes under investigation were committed 'not by abstract entities but by men'.[1] This apparently commonsensical, but at the time revolutionary, idea has by now become central to international criminal lawyers' self-understandings (Robertson, 2005: 655).

Putting the individual at the centre of the international law project has been a distinguishing motif in much commentary in the field, but it is linked, too, to some other effects of the law of war crimes on the wider discipline. To take the most obviously significant, punishing individuals through criminal sanction is important because it promises the renewal, perhaps completion, of international law; because it links international law explicitly to international human rights law and anticipates the future enforceability of these norms; and because it contributes further to the recession of sovereignty (in the latter case, international criminal law is recruited as part of a wider process of globalization). Let me take each of these in turn.

First, international criminal law represents at least one possible future for international law (Mégret, 2003; Robertson, 1999). International lawyers have long been assailed by anxieties arising out of the apparent unenforceability of international law (chapter 6). This is, of course, partly a problem built into the very structure of international society. In a world in which many are sovereign, there is only an absence where sovereign authority should reside. Many international lawyers have accepted that the international system is an anarchical society (Watson, 1999) in which states must work to achieve certain global ends while at the same time preserving their freedom. To the extent that compliance is secured, it is done so through reciprocal sanctions (D'Amato, 1984/85; Kratochwil, 1984), through the establishment of coalitions of like-minded states (Tesón, 1992), through the self-identifications of states (Reus-Smit, 2004) or through the work of global networks of state and non-state actors (Slaughter, 2004: 14–44). Often, though, what appears to be missing from even the rosiest portrayals of international law's muscularity or relevance is the possibility of simple criminal repression or top-down enforcement. In the case of the Iraq War, the tragedy of international law for most international lawyers lay in the breach of the law by two of the Great Powers (Sands, 2005). The system of habitual compliance and institutional fidelity had been violated. The solution for one group of international lawyers was the reinvigoration of international society through confidence-building among estranged allies and institutional renewal (Brunnée and Toope, 2004). This, indeed, was the official response of the United Nations in its *High-Level Panel Report* (2004), and in the Secretary-General's *In Larger Freedom* (2005) document where the accent is firmly on avoiding future transgressions by strengthening the UN system and by elaborating principles that would make decisions concerning the use of force more transparent.

Among other lawyers, though, there was a sense that law could only function if there was some sort of *ex post facto* punishment meted out to those who violated the rules. In other words, this comprehensive system of rules elaborated over centuries was capable of completion only when it could offer the possibility of some form of retribution for those individuals who disregarded its most fundamental precepts. But who is to be punished?

The structure of international society makes it difficult to punish states. International law is largely auto-interpretive and states are beholden to no super-sovereign. As the ICTY said in *Blaskic*, '. . . under international law States could not be subject to sanctions akin to those provided for in national criminal justice systems'.[2] States make and enforce international law and they have shown a marked reluctance to devolve powers of punishment to international organizations. In any case, states may not be a suitable object of punishment. The project of completing international law, or making it more like domestic law, seemed to require, then, the punishment of individual violators. Bad men were to be incarcerated. This was the thrust of much commentary around the Iraq War. If the United States and the United Kingdom really were guilty of breaching international law then, surely, the natural consequence of this was the indictment of the war leaders. This approach was reflected in the questions asked by journalists, in the anti-war banners carried by protesters ('The war is illegal, Bush and Blair are war criminals') and by the various efforts to have US and UK officials indicted before the international criminal court. Only individualized justice could ensure the relevance and meaningfulness of international law. Abstract entities were out, flesh and blood human beings were in.

The personalization of international law through international criminal law is linked to a second broader trend: the emergence of human rights as a field. The move from thinking of international law in terms of 'abstract entities' to conceiving of it as a legal order about individual human beings is invigorated at Nuremberg, and transforms the soul of international law. No longer exclusively about states (or, to a much lesser extent, organizations), it now becomes fixated on the rights and duties of individuals. This is so much so that there is an equation in the public mind of 'human rights' with 'international law'. At least since Nuremberg, states have been seen as potentially self-destructive, rapacious and violent. Initially at least, the human rights system, while it attempted to place the security and integrity of individual human beings centre stage, still made respect for human rights a matter of state responsibility. The (perceived) early failure of human rights instruments can be traced to an erroneous assumption that states would hold each other responsible for any breaches of personal rights. This has happened only very rarely. Greece was taken to the European Court of Human Rights by Denmark, Sweden, Norway and the Netherlands, and the UK was sued by Ireland over the treatment of IRA detainees, but overall the record has been patchy. Even where mechanisms of individual petition were established, such as under the International Covenant for Civil and Political Rights, states found to be in breach of human rights obligations remained under only a weak obligation to remedy any abuses. And, of course, it was states themselves, despite the Nuremberg judgment, that continued to be the relevant 'entities' for the purposes of attributing responsibility even if it was individuals who were doing the torturing or killing (the International Law Commission had exercised itself with the question of state responsibility for almost half a century before its Articles on that topic were adopted by the General Assembly in 2001). The move to individual responsibility, then, in international criminal law, modifies this tendency and has also been hailed as a way of giving human rights law the bite it was thought to lack.[3]

Third, international criminal law promises to advance the demise of sovereignty. In this sense, the recent explosion of institutional innovation in criminal law is hitched to wider trends in the direction of globalization. As the state recedes in importance in the economic, cultural and political spheres, it seems appropriate that its centrality in international law should also disappear (Koskenniemi, 1991; Koh, 2001). Thus, the trials of Milosevic and Hussein, and the decision in *Pinochet*, seem to explicitly deny states some of the privileges they once held in the international order. This is why in encomiums to globalization, the ICC is frequently invoked alongside the WTO, the loosening of state ownership and the deregulation of trade and capital. Sometimes, too, international criminal law is associated with the triumph of global individualism or some form of cosmopolitanism; reposing in the Rome Statute of the International Criminal Court are the lineaments of a new global justice order (Hirsh, 2003). Daniele Archibugi makes this link explicit: 'For all their flaws, existing bodies [of international criminal law] are the embryos of more robust ones that will be needed to guarantee global legality . . . a fully-fledged international criminal court needs to be set up' (Archibugi, 2002: 36).

But it turns out that, despite the claims and promises made by its keenest proponents, international criminal law or the law of war crimes is not, and has not been at its origins, exclusively dedicated to this individualism that lies at the heart of much international justice rhetoric, human rights law and cosmopolitan enthusiasm for international criminal law. Instead, what we find, and what I want to discuss in the remainder of this chapter, is a perpetual tension between the collective and the individual.[4] This manifests itself in a number of different relationships. In the next section, 'State crime and individual responsibility', I discuss a series of institutional choices made throughout modern history between the criminalization of states (what I call, the Versailles Model) and the punishment of individuals (the Nuremberg Model). I conclude that these two models now coexist rather uncomfortably in the contemporary practice of international law with the paradigm instances in each case being the treatment of Iraq after 1991 (and, in particular, Security Council Resolution 687) and the establishment of the ad hoc and permanent Tribunals in The Hague (and Arusha).

Then, in section 3, 'The liability of men and things', I turn to the way in which collective responsibility is built into the doctrinal architecture of much of international criminal law even in its putatively individualistic mode. International criminal law, understood as the trial of individual violators by international courts, cannot escape into individualism entirely. It finds itself perpetually drawn back to group responsibility and communal guilt. In an analysis of the work of tribunals at Nuremberg and The Hague (and here I advert to the Rome Statute, too), I show how doctrines such as joint criminal enterprise, organizational criminality and conspiracy betray international criminal law's roots in, what George Fletcher has called, a romantic view of history and personality, i.e. one in which the individual's behaviour is motivated by, and can only be understood in reference to, larger communities of nation, state or tribe (Fletcher, 2000).

Finally, in the fourth section ('Three Eichmanns'), I turn to broader questions around the structure of war crimes trials and the way in which that structure itself reflects our moral intuitions about responsibility for mass atrocity as well as our apparent allergy to collective punishment (and our willing recourse to it). And I show, too, how implicated in all this is the relationship between individual evil, structural deformity and the tragedy of being human.

Ultimately, this chapter presents the field of international criminal law, or war, law and crime as a bargain (played out in institutional history, in doctrinal innovation and in the structuring principles of both international society and our moral intuitions) between individual blameworthiness and collective guilt.

2   State crime and individual responsibility

The modern institutional trajectory of international criminal law can be understood as a set of transitions between collective guilt and individual responsibility. This history begins at Versailles with the peace imposed on Germany following the Great War, a model of peace repeated to some extent in criminalization efforts at the end of the twentieth century in Iraq, in Libya and in Serbia (Bederman, 2002). The Versailles settlement represents the first such *de facto* criminalization of pariah states in international legal history. Previous post-war rearrangements had contemplated forms of demilitarization or sanctions imposed on defeated states (e.g. the Congress of Vienna in 1815, the peace imposed on France at the end of the Franco-Prussian war of 1872) but none before had placed a state under such intense levels of scrutiny nor applied a regime as punitive as that found at Versailles. Versailles represents the moment when the modern international law of institutions begins, and with it the possibility of applying the machinery of institutional oversight to whole nations. Narrow definitions of criminal law (requiring criminal courts (Higgins, 1995)) or incarceration (*Blaskic*) need to be modified when we contemplate the way in which certain states are stigmatized and punished by international society (Simpson, 2004a).

Under the nineteenth-century conception of international law, and it is a view that persists to this day, breaches of international law were understood as largely bilateral: one state's acts caused injury to a second or third state. Such breaches were dealt with at an inter-state level through a negotiated settlement of claims, or, occasionally, a form of arbitration or through the employment of countermeasures by the injured state.[5] Civil or private law is the appropriate model for understanding international law in this traditional mode. This legal order is composed of a matrix of bilateral relations with the civil suit being paradigmatic (represented by the inter-state dispute settlement mechanism at the International Court of Justice).

By the time of Versailles, though, the Great Powers had begun to see themselves as an incipient 'international community'. Serious violations of that community's dominant mores were no longer thought to be a matter of merely dyadic concern but were understood or reconfigured into a breach of the rights of all states or of international society. At least one of the conditions for the existence of the criminal law was now satisfied – the self-consciousness (and self-righteousness) of a moral community (albeit one largely directed by the Great Powers).[6] This self-righteousness translated into a new belief that victory and defeat in war were not simply a matter of luck or strategy but also implicated questions of collective virtue and criminality (Schmitt, 2003; Pal, 1955). This combination of institutional self-confidence, community self-awareness, and legalism produced the Versailles settlement and the criminalization of Germany. Germany was punished by the society of states, and the extent and intensity of its punishment was akin to that of the criminal sanctions found in many domestic legal orders. The Versailles model of state criminality was marked by a number of highly distinctive qualities.

First, the criminal state was adjudged to have breached one of the fundamental norms of the international legal order. It was never made absolutely clear which norm had been breached but there was general confidence among the statesmen of the time that the German state and its leadership were responsible for a war that the Canadian Prime Minister, Robert Borden, misleadingly but also rather presciently, called a 'crime against humanity' (Bass, 2000: 65). Second, the contractual relationship usually found in armistice and peace agreements with accompanying amnesties (Pal, 1955: 399) (between two private parties, *justi hostes*) was transformed into a relationship between representatives of the legitimate political order and the outlaw state (Schmitt, 2003: 262). Third, the state in question (Germany in this case) was deprived of some of its basic sovereign prerogatives. In Germany's case, the state lost some of its territory, was forced to pay highly punitive damages (in the Entente Note of 10 January 1917, the Allies declared that Germany's liabilities were without limit because it had engaged in an aggressive war) and was obliged to undergo a process of demilitarization underwritten by the international community and overseen by, often ad hoc, international bureaucracies (e.g. the Inter-Allied Commissions of Control charged with ensuring that Germany disarmed). In addition, the criminal state in this case was placed under notice that any breach of the enhanced regime of oversight could result in a resumption of hostilities or an enforcement of treaties of guarantee (Bederman, 2002: 128).

This Versailles model, of course, fell into serious disrepute shortly after it was imposed. Many contemporary critics blamed it for the breakdown in the European order less than two decades later. John Maynard Keynes famously predicted the dire consequences of criminalizing Germany, the United States displayed a marked reluctance to support the more punitive aspects of the settlement, and, of course, the effects of the peace on the German population at large were felt by many people to have been fundamentally unjust. Some of the fault for the rise of the Nazis and the onset of war was laid at the door of the Versailles settlement. It is little wonder, then, that when the Second World War ended, the Allies appeared to renounce the idea of state criminality and resorted to a rejuvenated model of individual responsibility. Nuremberg was a riposte not only to conventional international law with its relentless focus on states' 'civil' liability but also to the state crime model pursued without much success at Versailles.

The orthodox account, then, of the war crimes trials at Nuremberg and Tokyo argues that they were fashioned with a view to cleansing Japan and Germany of collective guilt. The absence of the Emperor from the list of defendants at Tokyo, for example, can be viewed as a symptom of this effort since he was viewed as a symbol of the nation rather than an individual capable of having committed a crime. At Potsdam on 26 July 1945, the Allies offered the following reassurance: 'We do not intend that the Japanese shall be enslaved as a race or destroyed as a nation'. At Nuremberg, too, there was a rhetorical tendency to shift responsibility from the German state to individual Germans and specifically Nazi institutions. The apparent exoneration of the Wehrmacht at Nuremberg and at the postwar Control Council Trials can be understood as part of this process of ridding Germany of the guilt of nations (Boxham, 2001: 178). The development of international criminal law after the Second World War was heavily influenced by the Cold War requirement that Japan and Germany be acquitted of any state crime. Alongside this, the failure to define and criminalize aggression during debates at the United Nations in the 1950s meant that the focus of war crimes prosecutions would return to crimes thought capable of being carried out by individuals (war crimes, crimes against humanity and genocide).

The above account does not quite accord with the historical record, though. In 1944, the 'Nuremberg solution' was still in some important quarters a minority position. Churchill and Stalin had favoured summary executions of large numbers of Germans who were to be deprived of the right of a trial, and plans were under way to occupy and emasculate Germany. The most developed of these proposals adopted an even more punitive version of the Versailles model. This was US Treasury Secretary, Henry Morgenthau's, Memorandum of September 1944. Here was a classic Carthaginian Peace (Beschloss, 2002; Bass, 2000). Under Morgenthau's proposal, Germany was to be deindustrialized and returned to a largely agrarian state denuded of military capability. This pastoralization of a great European state was to be accompanied by a series of 'political' actions against high-ranking Nazis (they were to be shot under summary procedure). The Morgenthau Plan was defeated by an unlikely coalition of American legalists (notably, Secretary of State Stimson) who wanted war crimes trials and Soviet officials who were happy to see the Nazis disposed of after some sort of show trial (Beschloss, 2002). The British reluctantly joined with the group seeking trials, and Morgenthau was left isolated and disappointed.

This defeat of the Morgenthau Plan is sometimes taken to represent the triumph of liberal legalism and individual responsibility over vengeful politics and collective guilt. However, elements of Morgenthau's Plan survived alongside Nuremberg. Most notably, of course, the state of Germany was divided into four zones and then two political entities. It was, in effect, temporarily extinguished as a state (this was accompanied by the brutal treatment accorded to German POWs (Bacque, 1999)). But, alongside this, there was the designation of Germany (and Japan) in the United Nations Charter as 'enemy states', against whom military action could be undertaken without reference to the UN's standard provisions restricting the use of force.[7] In any case, at least as far as the US Zone was concerned, the Morgenthau Plan was supplanted by JCS 1067 Directive and the Potsdam Protocol (1945). The Directive, which was recommended as practice for the other four controlling authorities, contemplated a highly intrusive programme of economic control, decentralization of indigenous political power and complete military and 'industrial' disarmament (indeed, the Directive cautions controlling authorities from taking any action that would enhance German economic power). The Potsdam Protocol (1945), meanwhile, set out the conditions for Four-Power Occupation. These included action to permanently prevent 'the revival or reorganization of German militarism' (Principle 3(a)) and the encouragement of primarily agricultural production (Principle 13). The Potsdam agreement, then, to a certain extent, undercut the apparent purpose of the Nuremberg Tribunal by setting out as its core principle the need: 'To convince the German people that they have suffered a total military defeat and that they cannot escape responsibility for what they have brought upon themselves, since their own ruthless warfare and the fanatical Nazi resistance have destroyed German economy and made chaos and suffering inevitable' (Principle 3(ii)). This was a long way from the IMT's move from abstract entities or collective responsibility to individual guilt. Here, the romantic idea of attributing agency to the nation had supplanted, or, at least, supplemented the liberal project of punishing individualized and autonomous moral behaviour.

The origins of contemporary international criminal law in post-war Germany, then, are found in both the 'stern [individualised] justice' (Moscow, 1943) meted out at the IMT and the broader notions of collective responsibility found at Potsdam. It is no surprise that the present period is one in which these two conceptions of accountability – individual responsibility and state crime – have both come to occupy prominent positions in the international legal armoury. By the time of the revival of international criminal law in the 1990s at The Hague, individual responsibility was an important means by which the Great Powers could respond to mass atrocity, and rogue states could be rehabilitated. In emphasizing the subjective roots of criminality and deviance, the turn to individual responsibility had the potential to cleanse the state of responsibility (and, at the same time, exonerate the state system). We need only think of the way the states drafting the statute for an international criminal court sometimes imagined their task. In order to proceed effectively, negotiators had to envisage themselves as acting on behalf of states and the state system against rogue individuals apparently disconnected from these same states. So, the call was for 'international cooperation' and for states to exercise their duty to punish perpetrators (Rome Statute Preamble). The field of struggle was to be between states applying the techniques of criminal repression (jurisdiction, coordination, detection) and rogue individuals determined to disrupt that system by committing gross violations of the public order (often on behalf of rogue groups or outlaw governments). In Security Council Resolution 1593, referring the Darfur human rights abuses to the International Criminal Court, the Council, in Operative Paragraph 2, called on Sudan to cooperate with and provide assistance to the Court in its investigations. International criminal law relies on the fiction of detachability; the state, whether it be Serbia or Sudan, is imagined as an entity distinct from its bad apples and rogue statesmen. For the Prosecutor, Carla Del Ponte, this was the message of the Milosevic trial. The Serbian people were the innocent dupes of a powerful criminal mind. Indeed, the Serbs, too, had been wronged by Milosevic. At the beginning of her opening statement, the Prosecutor provides a summation of the individualized version of international criminal law:

> 'The accused in this case, as in all cases before the Tribunal, is charged as an individual. He is prosecuted on the basis of his individual criminal responsibility. No state or organisation is on trial here today. The indictments do not accuse an entire people of being collectively guilty of the crimes, even the crime of genocide. It may be tempting to generalise when dealing with the conduct of leaders at the highest level, but that is an error that must be avoided. Collective guilt forms no part of the Prosecution case.' (*Milosevic* (Transcripts), 12 February 2002: 4)

She goes on to say however: 'I do, of course, intend to explore the degree to which the power and influence of the accused extended over others . . .'. It is this 'exploration' that is the subject of the next section where I consider those doctrines of international criminal justice that seek to situate the individual accused within a criminal enterprise or community of responsible persons. Historically, as I have noted, the attention given to collective guilt has resolved itself as a focus on the societal liability found, for example, at Versailles and at Potsdam. This inclination has not disappeared, and indeed, seemed newly invigorated at precisely the point when the idea of individual justice through international criminal tribunals was itself undergoing a revival.

This reinvigoration happened largely in three domains. First, at the United Nations the International Law Commission, the UN's law reform body, elaborated a set of principles that sought to distinguish ordinary wrongs committed by states with a group of breaches that appeared to be more fundamental than mere delicts. In doing so, the ILC considered whether to import the distinction between tort and crime from domestic law into public international law. As one commentator asked: 'Can a state commit a crime?' (Pellet, 1999). In its 1996 Draft Articles on State Responsibility, the Commission defined a series of acts that would give rise to criminal liability on the part of states. These included genocide, aggression and serious environmental offences (Article 19). More importantly, the Commission developed rules outlining the consequences to be attached to such criminal acts. The most significant of these, found in Articles 43, 45 and 52 of these Draft Articles, contemplate placing criminal states within a special juridical category whereby any reparations or sanctions imposed on them would have seriously deleterious effects on the sovereignty, immunity and dignity of such states (Simpson, 2004a).

These principles resembled, in some respects, the Versailles Model discussed earlier. States were to be subject to uniquely punitive quasi-penal sanctions and, in a rather unfortunate nod to the Versailles Treaty, Article 52 declared that sanctions directed against criminal states (or restitution claimed from the criminal state) would not be subject to the normal limitations set out in Article 43 (typically, and for cases involving mere delictual liability, restitution was only permissible to the extent that it '. . . would not seriously jeopardize the political independence or economic stability of the State which has committed the internationally wrongful act, whereas the injured State would not be similarly affected if it did not obtain restitution in kind'). Criminal states, under the system envisaged by the ILC, would be in a similar situation to post-Versailles Germany. As was the case with Germany, sanctions would be applied to contemporary criminal states regardless of the consequences on the internal politico-economic order. A critical attribute of state sovereignty, the dignity of states, would be denied the outlaw state in the name of enforcing a higher order international law.

Five years prior to the drafting of the 1996 Articles, the Security Council passed Resolution 687. From at least that point onwards, Iraq became a criminal state and its people subject to collective punishment. The second domain in which the idea of collective responsibility re-emerged was that of the Security Council. The Council deprived Iraq of part of its territory and prohibited it from acquiring certain types of weaponry. The people suffered seriously as a result of sanctions. The UN Population Fund released a report in 2003 stating that the number of women dying in childbirth had tripled between 1989 and 2002, and the respected British medical journal *The Lancet* published research in 1995 suggesting that 567,000 Iraqi children had died as a result of sanctions.[8] In the succeeding decade, the outlawry of whole states became a favoured technique of international administration in Serbia, in Afghanistan, in Libya and in Iraq. These states were confined within a system of surveillance and oversight, deprived of the traditional privileges of sovereignty and reduced to a state of impoverishment. This was the state system's equivalent of 'incarceration' (*Blaskic*), and, despite the protestations of the Great Powers and the international community, the result was a form of old-fashioned collective punishment directed at a population at large.

Alongside all this, and representing the third sphere in which state crime has emerged, the Great Powers themselves began to deploy the image of the criminal state in their rhetoric (e.g. Prime Minister Blair's 'irresponsible states' and President Bush's 'enemies of civilisation', each recalling

Roosevelt's description of the Nazi State as an 'international outlaw' (Woetzel, 1960)), in the work of government bureaucracies (the US State Department's 'states of concern'), in legislation (the US Anti-Terrorism and Effective Death-Penalty Act 1996, a statute suspending the operation of sovereign immunity in cases where a designated terrorist state is sued in the United States by (American) victims of acts of terrorism, placed a group of states on a terrorist list (s.221)), and in legal memoranda seeking to justify the illegal detention of enemy combatants at Guantanamo Bay (Gonzales Memorandum). These developments were reflected in turn by scholarship that sought to draw distinctions between civilized, democratic or decent states, and indecent outlaws (Tesón, 1992; Rawls, 1999), and in the turn to reparations in the UN's human rights system.[9]

The 1990s, then, was a decade in which the idea of individual responsibility certainly underwent an astonishing revival (the ICTY, ICTR and the ICC) in international relations.[10] But, at the same time, and less visibly and self-consciously, the system also was embracing, again, the Versailles Model of state criminalization. The institutional history of international criminal law is captured in the Commentary on the 1996 Draft Code on Crimes Against the Peace and Security of Mankind where the ILC notes: 'The state may thus remain responsible and be unable to exonerate itself from responsibility by invoking the prosecution or punishment of the individuals who committed the crime', and in Article 25(4) of the ICC Statute: 'No provision in this Statute relating to individual criminal responsibility shall affect the responsibility of States under international law'.[11] The enhanced status and moral appeal of individual criminal responsibility is undermined by the temptations of collective responsibility. It may be that the tension between state crime and individual responsibility (exemplified by the fact that on 27 February 2006 in The Hague, two cases were being heard simultaneously: one, *Prosecutor v. Milosevic*, concerning the *individual* responsibility of the former Serb leader; the other, *Bosnia v. Serbia*, also about genocide but this time *state* responsibility for the crime of genocide) cannot be resolved because the structure of international society and the suppositions of our own belief-systems rest upon that tension.

3   The liability of men and things

The co-existence of collective guilt and individual responsibility, identified in the discussion of institutional preferences in the field, is reflected at the level of doctrine even if, at first blush, international criminal law seems wedded to modes of liability that are highly individualistic. In some respects, it is a declaration of intent concerning personal liability – a turn from structure to agency – that marks off the international criminal law enterprise from the rest of the field of public international law. International criminal law's core instruments are concerned to advertise the centrality of individualized justice just as the key commentaries are keen to enumerate its virtues. The statutes of the ICTY, ICTR and ICC follow the Nuremberg Principles by placing individual accountability centre stage. The Charter of the IMT gives the Tribunal (in Article 6) jurisdiction over 'persons' who acting as 'individuals' commit any of the listed crimes. The ICTY Statute states at Article 7(1): 'A person who planned, instigated, ordered, committed . . . [a crime] . . . shall be individually responsible for the crime'. Article 6 makes clear that this jurisdiction is to be found over 'natural persons' not abstract entities. The Rome Statute, too, refers consistently to natural persons and individual responsibility (Article 25). The law of war crimes, then, seems to mark a switch from the abstractions of the general field of public international law to the flesh and blood corporeality of human culpability. As Antonio Cassese puts it, the central idea behind individualized liability is that a defendant ought not to be punished for acts perpetrated by other individuals. Collective responsibility, as he puts it, is 'no longer acceptable' (Cassese, 2003b: 137). These doctrinal efforts promise simplicity (it is no longer necessary to explain the reasons why crimes are committed – 'motive', as the Court in *Jelisic* noted, is not relevant to questions of intent), parsimony (the question of guilt is pared down to an investigation of one person's mental state and capacity) and depoliticization (the central questions become narrowly psychological rather than expansively political).[12]

These doctrinal projects, like the institutional ones discussed above, are frequently undone by the fact that the very acts criminalized under international law are those least susceptible to individualized justice. International criminal law's core offences are crimes against humanity, serious violations of the laws of war (war crimes), genocide and aggression. This is reflected in the IMT Charter at Nuremberg, and in the crimes included under Article 5 of the Rome Statute. In each of these cases, the typical crimes are, what José Alvarez called 'crimes of state', i.e. crimes arising from organizational tendencies or collective choices (Alvarez, 1999).

Indeed, the rhetorical attention international criminal lawyers devote to individual responsibility is ill-matched to the mood of the general public when it comes to questions of responsibility. An example of precisely this tension occurred in 2005, when the UK Government announced that it would begin prosecuting British soldiers for alleged war crimes committed during the occupation of Iraq in 2003. There was almost universal condemnation of this decision in the UK media. Many commentators and letter-writers, while conceding that the soldiers were accused of very grave crimes, could not imagine an international criminal law that applied to one-off acts of murder or assault committed by the personnel of states engaged in largely lawful combat. The commanding officer of the regiment most closely involved stated that: 'From the moment that Mr Baha Mousa lost his life while in our custody, the regiment has made clear that this was an isolated, tragic incident that should never have happened and which I and every member bitterly regrets' (Tweedie, 2005). In the House of Lords, similar sentiments were expressed:

> What is now hanging over him and other soldiers is that the case may be referred to the International Criminal Court. That court was not set up for that purpose. It was set up to deal with cases of genocide and with war criminals. That that gallant officer [Colonel Mendonca, the Commanding Officer of the soldiers accused of killing Baha Mousa in custody] could be in the same dock as that in which Milosevic has appeared must be wrong in itself. (Hoyle, 2005)

As I indicated in chapter 2, these commentators equate the idea of war crimes with the practice of mass atrocity. The Nazi genocide, and its contemporary variants, loom over the field as ideal types. The critics of the Williams and Mendonca investigations are responding to a legitimate sense that war crimes law, in its broadest sense, is about mass criminality. This is a well-founded intuition. International criminal law, it turns out, even in its individualistic mode, is very often deeply concerned with structure. At a very obvious level, the Rome Statute restates this in its Preamble, and elsewhere. The negotiators were at pains to emphasize that the Court would have jurisdiction over only 'the most serious crimes of concern to the international community'. But how were such crimes to be understood? In the case of aggression and genocide there is an in-built presumption against the idea that an individual can commit either of these crimes acting independently of a state apparatus. Aggression is an interstate crime, defined as such in countless international instruments, and capable of being committed only if a group of individuals captures the machinery of the state. The discomfort expressed in 1919 by the Commission on the Authorship of the War at Versailles is reflected in the continuing lack of agreement found in the negotiations for an international criminal court.

Likewise, the classic genocides of the twentieth century have been carried out either by states or state-like entities. One of the distinguishing elements of genocide is its sheer scale (in *Jelisic*, the ICTY discusses the possibility of the 'lone genocidal maniac' but this figure is more hypothetical than real and even the Court sounds unconvinced about the monster it has created). The mass killing of national, ethnic, racial or religious groups requires a degree of planning and organization typically beyond the capacity of all but state or state-like instrumentalities.[13]

Crimes against humanity and, in particular, war crimes appear on first glance to be quite different. The acts associated with these crimes – murder, torture, hostage-taking, improper use of a flag of truce – are capable of being committed by individuals acting in an individual capacity. These crimes appear, then, to represent international criminal law's true face: the face of individualized justice. However, even here, at the definitional level, there are qualifications and conditions that disclose again this co-existence of the collective and the individual.

The Rome Statute defines crimes against humanity as acts (including murder, extermination and rape) committed 'as part of a widespread or systematic attack directed against any civilian population'. An earlier draft had made 'widespread and systematic' conjunctive but even in their eventual formulation it is clear that a requirement of collective action is retained. A systematic or widespread attack, after all, is not something that can be readily undertaken by a single individual. The definition of war crimes comes attached with a similar qualifier. While war crimes are defined as grave breaches of the Geneva Conventions and other analogous offences, the ICC is to possess jurisdiction only over such crimes when committed 'as part of a plan or policy or as part of a large-scale commission of such crimes' (Article 8). This suggests that the ICC would lack jurisdiction over the likes of Mendonca and Williams (regardless of the substance of the accusations). Critics of the UK Government, then, are simply drawing on a tradition in international criminal law, reflected in the Rome Statute, which understands 'war crimes' and 'crimes against humanity' as references to organized mass atrocity perpetrated in the Balkans and in the Second World War rather than the aberrant behaviour of British soldiers in Iraq.

This tension between individual agency and collective responsibility has been a powerful influence on the development of international criminal law since its inception at Nuremberg. The Nuremberg Trial represents a particular paradox in this regard because at the very moment when individual responsibility (the accountability of, what Churchill called, the 'gang' of Nazis) was introduced onto the international scene in the form of individual trials, the American delegation was working behind the scenes to formulate charges that would imply a form of collective guilt. These ideas formed the back-bone to the IMT Charter. In Article 6, the crime of aggression included the offence of participating 'in a common plan or conspiracy' for the accomplishment of planning or prosecuting aggressive war, and the final provision of that Article charged that those who participated in the formulation or execution of the common plan or conspiracy to commit Charter crimes would be 'responsible for all acts performed by any persons in execution of such a plan'. The purposes of the trial began to work against each other. On one hand, in order to pre-cipitate the rehabilitation of Germany as a state, the Allies were keen to extract the poisonous elements from German society by identifying the ways in which the Nazi state had been captured and utilized for evil ends. On the other hand, the American conspiracy plan was meant to strike at the heart of that same society, and the broader the conspiracy claim became, the less plausible was its core proposition: that the conspirators were guilty of a massive organized conspiracy but the German people were innocent of participation in it. The idea that the leading German war criminals could be prosecuted with 'joint participation in a broad criminal enterprise' also contradicted one of the central pillars of the idea of indi-vidual responsibility because high-ranking Nazis would be prosecuted for acts committed by other individuals: 'Under such a charge there are admis-sible in evidence the acts of any of the conspirators done in furtherance of the conspiracy, whether or not these acts were in themselves criminal . . . .'.[14] The central core of individual responsibility, the mental culpability of the accused, was slowly stripped away by the drafters.

The turn to the collective gathered pace around the idea of criminal organizations, too. When Stettinius met Eden and Molotov in San Fran-cisco in the middle of 1945, the Americans had already formulated their plan to criminalize whole strata of German society: 'We proposed to put on trial the Nazi organisations themselves rather than the individuals and convict them all of criminal conspiracy to control the world . . . Once having proved the organisation to be guilty, each person who had joined the organisation voluntarily would ipso facto be guilty of a war crime' (Marrus, 1997: 35). The mass criminality outlined and envisaged in these plans, and in the core ideas of conspiracy and criminal organization, departed from Western standards of individual guilt and personal respon-sibility at the very moment of international law's apparent and much-trumpeted transformation from a body of law exclusively concerned with state responsibility to one in which individual humans and not abstract entities would be judged by the ideals of the international legal order.

International criminal law, then, is revealed at its origins as a composite of collective and individual notions of responsibility, and this carries over to the trials in The Hague where there are engineered a number of successor doctrines to those elaborated in the 1940s. At the ICTY, for example, the Court has developed a doctrine of 'joint criminal enterprise' (a phrase not even found in the ICTY's Statute). The Court deployed this in convicting Dusko Tadic where it conceded that many crimes committed in war, rather than being individual acts of wrong-doing 'constitute a manifestation of the collective criminality' (*Tadic* (Judgement) para. 191). Joint criminal enterprise is attractive to war crimes courts because it is sensitive to the reality of organized crime during periods of armed struggle (Osiel, 2005). More controversially, though, the doctrine is used by Courts to avoid the responsibility of determining who actually killed or tortured in specific cases. It is sufficient that the Court is able to show that the accused was involved in the system of criminality and had some knowledge of its ultimate criminal purpose. It has not always been necessary for the accused to have shared in that criminal purpose. As Verna Haan argues, joint criminal enterprise is useful in difficult cases '. . . where the accused had acted in the sphere of politics' (Haan, 2005). But this means criminalizing political behaviour as well as the corollary of this, the politicization of criminal law (see chapter 1).[15]

The scale of crime contemplated by international criminal law means that there is often likely to be present some element of organizational or mass criminality. Prosecutors and judges, particularly those concerned to steer a course between an absurd and ahistorical individualism (the idea that one person commits genocide or carries out ethnic cleansing) and a reductive structural determinism (the idea that the state or culture or people are guilty of these crimes at some collective level), are left with two awkward tasks. They must be satisfied that there is proof of personal guilt without ignoring the broader context in which crimes take place and they must limit the contextual investigations in order to secure the 'innocence' of the society from which the perpetrators emerged.

4   Three Eichmanns

The discussion up to this point has been concerned with the institutional and doctrinal responses to a complex relationship between individual guilt and collective responsibility. But this conflict, perhaps, reflects deeper tensions in the structure of international society and in our ethical predispositions. This is a book about international law and society not a philosophical treatise so I only have a limited amount to say about the latter question but it clearly animates and underpins the narrower questions of institutional (section 2) and doctrinal (section 3) choice. Who, or what, commits war crimes, crimes against humanity or crimes against peace? This is a question with ethical, legal and political answers. As I have argued, the Nuremberg and Tokyo war crimes trials represented an attempt to individualize responsibility for war. Of course, prior to Nuremberg, lawyers had developed rules on the proper conduct of warfare but only very few criminal prosecutions associated with this body of norms had, by then, taken place (e.g. in Leipzig after the Great War (*Llandovery Castle, Dover Castle*)) and these were highly unsatisfactory (Woetzel, 1960; Bass, 2000). Indeed, it was doubtful whether the existing legal rules anticipated or permitted criminal prosecution at all. Arguably, then, as we have seen, Nuremberg introduced into international law the conceit of individual responsibility for gross crimes. But it also, and even more contentiously, developed principles of organizational criminality. So, while the Tribunal convicted von Ribbentrop, Göring, Streicher, Keitel et al. of having committed individual offences against the law of nations, it also declared whole organizations, such as the SS and the SD, criminal. This declaration, in turn, created the possibility of 'fixing the criminality of its members' (IMT Judgement (1946)). However, this hardly solved what David Luban called 'the central moral challenge of our time, the problem of moral responsibility in a bureaucratic setting' (Luban, 1987: 13).

In thinking about criminality at the level found in the Nazi era or, to a lesser extent, during the Vietnam War and in Serbia, one is faced with a problem of structure and agency. The structural analysis of criminality inevitably focuses on processes, social behaviour, institutions, hierarchies and so on (i.e. deviance through the eyes of Kafka and Edelman). There are variations on this theme of structural explanation in Arendt's 'rule by nobody' (Arendt, 1970: 38), in Marx's bureaucratic mind (Marx, *Critique* (quoted in Luban, 1987: 68ff.)) and in Raul Hilberg's contention that: 'The killing . . . was no atrocity in the conventional sense. It was infinitely more, and that 'more' was the work of a far-flung, sophisticated bureaucracy' (Hilberg, 2002: 59). In the light of this, war crimes trials at best can appear as partial justice, at worst a form of scapegoating.

Structural analysis can yield important insights but it is not without its failings, particularly when translated into legal norms attributing structural responsibility. On one hand, collective responsibility might result in a situation where everyone is guilty and, therefore, no one is. Daniel Ellsberg, quoted by Sanford Levinson, speaks of the tendency to see Vietnam as 'a tragedy without villains, war crimes without criminals, lies without liars, a process of immaculate deception' (Levinson, 1973). On the other hand, the result of collective responsibility might be the criminalization of conduct that lacks the components of crime as traditionally understood by the liberal legal mind (*mens rea* and *actus reus*).

In approaching this dilemma, George Fletcher identifies a liberal bias in international criminal law's emphasis on agency or individual responsibility. This bias, he argues, 'obscures a basic truth' about war crimes. These are 'deeds that by their very nature are committed by groups and typically against individuals and members of groups' (Fletcher, 2002). For Fletcher, the tension between collective and individual notions of guilt or responsibility can be understood through a contrast between what he calls 'romantic' and 'liberal' views of war and guilt. The liberal conception of responsibility is, of course, familiar enough. Liberals focus on individuals as free agents capable of making political choices, consuming freely, and, crucially, of doing wrong as individuals abstracted from the social group to which they belong. Criminal concepts like 'intent' go to the heart of this liberal view of individual human agency. Yet, a less familiar, romantic ontology also pervades international criminal law. This emphasizes the role of the collective will and the idea of the people as the 'folk' or as an independent actor capable of greatness and, of course, great evil.

International criminal lawyers might be less surprised than Fletcher to discover that this romantic sensibility permeates their work. After all, international law is replete with assumptions about 'the collective will'. The creation of legal norms through customary practice, for example, involves an acceptance that there can be such a thing as 'state consent'. Group guilt, however, is an idea that has made international lawyers uneasy since Versailles, and criminal lawyers anxious since the onset of modernity. Fletcher wants to rehabilitate this idea but he does so with understandable caution. The individual and his or her responsibility 'remain central'. The dangers of collective guilt (its vivid historical and biblical connotations, and its ill-suitedness to criminal procedure and the rule of law) are obvious. However, Fletcher believes collective guilt has a role to play in mitigating the punishment of those individuals whose acts are both individual and also collective. To put it bluntly, an Eichmann or Milosevic who commits mass atrocities in the context of a diverse and decent society in which there is a clear possibility of self-correction is more culpable than the real historical Eichmanns and Milosevics. The 'climate of moral degeneracy' (Fletcher, 2002: 1541) produced by the 'collective' contributes to the crime.

International criminal law, though, seems to work in the opposite direction. The prosecution of Milosevic is a way of punishing him for *his* crimes *and* the crimes of the Serbian state. Instead of mitigation we have aggravation (at 1542). Because there is a desire to see Serbia rehabilitated (in international society, individuals are disposable but states much less so) and to ward off the dangers of Serbian revanchism, the emphasis is on producing some sort of closure through trial. Thus the oscillations of subjective and collective guilt were likely, prior to the former President's death, to resolve themselves, at least formally, through the conviction of Milosevic. But the credibility of this conviction from the perspective of international criminal justice would have depended largely on how well the prosecution and Court were able to uncover the criminality of the Serbian state. After all, mass murderers are known for their notorious reluctance directly to kill people. Eichmann was famously squeamish at the sight of blood, and Albert Speer found his visits to concentration camps impossibly confronting. Likewise it is possible that Milosevic had no history of direct killing. The emphasis, then, was on Milosevic's indirect responsibility, with the prosecution case resting largely on Milosevic's command responsibility for illegal acts committed by subordinates and for his leadership role in a joint criminal enterprise dedicated to the commission of genocide against Kosovar Albanians and Bosnian Muslims. Paradoxically, then, the more effective the Court was in building a record of mass atrocity and securing a conviction, the more likely it was to, indirectly at least, indict the Serbian state as a whole.

Coming to this dilemma from the opposite direction, Sanford Levinson, in an article written during the Vietnam War, argued that the problem lies not in a lack of mitigation but rather in the absence of any responsibility at all (Levinson, 1973). The dilemmas identified by Levinson are largely those of Fletcher though the problem is presented differently. How is individual culpability and responsibility to be secured in the context of bureaucratic enterprises? Levinson believes this can be accomplished through a teasing out of individual command responsibility in times of war. He begins by rejecting three other possibilities. The first is to engage in collective criminal punishment. This fails the test of fairness because of over-inclusiveness; innocent citizens would become criminally liable. A second possibility is to impose civil liability on the state. This is deemed unsatisfactory because tort-based remedies cannot capture the moral opprobrium associated with war crimes. The third possibility is to do nothing. Levinson worries about this option on the grounds that there would be no opportunity to 'restore a moral harmony which is dislocated when justice is done' (p. 273).

According to Levinson, then, the preferred model is to be derived from the existing jurisprudence at Nuremberg and in particular at the trials following Nuremberg. War criminality depends on finding and prosecuting discrete criminals (p. 251). The guilt of military and civilian leaders will be determined by their level of involvement in policy-making and implementation, the power they possess over that policy and the opposition they express towards criminal policies (see, e.g., the 'High Command Case'). Armed with principles derived from the substantive jurisprudence of the tribunals and the law of command responsibility, a reasonable effort can be made to secure individual responsibility. Of course, as Levinson knows, this will work best in judging a regime dedicated to the meticulous documentation of state policy and its enactment (e.g. Nazi Germany) and will work less well in relation to a system in which power is diffuse, commands are informal and constitutional authority is enigmatic (the United States in Vietnam). In the latter case, Levinson seems to argue for some informal procedures along the lines of the Russell Tribunal and the recently convened 'comfort women' trial (these trials have demonstrated that the failure of official criminal law to punish may not be fatal to efforts at stigmatizing those guilty of international crimes).

Perhaps this debate and international criminal law, itself, simply reflect a wider need in the culture to see war criminals as at the same time uniquely evil ('no one but Milosevic could have led the Serbs to such moral depths'), culturally representative ('Milosevic simply anthropomorphizes a system gone horribly wrong') and typically human ('what would I have done in Milosevic's shoes?'). In the Eichmann trial, these debates came to a head. If the law, war and crime dilemma at Nuremberg involved applying law to the problem of exceptional, unprecedented criminality, then the Eichmann Trial revealed another perhaps more disturbing symptom of modern industrial society: the figure of the unexceptional political mass murderer. At Nuremberg and Tokyo, there are traces of the idea of 'ordinary' criminality, but the trials were largely dedicated to proving the existence of a criminal enterprise dictated by a small, but powerful, elite within Germany's and Japan's heavily militarized and ideologically deformed society. Eichmann, though, presented a problem. Was he exceptional? Banal? Human?

In the most famous picture of Adolf Eichmann, he sits, inside the courtroom, in a glass booth staring impassively ahead. The evil of the Holocaust is heaped upon this Eichmann. This Eichmann was portrayed in his trial as a 'hater' (Poliakov, 1956), a man of exceptional evil who claimed he had not killed sufficient numbers of Jews, who disobeyed only one order – the command from Himmler telling him to cease the murders – and who charged Jewish children a half fare for the rail journey to Treblinka (Lacquer, 2004). This is the Eichmann who was, in fact, profoundly evil in some ordinary sense. He regretted not killing more Jews in Europe, he showed no remorse for the Holocaust and he often boasted about his important role in mass murder and deportation. In a variation on this, there are portraits of Eichmann in which he is neither banal nor ordinary but, instead, a bureaucratic genius. This is the Eichmann who had overseen the destruction of the European Jews from a relatively small office and with a relatively small staff. Eichmann has been described as a clown but he was a clown who played the violin and had read Kant's *The Critique of Pure Reason*. He applied his intelligence to a life shaped by his senior role in a system of governance that sought to undo the Enlightenment project. For him, the categorical imperative was the opposite of Kant's. The idea was to avoid putting oneself in another's shoes. Perhaps Eichmann was ordinary and representative but he was representative in a particular way. He was not one of Christopher Browning's *Ordinary Men* or, indeed, one of Daniel Goldhagen's *Willing Executioners*. Eichmann was exceptionally powerful. *This* Eichmann is alleged to have drafted the letter sent from Göring to Heydrich on 31 July 1941 authorizing a 'final solution' to the Jewish question.

Then, there is the Adolf Eichmann who perfectly captures the breakdown of a moral universe; neither better nor worse than a thousand other Nazi functionaries, he somehow belongs behind a glass booth and on trial. He is the bureaucrat in his transparent office, a former vacuum cleaner salesman who comes to be implicated in mass criminality: the accidental genocidaire. This is the 'banal Eichmann' that Hannah Arendt made notorious. He was certainly ordinary enough to escape indictment at Nuremberg, though this is hardly conclusive. Fritzsche and Sauckel were unexceptional individuals, too (Neave, 1978: 137). For Hannah Arendt, Eichmann was the petty bureaucrat, the clown who managed to work his way up the organizational ladder in the normal way: '. . . a German civil servant, absorbed in his work and getting no glory for it' (as Gerald Reitlinger put it) (Lacquer, 2004). This Eichmann is ubiquitous. This is the Eichmann who *became* Eichmann because of his trial. Prior to the trial there would have been very little to write about this 'obscure lieutenant-colonel' (Lacquer: 7). Since the trial, Eichmann has generated several biographies (the most recent of which is David Cesarani's *Eichmann: His Life and Crimes*) and numerous essays and articles.

Before his trial, Eichmann was interviewed on several occasions. One of his interlocutors, an examining psychiatrist, was quizzed by the press about his views on the accused. Was he normal, they asked? The psychiatrist replied: 'More normal, at any rate, than I am having examined him' (*Granta*, 1982: 25). When we look closely at the picture of Eichmann in his bullet-proof booth, we see a third Eichmann, represented in this case not by Eichmann himself but by the stenographer sitting in front of Eichmann; he is the very image of the original, a bespectacled doppelgänger. This Eichmann is, of course, the Eichmann of our nightmares. Not inhuman, he is supremely human. He is the representative *Homo sapiens* – no different, in some respects, from the man sitting in front of him. He is Tojo tending his garden (Maga, 2002: 49) or Hitler playing with his nieces. He is the man George Steiner describes who '. . . can read Goethe or Rilke in the evening . . . he can play Bach and Schubert and go to his day's work at Auschwitz in the morning' (Steiner, 1961: 699). Only circumstances change, man remains the same.

In 1961, Adolf Eichmann, in a Jerusalem prison, awaiting his trial for crimes against the Jewish people and crimes against humanity, would not have been aware of an experiment being conducted in the United States into a behavioural phenomenon with which he came to be associated. In that year, the *New Haven Register* carried an advertisement asking for volunteers to participate in a memory experiment. They were to be paid $4 an hour to take part in a series of tests involving the application of electric shocks to a number of subjects. The volunteers were positioned in front of a fake shock machine that appeared to administer electric currents to the subjects (who, themselves, were insiders, part of the experimentation team). The electric shocks, increased in 15-volt segments reaching a maximum level of 450 volts, were applied to 'wrong' answers given by the subject. The volunteers could hear, but not see, the subjects. The levers used to apply the shocks were marked from slight shock through to severe shock to potentially fatal shock. Severe shock began at 315 volts with death or severe injury reached at the maximum of 450 volts. As the shocks reached the 300 mark, the subject would often begin crying out in pain and desperation. Sixty-five per cent of volunteers applied the full 450 volts, often in distress themselves and often in response to insistent assertions from the experiment leaders that the experiment continue. Stanley Milgram claimed to have conducted the experiments because he was curious about whether there were sufficient numbers of people in the United States who might have been capable of running a Nazi-style laager in the United States. After the experiments, he concluded, wryly, that there were enough people in New Haven, Connecticut, to operate the camps (Diski, 2004; Blass, 2004). The third Eichmann, then, is the most disturbing; he is unexceptional, an ordinary man receiving extraordinary orders.

In the end, there is an inescapable tendency to see mass criminality as a uniquely individualized expression of criminal psychopathology ('Hitler's evil mind'), a matter of socio-political joint responsibility (the failures of Versailles and the League), historical inevitability (the trajectory of modernity) or national temperament ('the German people'). The constitution of international criminal law has reflected these apparent tendencies at three different levels: in the institutional oscillations between state crime and individual responsibility, in the doctrinal ambiguities of a juridical order concerned with personal agency and collective conspiracies, and in the way the field is structured around the problem of the moral responsibility of groups and persons.

4

Law's Promise
Punishment, Memory and Dissent

I don't want anyone to forget what happened to us.

R. McCarthy, 'They must be brought to court'[1]

1 Teaching history

War crimes trials infiltrate and shape political life and collective consciousness through the 'judicial memory' (Bloxham, 2001: 2) they produce and
reproduce, and through the 'dissident histories' (Simpson, 1997) or 'dissenting judgements' (Simpson, 2004b) engendered by the trial. This chapter
is about these didactic and dissident functions, and their compatibility
with, what many take to be, the primary function of a war crimes proceeding: the trial of an individual wrongdoer. In two prior chapters, I discuss
the ways in which international criminal law, or the law of war crimes, is
constituted by two sets of relations. In chapter 2, I advanced an argument
about the conjunctions and disjunctions of domestic and international
space in the field. Chapter 3 was concerned with the tension between
individualized forms of culpability and communal wrongs. In this present
chapter, I investigate the idea that war crimes trials narrate an episode of
national or world history with a view to educating a particular population
(Douglas, 2001; Hirsh, 2003), and I discuss the tension between this function and other effects or imperatives of trial.

The use of law as an idiom for responding to and shaping traumatic
history raises some dilemmas. The discussion here is divided into six sec-
tions. At the core of the chapter is a consideration of three problems and
one 'promise' of law and pedagogy. I call these three problems the problems of *proportion* (section 2) (is law capable of developing languages and
mechanisms responsive to the horrors of mass atrocity?), *incompatibility*
(section 3) (can law teach history and, at the same time, do justice?), and
legitimation (section 4) (are the histories produced by trial largely intended
to lend authority to the prosecuting institution or state?). Part of the
promise of war crimes trials lies in the possibility of dissent – the capacity

of the trial to generate unexpected histories and conceptions of justice. This is discussed further in section 5. These central discussions are framed by an initial account of law's commemorative or didactic function ('Teaching history', section 1) and a concluding section on law's tendency to erase some histories at the moment of invoking others ('Forgetting', section 6).

What can war crimes trials show us? Can they illuminate our understandings of trauma and tragedy? Of what would such an illumination consist? What is the relationship between evidence and truth, between the commitments of history-making and the procedures of law-making (Osiel, 1997; Felman, 2001; Minow, 1998; Luban, 1987; Bloxham, 2001)? Alice Kaplan, in her introduction to Alain Finkielkraut's book on the 'Barbie' trial, *Remembering in Vain*, describes the trial as a 'pedagogical event' (p. xvi) which she claims 'resuscitated history and made it into a current event' (p. xvii). Finkielkraut, himself, remarks that the 'historical past [was] transmuted into a judicial present' (p. 2). This indeed is a relentless theme of all war crimes commentary and rhetoric. Robert G. Storey, executive trial counsel at Nuremberg, spoke of the need to make 'a record of the Hitler regime which would withstand the test of history' (Arendt, 1994: 252; Minear, 1971: 126). Before the Eichmann trial began, Israeli Prime Minister Ben-Gurion reminded Israelis that: '. . . it is necessary that our youth remember what happened to the Jewish people. We want them to know the most tragic facts of our history' (Arendt, 1994: 10). The District Court in Jerusalem, itself, acknowledged 'the great educational values implicit in the very holding of a trial' (Arendt: 19). A quarter of a century later, an amendment to the Australian war crimes legislation came into force, with parliamentarians speaking of the need to tell the story of the Holocaust to future generations,[2] and in advocating a war crimes trial in the Persian Gulf, Anthony D'Amato warned the Congressional Committee on Foreign Relations that '. . . a war crimes trial should not be today's news forgotten tomorrow. Rather, it should be one of the most fundamental lessons in civics that can be taught to the people of the world, especially the young people.'[3] In *Eichmann*, what was important was not the conviction and execution of the accused but the sheer weight of evidence about the existence of the Holocaust itself. Witness after witness testified to the terrible things *they* had seen. Accordingly, the trial would recount a history of human depravity and bureaucratic deformity, the larger purpose of which was the valorization of heroic memory.

This didactic function can be seen, also, in the reports and rhetoric around more recent trials. In its *Erdemovic* judgment, the ICTY referred to its work in the following terms: '. . . the International Tribunal sees public reprobation and stigmatisation by the international community, which would thereby express its indignation over heinous crimes and denounce the perpetrators, as one of the essential functions of a prison sentence for a crime against humanity.'[4] The *Christian Science Monitor*, more recently, reported that the trial in Baghdad of Saddam Hussein would re-educate the Iraqi people about the virtues of the rule of law: '. . . the tribunal, an ad hoc court under Iraqi law created to mete out justice to the *ancien régime*, will foster a rule-of-law culture; train a generation of Iraqi judges and lawyers in criminal prosecution; and set new standards for detentions, interrogations, and trials.'[5]

Conversely, the failure to hold trials can result in the loss of this memory. In a speech on the tenth anniversary of the massacre at Srebrenica, Theodor Meron, a judge at the ICTY, warned: 'The Tribunal's work in bringing justice and contributing to reconciliation in the region will go unfinished, and the record will remain incomplete, so long as the most prominent indictees remain at large.'[6] Indeed, Carla Del Ponte, the Chief Prosecutor at The Hague, declined to attend the ceremonies at Srebrenica because, for her, commemoration could only occur after a full judicial accounting and not before.[7] Political memory was indulgent or tactless in the absence of didactic legalism.

Four decades earlier, during the 1970s, the French Fifth Republic debated whether to continue applying the death penalty to the gravest crimes against the social order. In the end, the abolitionists prevailed, and the death penalty was removed from the statute books. The then French Minister of Justice, Robert Badinter, had been a prominent advocate of abolition; he had argued that there was no place in a modern France, a France dedicated to the project of modernity, for the barbarism of state execution. Badinter's father, Simon, had been working in a welfare office in Lyon during the Second World War and had perished in a famous Gestapo raid on his office on Rue Sainte-Catherine: a raid instigated, organized and executed by Klaus Barbie. When Barbie was returned to France from Bolivia in 1983, cries for him to face death were stilled by the realization that France had renounced capital punishment. Ted Morgan called this 'vengeance in reverse, where the son of one of Barbie's victims had saved him from the guillotine' (T. Morgan, 1990: 24). But Badinter's civilized liberalism might be viewed, also, as the best possible 'revenge'; a vindication of law's majestic detachment in the face of profound evil. Indeed, the point of Barbie's trial may not have been punishment at all but instead the assembling of edifying histories and the promotion of cosmopolitan values (see chapter 2).

Certainly, war crimes suspects have often favoured a sort of amnesia. General Alfredo Blandon, in El Salvador, called for a little forgetting to be thrown on the past (Simpson, 2005), Barbie himself declared: 'It was wartime, and today the war is over' (E. Morgan, 1988: 26) and Himmler in 1945 implored Jews and Nazis 'to bury the hatchet'. The purpose of the typical war crimes trial, then, can be to provide an antidote to such forgetfulness. Trials, on this view, take place in order to enlighten the present-day innocents through the enactment of history as well as to punish the historical criminals. War crimes trials offer exemplary performance, classical retribution and commemoration all at once (Morgan, 1988). This idea of telling histories through war crimes trials requires courts to uphold or demonstrate fealty to the requirements of procedural justice and the sovereignty of law while at the same time transmitting an authoritative account of history, and an attractive version of politics (Morgan, 1988). For some commentators, it is this latter function that is the most significant. In *The Memory of Judgment*, Lawrence Douglas (taking an ecumenical approach to the subject of war crimes trials by including, alongside *Eichmann* and *Demjanjuk*, a trial that was not a war crimes trial at all but rather a case involving Holocaust denial, that of Ernest Zundel, the Canadian photojournalist) constructs around these trials a theory of the limits and possibilities of didactic legalism (or, what David Hirsh calls 'cosmopolitan memory' (Hirsh, 2003)) in war crimes proceedings. Of course, these functions may not be themselves consistent and, in addition, can clash with others. 'It's not about remembering' as Hannah Arendt argued after the Eichmann trial (Arendt, 1994).

There is, in particular, a tension between law in its history-making mode and law in its judicial, probative mode. This tension is a recurrent motif of war crimes proceedings and it expresses itself in several ways. First, the law, with its commitments to precedent and its reliance on procedural rules and technical language, may produce bathos in the face of great evil (the problem of proportion). Second, it may be that legalism is subject to compromise when the needs of history occupy a central place in the choreography of a war crimes trial. Carla Del Ponte, worrying about precisely this possibility, offered Serbs the following reassurance: 'The Serbian people are not on trial here. The history of Serbia is not under examination. It is Slobodan Milosevic as an individual'. But it was *this* history that *amicae* for the Defence wished to uncover in order to capture the full context for Milosevic's actions (the problem of incompatibility). Third, the history-making engaged in by a court or state may be designed to buttress or consolidate a particular ideological programme or 'necessary illusion' (the problem of legitimation). Fourth, these illusions themselves and, indeed, legalism's pretence to neutrality, may be challenged by dissenting views or unauthorized histories conveyed through the trial procedure (the promise of dissidence). Finally, the relocation or displacement of history into legal settings has the potential to distort the story. Law must discriminate between relevant history and irrelevant or inadmissible evidence. But for the storyteller the production of history or the story of an event like the Holocaust is dedicated to a different mission. The Nuremberg Trials may have resulted in the conviction of nineteen high-ranking Nazis and inscribed the Holocaust on post-war minds but its version of history was patchy and elliptical.[8]

2 Proportion

International law had brought criminality in from history at Nuremberg (*Göring et al.*) only to find it pulled back towards history and structure and the human condition in Jerusalem (*Eichmann*). At Versailles, the Commission on the Authorship of the War worried over the idea of aggression as a crime. For the majority there, aggression was a wrong to be judged by history or by conscience (or, they might have said, by social psychology) but not by law. The dissenting views expressed by the Americans, Lansing and Brown Scott, meanwhile, wanted to confine also the laws of humanity and the idea of command liability to the realm of moral and political responsibility. Such acts of criminality were deemed too large for the law.

According to Karl Jaspers, too, there was something rather measly about using law to confront the unspeakable horrors of the Shoah: 'Something other than law was at stake here and to address it in legal terms was a mistake' (Koskenniemi, 2002; see Arendt, 1994: 271). Hannah Arendt famously pronounced that hanging Eichmann was necessary but totally inadequate (Arendt, 1994). Law seems to belong to an everyday of traffic violations and house sales. Could it be of any help in understanding the metaphysics of evil? If, as Adorno argued, writing poetry is barbaric in the light of the Holocaust, what of law and remembrance?[9] This question goes to the heart of a genuine concern about the incongruity of legal language and unimaginable evil. This alleged lack of proportion has taken two forms.

The first form appeared when it was discovered in the 1940s that there was no legal language available to confront the horrors of mass atrocity. What Primo Levi, the Italian chemist and Auschwitz survivor, feared most of all on his release from the death camps was disbelief. He dedicated the remainder of his life (Levi committed suicide in 1987) to recording and retelling the story of the camps in *If This is a Man* and *The Truce*. In one of his earliest books, he describes a meeting with a lawyer shortly after the liberation of Auschwitz. The interview is marked by awkwardness and, one suspects, on the lawyer's side, incredulity. At the conclusion of the meeting, the lawyer gets up, shakes Levi's hand and 'urbanely excuses himself' (Levi, 1966). Gideon Hausner, the Chief Prosecutor at Jerusalem in 1961, captured some of this awkwardness or lack of fit when he said: 'all precedents and examples originating from serious "peacetime causes" sounded hollow and inappropriate in this case' (Hausner, 1966: 392). It is not uncommon, after all, to hear the Holocaust described as 'unprecedented'. Precedents, though, are the life of the common law. Without them, the law in some of the early war crimes trials, at least, seemed incapable of dealing with the exceptional nature of administrative massacre (Arendt, 1994: 294). Such massacres 'explode[d] the limits of the law'.[10]

The second form of lack of proportion arose as a result of attempts to find a solution to the problem of the first. As law began to cover the field with procedure and precedents, the crimes themselves threatened to disappear in a welter of process. In 1998, I was a legal adviser at the Rome Conference to establish a permanent international criminal court. I was struck by the ease with which the images of evil became the nomenclature of bureaucracy and diplomacy. 'Genocide', 'crimes against humanity' and 'serious violations of human rights', in the face of our best intentions, became terms of technical art to be debated and reinvented. A number of international legal theorists have hinted at a gap between the words used by lawyers and the experiences of victims of mass atrocity (Koskenniemi, 1999). These experiences are in some way diminished when articulated in jurisprudential language. Ralph Lemkin gave the world the word 'genocide' to describe what happened to the Armenians, the Gypsies, the Jews and the Slavs but in coining the term he may have transformed the unspeakable into the routine. Could it be that the human heart loses some of its capacity for indignation when evil is judicialized, that 'genocide' somehow means less in Darfur than it did in Rwanda and less in Rwanda than it did in Bosnia and less in Bosnia than it did in 1961 during the Eichmann trial? These are each undoubtedly genocides but their capacity to inspire outrage or response may have deteriorated as the term 'genocide' has insinuated itself into diplomatic language. In trials, too, there is a disassociation between the description of these horrendous acts and the legal language in which the debates about them are framed. Hrant Dink, an Armenian journalist, discussing the massacres of Armenians in the early twentieth century, asked recently: 'What is its name? The discipline of law can be preoccupied with this question, but whatever it decides we know exactly what we have lived through' (Dink, 2005). Law's preoccupations begin in 1945 with a sense that it is unable to confine or limit the sheer horror of mass atrocity. Existing categories hardly seem adequate. By the 1990s, the categories had expanded and the language of mass criminality was ascendant and ubiquitous. But had law, by now, explained too much?

3   Incompatibility

In *Operation Shylock*, Philip Roth's novel about a visit made to Israel by a character called Philip Roth, the subject of the Demjanjuk trial is pervasive. In 1988, John Demjanjuk, a Cleveland car-worker had been extradited from the United States to stand trial in Israel on suspicion that he was Ivan Marchenko, Ivan the Terrible, the notorious Treblinka concentration camp guard (Sheftel, 1994). The Demjanjuk trial was the most celebrated war crimes trial since the 1961 trial of Adolf Eichmann in Jerusalem. Indeed, it was something of a counterpoint to that trial because it sought to show that the Holocaust was personal as well as structural and that though the killing had been organized by office bureaucrats, it was carried out by 'ordinary men' with sadistic inclinations. If Eichmann had passed into history as the faceless, bespectacled, bureaucrat responsible for making sure the trains ran on time, then Demjanjuk was intended to be the vicious petty criminal who made life intolerable for those whose destination was the camp. Demjanjuk was eventually acquitted in a case of mistaken identity, but in the conversations around the trial between the Roth character and various friends and accomplices, the trial is characterized as an effort on the part of the Israeli State to educate the Israeli public. At one point, a character called George Zaid exclaims: 'But to try him here in the courtroom and over the radio and on the television and over the papers, this has only one purpose – a public relations stunt. . . . The criminal-justice system has a legal purpose, not a public relations purpose. To educate the public? No, that's the purpose of an educational system' (p. 132).

Zaid's tirade expresses the common thought that there is some fundamental mismatch between the impulse to educate, and the requirements of trial and conviction. This problem of incompatibility is captured in Hannah Arendt's indictment of the Eichmann trial (and rather peculiar nostalgia for the Nuremberg Trials). Arendt argued that law and pedagogy were fundamentally at odds (at least in the context of *Eichmann*) (Arendt,

1994). A trial that had one eye on educating the public was bound to fail as law, she claimed. Such trials were too concerned with pedagogy to properly perform law. According to Arendt, in Jerusalem, the prosecution (and the State) saw the trial as an opportunity to chronicle the Holocaust and the suffering of its remaining witnesses. The judges were reluctant to abbreviate the testimony of these survivors, and even the defence failed to object when obviously extraneous evidence was presented. Instead, a picture of the Holocaust was offered for the education of the people of Israel and the international community. The trial's integrity, she argued, was mortally wounded by an insistence in teaching the Holocaust when its job was the conviction of Eichmann. For her, the trial was rendered 'stinknormal, unworthy' by its association with, what she believed to be, Zionist myth-making.

It was this tendency also which so enraged Klaus Barbie's lawyer, Jacques Vergès, on several occasions during that trial and produced a mountain of criticism and reportage on the Nuremberg and Tokyo trials.[11] At Tokyo, Bruce Blakeney, the Senior Defence Counsel, complained about the Chief Prosecutor's theatrical storytelling, and the repeated use of testimony unconnected to individual guilt (Maga, 2001: 126, 120). For these lawyers, there was too much history, and the trials threatened to lapse into show trials (chapter 5). This conflict, though, exists even in trials which are not obviously dedicated to finding people objectively guilty (even if subjectively innocent) or eliminating political enemies or enforcing particular histories. The possibility of a trial's didactic purpose overwhelming its judicial task is an inevitable part of war crimes proceedings freighted, as they tend to be, with political meaning and historical significance.

There also is the converse problem of the judicial imperative undercutting the claims of history and pedagogy. It is not always the case that courts can produce compelling historical documents. In *Demjanjuk*, the failing memory of living witnesses began to affect the credibility (or at least utility) of their testimony. Law, unable to produce its own memories, could not engage in the acts of remembrance so fervently wished upon it by those who had advocated war crimes trials. In *Sawoniuk*, there was a tension between the truth-telling imperatives felt by the main witness, Ben-Zion Blustein, and the constraints on evidence imposed by the court (Hirsh, 2003). Meanwhile, in the Irving defamation case, the very subject matter of the legal proceedings was the status of history, and the nature of collective memory, historical truth and professional credibility (Lipstadt, 1993; Guttenplan, 2001).

The effects of these trials, and the idea of teaching history are not, of course, unconnected to the problem of Holocaust denial, which, after all, seeks both to question the authenticity of the testimonial evidence for the existence of the Holocaust and produce a version of the persecution of Europe's Jewish population that significantly underplays its severity and consequences ('it did not happen and if it did, worse things have happened, for example to Germans in the USSR' (paradoxically one of the early Holocaust denial statutes in Germany played into the hands of the very revisionism it sought to prevent by making it an offence either to deny the existence of the Holocaust *or the forced migration of ethnic Germans from Silesia*) (Douglas, 2001: 235–40). What happens, then, when law, instead of telling a story en route to the prosecution of an accused, enforces the story itself, i.e. does literally what Arendt believed the Eichmann trial was attempting figuratively? In a Canadian case called *Zundel*, the accused, a Canadian photojournalist and retoucher, had been active among Canadian neo-Nazis in writing and distributing material denying the existence of the Holocaust. This material brought him to the notice of the Canadian authorities who prosecuted him under Canada's Holocaust denial legislation (ultimately, there were two trials, and a constitutional appeal resulting in an eventual acquittal). In the two trials, Zundel's lawyer, Douglas Christie, managed to convert the proceedings into a trial of the Holocaust itself.

Lawrence Douglas describes how, in *Zundel*, survivor testimonies could be discounted as unreliable *because* traumatic, films were challenged as hearsay (indeed, much of the testimony fell into this category as well; hearsay rules had been relaxed at Nuremberg) and professional histories were relativized. Thus, even giants of Holocaust scholarship such as Raul Hilberg were subjected to demoralizing cross-examination and were positioned as mere expert *opinions* (along with those of Holocaust deniers such as Robert Faurisson). Christie adopted a version of radical hermeneutics to suggest that Holocaust history was in the process of constant revision and reinvention, and that the work of Holocaust deniers was a respectable part of this professional ferment (Douglas, 2001: 235). Initially, this did not succeed in the legal sense (Zundel was convicted) but it prompted the following headline in the *Toronto Globe and Mail*: 'No gas chambers in Nazi Germany, expert witness testifies' (Douglas: 242). In the end, the Supreme Court of Canada decided that the statute under which Zundel was prosecuted was itself unconstitutional because it breached rights to freedom of expression protected in the Canadian Charter of Rights and Freedoms. The law in the court, and in the Constitution, in different ways elevated Holocaust denial into a position of equivalence with other histories of the mid-twentieth century. The courtroom proceedings treated each party impartially and each view was subject to a degree of neutrality. The Charter, meanwhile, protected the rights of deniers (along with the rights of those who asserted the existence of the Holocaust). The legal domain, alone, afforded Holocaust denial equal status as expression. In the Zundel trial expert witnesses took the stand in the one case to deny the veracity of the Holocaust (Faurisson) and in the other to assert its existence (Hilberg). Only in judicial settings could these views be characterized as 'versions of history'. This pedagogic effort, then, can be deemed a failure from the perspective of 'telling' the Holocaust.

Many observers, including Douglas, conclude, though, that despite these failures law *can* be enlisted in the project of creating responsible memory (Arbour, 2002: 32–3). They argue that the dramatic potential, social space and material resources offered by legal proceedings can provide a sort of provisional closure. Some trials fail as history, just as some trials fail as law but for Douglas, war crimes trials, when undertaken with vigilance and honesty, can provide telling, instructive and just outcomes (in Jerusalem in 1961, episodically at Nuremberg in 1945–6). For all its failures of didacticism and legalism, he argues that the law (and many lawyers and judges) has approached mass atrocity with a sensitivity to the requirements of the historical record.[12] Georg Schwarzenberger, too, rejected Arendt's critique of the Eichmann trial, dismissing those who did not recognize that all trials have meta-legal objectives, and that in trials involving sedition or national survival these objectives can become dominant. As he put it: 'In its [the trial's] deterrent and corrective aspects it fulfils social functions of an essentially educational nature' (1962: 250).

The relationship embodied in the phrase 'didactic legalism' is a complicated one. Law and pedagogy are not incompatible. A trial conducted with scrupulous adherence to natural justice may also convey powerful historical truths. It is true, too, that war crimes trials have greater therapeutic or didactic potential than many other trials. This potential has been realized in a number of cases. Didacticism, though, as I now want to show, can be deployed in the service of a legitimating script (*Barbie*, for example, was prejudiced not by teaching history but by using history to buttress myths about French identity), it can be undercut by dissenting narratives and it can both sustain and erase histories (Morgan, 1988).

4   Legitimation

On 3 August 2001, three Israeli soldiers were detained on suspicion of having forced Palestinian civilians to beat each other. An Israeli military spokesman announced that: 'It really appears that there was bad intent on the part of these soldiers, that they did these things knowingly. In a lot of cases it is simply not the case. It can be bad judgement, or a mistake. Here it appeared they did this knowingly and wilfully and these sorts of actions are unacceptable'.[13]

Trials have purposes other than the neutral teaching of history or the prosecution of the accused. They also can be convened as demonstrations of the prosecuting party's virtue or innocence. In some cases, the trial is intended to purify state policy by distinguishing a policy from the particular and 'isolated' abuses that are committed by individuals in support of that policy (see e.g. *US v. Calley*). In other cases, a war crimes trial is intended to expose the chasm between the behaviour of an enemy, represented by the accused, and that of the state holding the trial. The very fact of having a trial discloses a gap between the prosecutors (merciful, lawful and open) and the accused. More generally, the conduct and nature of the trial is intended to reveal the rectitude of the prosecuting party. In *The Winter's Tale*, when Leontes tries his wife for crimes she did not commit, he opens the proceedings by exonerating himself: 'Let us be clear'd, Of being tyrannous, since we so openly Proceed in justice.'[14] In war crimes trials, bad men are tried for gross crimes but, at the same time, the prosecuting party often is attempting to clear itself of tyranny.

In the first set of examples, trials or courts-martial isolate the aberrant behaviour of a few rogue personnel thus ensuring that the larger operation or political strategy remains untainted. The courts-martial of US prison guards at Abu Ghraib have the effect of abstracting this behaviour from the practices of violence accompanying the US-led invasion and occupation of Iraq. Forcing groups of Iraqi soldiers to simulate sexual congress will be shown to have nothing to do with the President's description of the Iraqi resistance as 'terrorists'. Instead, these trials attempt to decontextualize the violence committed against Iraqi prisoners and symbolize the worthiness of the invasion and the subjective wrongdoing of the guards. These horrendous acts, which can be safely condemned by all, serve to distinguish the occasional, unrepresentative consequences of occupation (clearly illegal) with the occupation itself (lawful and, by contrast with these acts, humane). It is not so much that '. . . the appalling behaviour of a few does not undermine the moral correctness of the coalition's mission';[15] rather, the crescendo of righteous condemnation and subsequent legal proceeding helps legitimize the mission. These are show trials but the guilt of the perpetrators is a side issue. What is important is the innocence of the prosecutors.

The 'Barbie' trial is an example of a broader policy of legitimation. At its most explicit, the Barbie prosecution was intended simply to present Barbie as the Nazi embodiment of evil and a moral counterpoint to French humanism (Binder, 1989). However, the trial was also engineered to celebrate the struggle of the French nation against the Nazis and atone for the collaborationist history of the Vichy Regime. More specifically, and by no means incompatibly with this story, there was the decision to narrate the history of the French resistance as a tale of leftist / socialist struggle at a time when François Mitterrand was the first Socialist President of the Fifth Republic (complicating the motives of the actors, further, was the fact that Barbie was implicated in indirectly assisting the killing of Che Guevara whose companion at the time of his capture was Régis Debray, Mitterrand's adviser at the time of the trial) (Finkielkraut, 1992). The trial was important for Israel, too. The Israeli Ambassador to France, Ovadia Sofer, did not miss the opportunity to recall Ben-Gurion when he said, on the steps of the Court house, 'terrorists are today's Nazis and S.S.' (Binder, 1989: 1343).

Similar legitimation functions were at work in the Eichmann trial. First, the trial was an indictment of the Western nations who had failed to save European Jews from the Final Solution or give them refuge prior to its enactment. Secondly, the trial, by retelling the story of the Holocaust, reaffirmed the legitimacy of Israel's existence as well as many of the measures the Israeli state deemed necessary to ensure that continued existence. Thirdly, and most controversially, Ben-Gurion's statements prior to the trial indicate that he intended the lesson of the trial to be one salutary not just to Jews, Israelis and Europeans but also to Arabs: 'They should be taught the lesson that Jews are not sheep to be slaughtered but a people who can hit back – as Jews did in the [1948] War of Independence' (Young-Bruehl, 1981: 341).

Many writers have been critical of this tendency of law to skew history or legitimize structures of authority. Hannah Arendt's target was, of course, the Israeli state and Jewish exceptionalism in the Eichmann trial. Lawrence Douglas reserves his ire for the misplaced didacticism of *Barbie* and *Demjanjuk*. But it is not always the prosecuting state(s) that are legitimized. Sometimes, it is prospective allies. Donald Bloxham in *Genocide on Trial*, shares some of Douglas's concerns about Nuremberg (its failure to make central the Holocaust, its awkward imported American legalese, its reliance on a rather muddy theory of conspiracy) but he offers, too, some intriguing elaborations of the jurisprudential efforts to exculpate the Wehrmacht, the domestic political shenanigans that influenced attempts to try industrialists (American capital was uneasy), the British focus on crimes committed against their own personnel (confirming Bass's theory of self-interested prosecution), the anti-Bolshevism and anti-Semitism that undermined some initiatives, and the breakdown of international criminal law with the onset of the Cold War. He recognizes then that the Nuremberg Trials created a big story about international law (Luban, 1987), i.e. the establishment of a new category of crimes, crimes against humanity, but that an even bigger story, the criminalization of aggression, undermined the crimes against humanity initiative. It was not just that Nuremberg downgraded the Holocaust (while at the same time gathering the evidence that would enlarge its status in the public imagination via history and via *Eichmann* and other trials) but that the American focus on structural guilt (a curiously Marxist idea, after all) led to a trial in which a large-scale conspiracy to commit an aggressive war became the primary motif of the trial. The conspiracy charge framed the Nazi experience as an attempt at world conquest, with ancillary human rights violations, directed from above with the reluctant or unthinking support of a mass population. The Nazi elite had directed the war, and their subordinate organizations did the killing at its behest (the SS, SD, Gestapo, Einsatzgruppen).

This historical method had the effect of mitigating the responsibility of the German people as a whole (ignorant about the Holocaust and incapable of resisting the structures of National Socialism), the Wehrmacht (fighting the war under orders and uninvolved in atrocity) and the individuals active in the mobile killing units and concentration camps (cogs in a large machine). Both Bloxham's study and others (Goldhagen, 1996; Browning, 1992) suggest that this was a misrepresentation of a 1933–45 period marked not by passive obedience but, often, rabid hatred and intense individual cruelty. Nonetheless, the Nuremberg Trials and the strategy employed at them were critical in legitimizing, not just the Allies, but the new German state(s) after the Second World War.

The legitimation effect of trial tends to be a less well-advertised function of war crimes trials but it accounts for at least part of the enthusiasm for such trials. Here the state involved is trying not only to illuminate the past but also to justify the present. Louis René Beres, in an article calling for the punishment of the Iraqi leadership, claimed 'the Nuremberg obligations reflect perfect convergence of International Law and the enduring foundations of our American Republic' (Benes, 1993). As Guyora Binder remarked, in relation to the 'Barbie' trial, '[e]very noble ideal attributed to France in such a trial served to distinguish France's repression of Algeria as mere crimes of war because, after all, the French were not Nazis' (1989 at 1339). Perhaps, in the end, all war crimes trials are saying this of the prosecuting state.

5   Discordant notes

War crimes trials may often legitimate the prosecuting state or the existing legal order but they also create space for the expression of unauthorized views and iconoclastic histories. The District Court in the Eichmann trial used the phrase 'discordant notes' to describe elements of Dr Servatius's concluding speech for the defence.

> . . . we wish to express our appreciation to counsel for the defence, Dr R. Servatius . . . who stood almost alone in this strenuous legal battle . . . and refrained from unnecessary controversy over matters which did not seem to him to be essential for the defence of his client. . . . Not even the few discordant notes in his concluding speech could detract from the worthy and serious impression made by his defence as a whole. (*Eichmann*: 20)

I use this judicial expression of anxiety as the organizing idea of this section. There is a tension in the conduct of, and commentary around, war crimes trials between a conception of them as acts of remembrance and/or legitimation, and the dissident effects of, or 'discordant notes' struck in, these trials. The aim here is to show how the authorized versions of history and legality in such trials are haunted by the presence of dissenting counter-narratives.

Chris Black, the Canadian lawyer seeking to represent Slobodan Milosevic, claimed that 'the trial will be no more than an exercise in "victor's justice" fixing in history the west's partisan version of events' (Bowcott, 2001). However, in some ways, the trial was the one significant, visible opportunity for this version of events to be challenged by the defendant. Sometimes, the discordant notes are struck outside the trial in commentary around it. In the Eichmann trial, it was not Servatius who provided the primary dissenting voice but rather Hannah Arendt in her startling critique of the trial. Sometimes, the discordant notes are provided by, what Klinghoffer and Klinghoffer call, 'the counter-trials': those trials or proceedings, usually unofficial expressions of civil society, that seek to provide a point of resistance or 'corrective mechanism' to the official trials (Klinghoffer and Klinghoffer, 2002). Finally, there are those instances where the proceedings produce actual dissenting judgments. The most famous examples of this are found at Tokyo where the three dissenting judges, Pal, Bernard and Röling, each challenged, to varying degrees, the very basis of the trial with Pal ending the most sensational dissent in the history of war crimes trials in the following terms: 'For the reasons given in the foregoing pages, I would hold that each and every one of the accused must be found not guilty of each and every one of the charges in the indictment and should be acquitted of all those charges' (Pal, 1953: 697).

It is at these points of resistance that war crimes trials become more than simply expressions of a dominant political morality or the technocratic application of rules of warfare or vindications of the international community. Legalism and, in particular, the criminal trial allow room for the alternative history or the critical project or the dissident act. In Mexico City, Leon Trotsky called on a Commission of Inquiry into the Moscow Show Trials, vowing to 'make the accusers the accused' (Klinghoffer and Klinghoffer, 2002: 56).[16] Trials retain at their core a symmetry that can never quite be dissolved by the political elites who convene the trial (Koskenniemi, 2002). It is this symmetry (only occasionally an equality of arms) that permits the articulation of histories and futures that are more readily erased in non-judicial settings.

The 'politics' of such trials are constituted by a contest between authorized and bastard versions of history, law and politics. Law and, in particular, trials allow for forms of political engagement and rebellion that may in other domains be closed off. Law's adversarialism, its commitment to equality of participation, and its openness mean it creates the occasional space for hitherto obscured 'dissenting judgments'. Indeed, law's procedural openness can extend to providing space for a challenge to the very legitimacy of the legal form itself. It is possible, of course, to enter into substantive disagreement over political projects in Western democracies (at least within circumscribed limits) but challenges to the competence of Parliament or the Executive are more difficult to mount. Similarly, the media purports to offer space for political controversy but challenges to the authenticity or validity of the media itself are often excluded or sidelined (Herman and Chomsky, 1995; Chomsky, 1989).

The juridical form comprises both a substantive and a procedural element. There is room for contestation over the content of particular claims but, also, crucially, the appropriateness or otherwrse of particular institutions in resolving these claims. Law contains within it the possibility of its own negation (to paraphrase Bukharin, at his own show trial, quoting Hegel (Kadri, 2005)). Indeed, it is the possibility of negation that makes it law. It is the possibility of delegitimation (or negation) that caused Roosevelt such concern during the negotiations over the post-Second World War war crimes trials (Kadri, 2005). Law's promise (its capacity to convert political gains into legally binding commitments) is also law's radicalism (its legitimacy is bought at the price of permitting attacks on this legitimacy, see e.g. unsuccessful investigations and proceedings in Australia concerning alleged Nazis).

There are two distinct genres of dissenting texts. In *justice arguments*, the trial or background institution or state is called into question for its failure to apply law or justice equally or universally or sensitively. The justice argument has its technical equivalent in the *tu quoque* defence raised at Nuremberg, for example, but it encompasses a broader network of reservations (about the absence of particular defences or crimes from the body of rules that makes up international criminal law). Sometimes, too, this takes the form of a challenge to the whole idea of using legal forms (or particular legal forms) to try individuals who have acted in what might be perceived to be a 'political' manner. *History arguments* are found in dissenting texts that challenge authorized versions of history transmitted during and beyond the trial. War crimes trials, and institution-building projects, have produced rather unexpected historical accounts. These arguments are sometimes correctives to historical orthodoxies; sometimes they tell histories from the margins, sometimes they lay bare the mechanics of history-making itself. War crimes trials are historiographical dramas. They enact a tension between the reproduction of conventional images of the past, and the making visible of obscured or disconcerting vectors of history.

5.1   Justice arguments

War crimes trials involve a formal procedure designed to acquire legitimacy through the equal and universal application of properly authorized rules: '. . . no one is above the law or beyond the reach of international justice'.[17] This formalism precisely is what allows defendants to challenge the idea of justice perpetuated in trials. Justice arguments of this sort were pervasive at Nuremberg, where some of the defendants possessed a keen eye for the hypocrisies of the Western Powers and the Russians, in particular, were assailed by a series of discordant notes. A trial intended to document the evil of Nazism, as well as confirm the moral gulf between the Allies and the Germans, contained several awkward moments. Albert Speer was particularly adept at deploying justice arguments in order to suggest an equivalence between the Allies and the Axis Powers. When badgered by a Soviet prosecutor into admitting that he must have known of Hitler's plans for a world war of aggression from an early reading of *Mein Kampf*, Speer responded that he had not taken such plans seriously, and was, he remarked, '. . . particularly relieved in 1939 when the Molotov-Ribbentrop Pact with Russia was signed'. After all, he continued, tartly, 'your diplomats too must have read *Mein Kampf*; nevertheless they signed the Non-Aggression Pact' (Raginsky Cross-Examination of Speer, 21 June 1946 (Marrus, 1997: 98)).

Hermann Göring was even more effective in exposing Allied double standards. When asked about 'lebensraum' (living space for the German people), a concept used to justify the expansion of the Reich into Russia, Göring retorted: 'I fully understand that the four signatory powers [to the IMT Charter] who call three quarters of the world their own explain the idea differently' (Testimony on the Nazi Party, 14 March 1941 (Marrus, 1997: 104)). Göring also managed to suggest that there was nothing unique in the way the Nazi Party had organized itself. A tribunal prosecutor, by implying that the Leadership Principle (present, after all, in the Catholic Church and the Soviet State) or secret mobilization plans (a practice common to the Great Powers) were somehow elements of a criminal enterprise, risked over-inclusiveness. Robert Jackson so disliked this tactic of Göring's that he tried to have the Luftwaffe Head's discordant notes struck from the record altogether. This prissy appeal to the bench simply underscored Allied sensitivities. Even the Ruling Judge in the matter quietly admonished Jackson (Marrus, 1997: 115).

Much more compelling and less obviously self-serving (or obnoxious) justice arguments, though, were made by Röling and Pal at Tokyo. Reflecting on his dissent some years later, Röling indicated his discomfort with the thrust of the Tokyo judgment. In particular he worried about '. . . the inflation of the concept of what it is to be criminal' (Röling, 1993: 94). Chief Justice Webb, Röling reported, was intent on producing a 'nice' unanimous opinion finding the Japanese leadership guilty of aggressive war, and tracing the roots of the crime of aggression back to the writings of Grotius. Röling could see the hypocrisy in this, noting wryly that Grotius had developed the aggressive war doctrine at precisely the same time that the European powers were establishing, sometimes through brute force, their huge Asian empires. The crime of aggression, he feared, was a concept that would be experimented on 'the underdog' (p. 99). And he was under no illusion that this was an experiment in law-making by the drafters of the tribunal Charter and by the judges. The effort to ground the decision in long-standing traditions and doctrines of international law was delusory (Röling, 1998: 1–249).

Along with those of Bernard and Röling, Justice Pal's dissent was excluded from the official published judgment: an Indian firm eventually published the lengthy dissent in 1953 (Pal, 1953) (the other dissents were made available in Pritchard's multi-volume sequence (Pritchard, 1998)). Justice Pal's dissent was, in effect, a comprehensive critique of the post-Second World War war crimes machinery and jurisprudence (Kopelman, 1991). The Court, of which he was a member, was, for him, an *ex post facto* mechanism for vindicating the Allies and punishing innocent Japanese statesmen and soldiers. In particular, he challenged the Court's claims to represent lawfulness, community, progress and universalism. The Court's aspirations to lawfulness were undercut by the adoption of procedures that were pale imitations of standard legal process (Pal, 1953: 139–77), by the punishment of prisoners of war in violation of existing legal rules (p. 29) and by the application to the accused of newly created legal norms (p. 26). The law enunciated by Allies and developed by the Tribunal did not derive from a sense of common humanity because this community of states did not yet exist. In its absence, the law applied at Tokyo was simply the emanation of a small coalition of states and its highly particular political and legal philosophy (pp. 57–62). The Court's pretensions to represent 'progress', meanwhile, were undermined by its resort to a punitive method for dealing with fallen enemies that more closely resembled the vindictiveness of the medieval era than the humanism of the nineteenth century (p. 20). Finally, the IMTFE's apparent universalism was a charade. Pal included, as an appendix to the Indian publication of his Opinion, some gruesome photographs of the after-effects of the Hiroshima and Nagasaki bombings. These were there to point up the gulf between the reliance on the conscience of the civilized world in the prosecution of the Japanese leadership and the degradation of this conscience in the use by that world of the atom bomb. Furthermore, the universal 'sense of humanity' underscoring the Tribunal's work was seriously destabilized by its failure to apply the laws of humanity generally and universally. The criminalization of domination was an entirely specious juridical move given that domination (i.e. colonialism) was a practice from which virtually no major power had desisted in the long period prior to the Second World War (p. 63). This aspect of Pal's dissenting judgment was the basis for a highly effective critique of international criminal law and the partial inspiration for the anti-colonial efforts at the United Nations. In the end, it was Pal and Röling who were vindicated and not the Tribunal. Decolonization became a major UN project a decade after the Tokyo Trials while in international criminal law, the project to render aggression a crime, against which Pal had agitated, fell into disrepair.

So far, I have referred to largely explicit efforts to call into question the justice of particular trial proceedings. These efforts are undertaken consciously (by defence lawyers, by judges and by commentators). However, quite often, the dissenting texts produced in such trials are the unintended consequences of the process. When the US delegation to the Commission on Authorship of the War rejected the application of crimes against humanity to the War defeated Germans (after the First World War), it could not have known that it was providing a foundation for the defence of Nazis in 1946, establishing a forerunner to the objections made by the Americans at the Rome negotiations in 1998 and, more broadly, elaborating a critique of war crimes trials that continues to resonate today. At the IMT itself, one of the Soviet Prosecutors, Roman Rudenko, in his opening address rails against the doctrine of preventative war developed by the Nazis: '. . . the Hitlerite clique . . . proclaimed that the predatory war which it started against the Soviet Union with aggressive purposes was a "preventative war". A pitiful effort' (Marrus, 1997: 96).

Such 'pitiful' efforts were to be repeated soon after in successive Soviet invasions of its Eastern European satellites, and continued to influence Soviet strategic policy through to the invasion of Afghanistan. The *United States National Security Strategy* (2002) is the latest attempt by one of the hegemons to elaborate the very doctrine comprehensively rubbished by them at Nuremberg. Nuremberg, in other words, has created an unexpected counter-text: a resource for challenging hegemonic dealings using the language of the Great Powers themselves. And, of course, the whole idea of crimes against peace at the core of the Nuremberg war crimes trials was hugely important in buttressing opposition to the Iraq War in 2003. The UK's Foreign Office Deputy Legal Adviser, Elizabeth Wilmshurst, resigned from the Foreign Office, stating in her letter of resignation that 'unlawful use of force [such as that contemplated in Iraq] on such a scale amounts to the crime of aggression'.[18] The Great Powers have been unable to cabin the idea of criminal law. Nuremberg may have been an example of victor's justice at the time but it has now come to have other effects. Crimes against peace and crimes against humanity have proved to possess radical as well as hegemonic (chapter 6) potential.

Robert Jackson understood this very clearly when he discussed crimes against humanity prior to the trial. The category, he understood, could result in unintended consequences. It was quite capable of turning on its makers who often had 'some regrettable circumstances at times in our own country in which minorities are unfairly treated' (Marrus, 1997: 45). But in order to avoid the implications of this novel category, the Allies placed some jurisdictional limits on its application (crimes against humanity could only be committed by aggressors). This had the immediate consequence of revealing that the trial was not essentially about Nazi crimes at all or, especially, the genocide of the European Jews but was about a war of aggression (containing 'the accumulated evil of the whole'). The ultimate consequence was that the contradiction of developing a principle invoking humanity and then dividing humanity into protected and unprotected classes could not be sustained (chapter 2).

This contradiction was removed at the ICC Conference (following on from the Control Council Law No. 10 and the *Tadic* Decision). The Rome Statute marked the final stage in untethering crimes against humanity from war.

5.2   History arguments

Tony Judt, in his 2005 book on Europe since 1945, *Postwar*, sets out a bleak picture of collective amnesia in the immediate aftermath of war. According to Judt, the Holocaust had barely established itself as a historical fact by the 1960s. As I write this, David Irving, author of *Hitler's War*, has just been sentenced to three years in an Austrian jail for the crime of historical denial. Yet much of Europe was in denial in the 1940s and 1950s. The Europeans memorialized the victims of Nazi barbarism but Jewish victims were simply assimilated into this broader category of victim. Surviving Jews were maltreated by post-war authorities (e.g. Jews were denied citizenship in Belgium after the war) and subject to a hostile public reaction (Jews were still being attacked in Germany at the end of the 1950s (Judt, 2005: 810)).

The Holocaust came to occupy a central place in European life only after some major political and cultural events, and the geo-strategic convulsions of the late 1950s and 1960s. And war crimes trials played a role in all this, too. The Frankfurt trials of concentration camp guards and the Eichmann trial electrified public opinion in the West and moved the Holocaust centre stage. To a certain extent, these trials galvanized opinion in Western Europe because the law's forensic accounting of culpability and dramatic reckoning meant that the large-scale occlusion of historical experience was no longer possible. These trials were one aspect of a generational transition from forgetting to remembering. But this remembering retained a particular quality. So, while trials often sought to establish a new historical orthodoxy (the centrality of the destruction of the Jews, the pedigree of the crime against humanity category), they left obscure, or attempted to obscure, other strands of history.

In the trials of Adolf Eichmann in Jerusalem, and the later trials in France of Paul Touvier and Maurice Papon, there is a sense of mainstream historical assumptions being exposed to dissident histories for the first time. The trial of Klaus Barbie in Lyon is the critical text here, though. By 1987, French history had found a secure place for the Holocaust. Crimes against humanity, elided in de Menthon's opening speech for the Prosecution at the IMT, had become central to French self-understanding. The Second World War was by now a narrative of Nazi atrocity and French resistance. The role of Vichy, and the French authorities in the North, in processing and deporting French Jews to the camps was significantly underplayed. Official statements by French leaders avoided commenting on Vichy altogether (the town itself remains proud of its spas but makes no reference to its past in the official guide to Vichy). The trial of Maurice Papon and the indictment of René Bousquet did much to erase the assiduously cultivated distinction between Vichy and France, and between Vichy and the Nazis. But the trial that produced an astonishing counter-text was that of Klaus Barbie. The 'Barbie' trial 'made' history but this was not quite the history its engineers had in mind. The trial was intended to demonstrate France's willingness to prosecute those guilty of crimes against humanity on French soil, enact the chasm between French Enlightenment values and Nazi ideology, and provide a sort of juridical memorial to the heroism of the French resistance. Much of this work was undone by painful contradictions of the French wartime experience, and the manipulations and conflations of Jacques Vergès, Barbie's trial lawyer (and what he called his 'defence of rupture').

Barbie's defence, in effect, offered two particular and familiar forms of dissident history. In the first, it is the alleged crimes that are rendered universal and not their condemnation. All states really are cold-hearted monsters, Vergès seemed to say. Barbie admitted that he remained a Nazi but his defence rested on an equivalence between Nazism and state ideologies in general. For him, all states utilized violence to advance their self-conceptions. And, not accidentally, Barbie invoked Israel here: 'Israel is in the same situation that we have been during the war in the occupied countries . . . And the Israeli people must defend. And that's the same thing that made the SS' (Wilson, 1984: 92). This is a reversal or inversion of Ben-Gurion's comments at the time of the Eichmann trial. For Ben-Gurion, as we have learned, the trial was partly intended to draw parallels between the enemies of the Jewish people (the Nazis) and enemies of Israel (the Arab states). For these purposes, Arafat was Eichmann (both wished to destroy the material conditions for Jewish identity). Barbie, on the other hand, draws parallels between the Nazis and the State of Israel. Both efforts are deeply ahistorical (and in the latter case, abhorrently so), of course, but they each tap into a desire for edification. What both strategies share (no matter their differences) is a willingness to see trials as an opening to retell history or place historical reckoning at the service of current ideological needs. It is precisely this that leads Binder to warn against 'permitting ourselves to be edified by atrocity' (Binder, 1989: 1322).

The second form of dissident history was directed at the particular historical responsibility of the prosecuting state, France. In the trial of Klaus Barbie, proceedings intended to document the superiority of Western liberal culture over Nazi totalitarianism were converted by a clever, opportunistic defence counsel into a conflict between Third World anti-colonialism and French imperialism. This counter-narrative challenged and eventually threatened to undo the main thread of the story. The possible lessons of the trial could not be contained in the face of this strategy. Vergès undermined the prosecution strategy by suggesting painful analogies between Nazi rule in France and the French occupation of Algeria. As a consequence, the authorized historical lessons were tainted by stories of French collaboration in occupied France and torture in occupied Algeria. This tactic was so successful that it led the former resistance leader and National Assembly President, Jacques Chaban-Delmas, to declare, 'France will be acquitted before the Tribunal of the World', as if Barbie were no longer the defendant. Vergès had situated the Holocaust among dozens of crimes of colonialism before and since as well as linking it to the collaborationist history of the Vichy regime. The pedagogical efforts of the French state were somewhat lost in this welter of anti-colonial rhetoric. On the other hand, Vergès' own teaching produced one of war crimes law's least palatable but most powerful dissenting readings.

Each war crimes trial operates at the behest or the sufferance of the Great Powers but each trial has the potential to shift social practice in a particular direction sometimes towards cosmopolitan justice (Hirsh, 2003), sometimes in the direction of edifying history (Douglas, 2001), sometimes dissident history (Simpson, 1999). No doubt, the trial offers a sort of equality among the participants, and it constrains myth-making even in the moment of making new myths (Nuremberg sanctified the Western Allies but it also opened space for the creation of a human rights system that would, at times, undermine hegemony and make the job of Holocaust deniers so much harder).

With good luck and better management, the trial of Saddam Hussein might have offered some sort of vindication for the invisible thousands who suffered under his rule. But trials create less predictable histories. The Soviets were terrified that Nuremberg would expose their close relationship with Nazi Germany as well as their own crimes against humanity and war crimes (at Katyn, for example), and, to an extent, this occurred. The Soviet Prosecutor was embarrassed on more than one occasion by his Nazi interlocutors. As I described earlier, the Allies, too, invented a category of criminality, crimes against humanity, that they worked hard to entwine with the war of aggression, but crimes against humanity returned unencumbered in later trials and provided a partial inspiration for the anti-colonial movement. The trial of Saddam would have been more controversial had the invasion of Iran and the use of chemical weapons against the Kurds been part of the prosecution's case. As Austen Chamberlain said of the plan to prosecute the Kaiser in 1919: 'His defence might be our trial' (Bass, 2000). The focus on a relatively minor incident, at Dujail in 1982, may have been a way of avoiding the appearance of potentially embarrassing 'dissenting texts'.

6   Forgetting

In section 4, I discussed the apparent incompatibility of legal procedure and didactic memory. Typically, this is presented as a problem because the desire to teach history undermines the enactment of procedural justice. But, perhaps, war crimes trials do not offer enough 'show'. What if these trials can indeed do justice to law but utterly fail in their duty to history? What if trials offer up a deliberately (but ahistorically) parsimonious account of history in order to do justice to the immediate participants in the courtroom drama? Critics have averred that war crimes trials are meagre tools for advancing the claims of traumatic history, being essentially reductive and individualistic. Nuremberg is a monument on the topography of international criminal law but, as political history and as international law, it leaves much to be desired. The conspiracy charge, for example, complicated the proceedings without providing the benefits of an extended reading of what constituted a breach of international law; the impact of the crimes against humanity charge (the great innovation of the hearings) was severely curtailed by the Charter's, and the Tribunal's, insistence that such crimes be linked to the war of aggression or to the more conventional charge of war crimes, and the Holocaust itself was, for a large part of the proceedings, rendered incidental by legal obfuscation, national deformities (the French Chief Prosecutor's failure to mention the Jews at all in his opening statement on crimes against humanity) and the Soviets' implicit anti-Semitism (Rudenko at one point spoke of 'excessive anti-Semitism'). The Holocaust was obscured by the Nuremberg Trials but some crimes under international law were erased altogether. Bombing 'undefended' cities from the air was illegal prior to the Second World War yet neither the arguably otiose fire-bombing of several German cities towards the end of the war (Grayling, 2006) nor the German attacks on Coventry or London formed part of the charges made at Nuremberg. In forgetting these acts, the tribunal may have been implicitly endorsing them (af Jochnick and Normand, 1994).

In the Milosevic trial, the judges made it plain early in the proceedings that the purpose of the trial was to determine the question of individual guilt. This involved an early and self-conscious screening out of the Balkan history. The Trial Chamber, after all, was not ideally equipped to untangle the threads of inter-ethnic rivalry and Great Power interference in the region. Any court would have found it difficult to ground the verdict in a comprehensive or even nuanced version of Balkan history. For the sake of expeditiousness, justice and reasonableness, the Chamber was summarizing and deforming history. This is not a criticism of the trial but a recognition of the limits of law. History is (sometimes) about remembering where law is, about resolving or vindicating and even forgetting. In the Eichmann trial, for example, the judges were under a duty to forget the facts of the Holocaust and their knowledge of Eichmann.[19] It seems that war crimes trials can only meet the requirements of legality if the crimes themselves are extinguished from memory prior to the trial. The trial, as it were, retells a seriously attenuated story from scratch. It attempts to understand the Shoah through the psychopathology or *mens rea* of one man, Adolf Eichmann. It may be that the trial has come to dominate to too great an extent the field of remembrance. When it comes to memory, Primo Levi may have more to tell us than the District Court of Jerusalem. Or better still, if one insists on official sanction and form, the South African Truth and Reconciliation Commission may be the preferable model in some situations. This was certainly the view, too, on the Commission on Authorship convened in 1919 to decide whether the Kaiser and high-ranking Germans should stand trial for the crime of having initiated the Great War. The US delegates, James Brown Scott and Robert Lansing, made the case that the so-called crime of aggression was a matter to be judged by history and conscience. No judicial proceeding, they argued, could capture the complex politics and history of the decision to use force. Ultimately, this would involve a trial of imperialism or, of what Woodrow Wilson called, 'the whole European system . . . of alliances and agreements, a developed web of intrigue and espionage', a system which he believed bore 'the deeper guilt of the war' (Wilson quoted in Schmitt, 2003: 268). It is the view of some commentators on the proposed Cambodian Trials (arguing that the healing had occurred in other ways, rendering the trial unnecessary (Maga, 2001: 148)), and it is a view given some credibility by the Human Rights Committee in 2004 when it stated that 'where appropriate, reparation can involve restitution, rehabilitation and measures of satisfaction such as *public apologies, public memorials . . .*' (my italics).[20]

The moment of juridical remembrance is often a moment of amnesia, too. The IMT Charter was signed the day before the bomb on Nagasaki was dropped, the French massacred 15,000 Algerians on the day the war ended in Europe and peace was proclaimed (only to exclude that massacre from subsequent definitions of crimes against humanity) and the Argentinians opened their files on the Nazis only two years after granting amnesties to those army officers who had participated in the Dirty War during the 1970s (Reid, 1994).

Barbie's trial may have been a triumph of remembering ('I want to look him in the eye' as one of Barbie's victims said during the trial) but there was much to forget, too: notably France's collaborationist history in the 1940s and some unsavoury aspects of its colonial past. Crimes against humanity, here, were again revised in order to forget these historical experiences. In the 'Barbie' trial, the defendant was charged with having committed '. . . inhumane acts and persecutions, which are carried out *in the name of a state practising a policy of ideological hegemony*' (my italics). Invocations of universal justice themselves attempt to obscure the counternarrative which threatens the coherence of these invocations. In the case of Barbie, Binder describes how the French reaffirmed an amnesty for all French military infractions committed in the Algerian war only days before enacting a statute declaring crimes against humanity imprescriptible under a Statute of Limitations (Binder, 1989).

War crimes trials tend to remind us of the evil committed by war's losers. But war's winners are capable of doing wrong also. Some of the same states that established Nuremberg in a triumph of legalism and self-righteousness rejected persecuted Jews in the 1930s as unwanted refugees. Today, we remember the war crimes committed in Central Africa in elaborate legal rituals but, too often, disdain the wretched from these same lands arriving on our shores asking for help. We can do justice to the living as well as the dead.

The relationship of the war crimes trial to history, then, is deeply problematic. The performance of a war crimes trial is both situated in a history and yet seeks to transcend it. The trial renders a historical moment abnormal but wishes to make its lesson universal. The history of genocide is presented as an aberrant and unique series of disparate events detached from the progress of history itself. One writer, for example, discussing war crimes in the former Yugoslavia, is careful to distance the commission of war crimes from the progress of Western civilization by consigning such crimes to 'a dark and seemingly remote past' only to have them 'once again haunt the conscience of humankind' (Akhavan, 1993: 262). But humankind has been 'haunted' in the recent past by 187 million dead as the result of human decision since 1900.[21] In the end, the trial of a war criminal is undoubtedly an act of remembrance. Nuremberg is a historian's treasure trove and the Eichmann trial provided the dramatic context for some of the most shattering testimony by Holocaust survivors. Yes, this testimony is preserved in Yad Vashem, but the District Court provided a crucible for its moment as living history. Frequently, though, war crimes trials are attempts also at closure or resolution and an inducement to extinguish other crimes of history.

5

Law's Anxieties
Show Trials

The answer again must be that there is politics and politics. It is the persecution which political trials serve that is the real horror, not the fact that
courts are used to give it effect. There are occasions when political trials
may actually serve liberal ends.

Judith Shklar, *Legalism*

I do not respond to this so-called court . . . what is built on illegitimacy is
illegitimate.

Saddam Hussein[1]

I was told by priests of the Serb Orthodox Church before arriving here that
the uniforms worn by the judges here resemble the uniform worn by the
former Catholic inquisition. The way you bow when you enter the courtroom reminds me of a satanic ritual. I'm afraid that should I bow to your
ceremonial, my consciousness might be affected by forces I cannot control.

Vojislav Šešelj[2]

1   The antithesis of legalism

The US infantryman who decided not to shoot the dishevelled figure
emerging from his refuge in Tikrit at the end of 2003, or lob a grenade
into that hiding-place, set in train a sequence of events that might have led
to the greatest trial in recent history (to paraphrase Norman Birkett's
description of Nuremberg). Saddam Hussein, hanged on 30 December
2006, was charged with a number of offences related to the killing of suspected assassins in the town of Dujail in 1982. The Iraqi Special Tribunal
Statute, enacted in December 2003, possesses jurisdiction over the classic
war crimes offences: crimes against humanity, war crimes and serious
violations of the laws of war committed between 17 July 1968 and up and
until 1 May 2003. The indictment, though, failed to encompass also the
gassing of the Kurds at Halabja (as well as other atrocities associated with
the Anfal Campaign, the subject matter of initial charges), the murder of
leading Shia clerics, the torture of inmates at Abu Ghraib, the violations

of human rights committed by Iraqi troops in Kuwait during their brief residency there in 1990–1 or the adoption of policies threatening peace between Arab states (Article 14(3)).

The prosecution's case was no doubt muddied by the requirements of political sensitivity. To what extent was the prosecutor's office willing to pursue convictions in relation to aggressive wars (in one case, at least, a war encouraged by the Western powers)?[3] How much of the current Iraqi state apparatus was implicated in, say, crimes against the Kurds? To what extent would the trial have become a trial of Iraq rather than Saddam? These, and other delicate issues, confronted the prosecutor. The defence case was much more obvious, at least rhetorically. The trial of Saddam Hussein was presented as a 'Show Trial', a proceeding which is more show than trial. In April 2005, newspapers around the world carried a report that members of Saddam's family had approached Jacques Vergès to act as legal representative for the former President.[4] Vergès is famous in the field for having defended Klaus Barbie in Lyon in 1988 where he turned the trial of a leading Nazi murderer and Gestapo chief into an orgy of recrimination directed at French colonialism (in Algeria) and collaboration (during Vichy) (chapter 4). The trial was intended to reframe the Vichy experience and French resistance to the German occupation, reconfigure national history and satisfy the leftist inclinations of the then current French Government. Vergès undercut all this. In the end, the innocence or guilt of the accused became somewhat marginal to the show planned by the French authorities and the alternative show conjured by Vergès (chapter 4). Vergès used similar tactics in two cases at the World Court: in one he acted for the Democratic Republic of the Congo in its successful suit against Belgium, the result of which was the partial gutting of Belgium's war crimes legislation; and in the other, a case was brought by the Republic of the Congo against France. In the latter case, concerning the exercise of jurisdiction by French courts over DRC government ministers, Vergès focused in his opening statements on the nature of French colonial rule, the failure of the French authorities to indict President Chirac for alleged crimes of corruption, and the racial motivations underlying the French judicial system.[5] Vergès, then, if indeed he had come to act for Saddam, would have had little hesitation, not to mention vast experience, in making some links between Saddam's alleged crimes and those of his enemies. If this had indeed turned out to be the case, we should not be too surprised. Saddam himself has already described the trial as a show trial: 'I do not want to make you feel uneasy,' he said at the beginning of the trial in July 2004, 'but you know this is all theatre by Bush' (Tisdall, 2005).

This is a relentless theme in defence statements, judicial anxieties and critical commentary around war crimes trials. In the previous 'greatest' war crimes trial in history, that of Slobodan Milosevic in The Hague, the accused began his Opening Statement before the ICTY by promptly denouncing the trial as an illegitimate sham: 'I never heard of indictments that resemble political pamphlets with poor, bad intentions'.[6] And this image of the war crimes trial as a bad trial infected with politics has a lengthy history. At Nuremberg, Speer and Hess each protested the legitimacy of the trials, with Hess describing them as direct descendants of the 'trials between 1936 and 1938' (in Moscow).[7] Even earlier, in the debates at the Commission on Authorship in Versailles, the US delegation worried that any trial of the Kaiser would be a misuse of judicial resources, combining the worst of ex post factoism and politicization.

This criticism was given a subtler twist in the Tadic case where the defence challenged the legality of the trial by dismissing the Court as the product of Great Power whim. In doing so the defence focused on the Security Council's role in creating the Court and the resultant lack of legitimacy. Defendants have been quick to conflate the show trial with the idea of victor's justice. The show trials charge was raised recently, too, again in relation to the decision to begin war crimes investigations in relation to UK soldiers involved in Operation Telic in southern Iraq. During a debate in the House of Lords, one of the peers accused the Army Legal Services of engaging in a politically motivated process inspired by 'extraneous reasoning' irrelevant to the guilt or innocence of those under investigation. He ended by inquiring of any future proceedings: 'Was that to have been a show trial on that reason?'[8]

Many advocates of war crimes trials are lawyers. These are individuals who believe in exporting constitutional and criminal procedures from the domestic to the international sphere. These lawyers want to domesticate the international state of anarchy using legal techniques. However, also drawn from the ranks of the legal profession are men and women (often judges) who have no wish to compromise the purity of legal procedure by exposing it to a world of political machination. They are legalists who believe legalism belongs at home. For some of them, international war crimes trials are perversions of justice rather than exemplars of it: a matter of regret not celebration. Such trials, they argue, dress the visceral impulse for revenge in the forms of legal procedure. For example, Justice Rutledge of the US Supreme Court described the post-war trial of General Yamashita as the 'uncurbed spirit of revenge and retribution, masked in formal legal procedure for purposes of dealing with a fallen enemy commander' (*In Re*

Yamashita, 1946). Justice Pal at Tokyo remarked that such trials allowed the Western powers to 'repent of their violence and permanently profit by it' (Kopelman, 1991: 187). And throughout the war and post-war era, Supreme Court Chief Justice Harlan Fiske Stone maintained a withering opposition to the idea of trials for the Nazis, believing that the Nuremberg Trials were a misuse of legal procedure.

Meanwhile, there has been ongoing critique of war crimes trials from outside the legal profession. Hannah Arendt's *Eichmann in Jerusalem* is perhaps a key text in this regard. She, famously, went to Jerusalem in 1960 enthusiastic at the prospect of observing the trial but ended up deploring the proceedings. For Arendt, what began, with some excitement, as 'an obligation I owe my past' was transformed into a feeling that 'the whole thing is *stinknormal*, indescribably inferior, worthless' (Young-Bruehl, 1981: 329–31). For some critics, show trials are a consequence of projecting legalism into an anarchic and irremediably politicized space, i.e. international society. Accordingly, these trials are a form of, what I called in chapter 1, *deformed legalism*.

These are minority opinions, however. For supporters of war crimes trials, totalitarian states are 'accustomed to running domestic show trials'; but such trials are avoided in the 'serious pursuit of international justice' (Bass, 2000: 8). Totalitarian states convene show trials, liberal states favour legitimate war crimes trials (Bass, 2000: 8). These trials may be defective but they are at least legitimate and worthwhile. As Antonio Cassese, former Judge at The Hague Tribunal, put it: 'half a pie is better than no pie' (Cassese, 2003). Tribuals operate at the behest of the Great Powers, perhaps, but, after all, this is a primitive legal order and what we are witnessing are the 'early glimmerings of international criminal justice' (Akhavan, 1993: 31) or the beginnings of cosmopolitan justice (Hirsh, 2003).

Show trials, on the other hand, are defined as procedures that seem to have exceeded the limits of legality itself. Such trials are all show, no trial. In this sense, the term is used to signify a place beyond law where all that remains is a theatre of the macabre (their purpose was elimination, terror and intimidation). The paradigm show trials in Western legal culture remain the Moscow and Prague show trials. At Moscow between 1936 and 1938, the last of the old Bolsheviks were tried and subsequently shot. These included the remaining members (Stalin and Trotsky apart) of Lenin's original Central Committee Politburo, among them: Kamenev, Zinoviev and, most famously, Bukharin.[9] Over a decade later, in Prague, Sofia and Budapest (as well as in other Eastern European capitals) the party elite was decimated in show trials. At a show trial, then, men clutch their unbelted trousers as state prosecutors harangue them for having committed vaguely defined but hysterically denounced crimes against the people or against the revolution. At show trials, defendants cheer hysterically when the death sentence is handed down. These trials are important because they have come to represent the ultimate perversion of legality.

For Judith Shklar, the primary purpose of a show trial is liquidation: 'What, after all, is a political trial? It is a trial in which the prosecuting party, aided by a co-operative judiciary, tries to eliminate its political enemies' (Shklar, 1964: 149). In show trials, as Goebbels once said, 'the man must go' (Shklar: 152). The show trial's features are largely deformities; they are typified by a bullied defence, a craven judiciary and a rabid prosecution. The trials are either staged (Lenin's show trials) or scripted (Stalin's) and often decisions are made in advance by the State (Ellman, 2001). As Shklar, again, notes (p. 152) the show trial usually involves the trial of a person for committing an act for which there is no crime (the conviction is secured through hostile judges and perjured witnesses) or the prosecution of a crime lacking an accompanying act (there is only danger in the future or 'historical' responsibility) or the use of a particular legal provision to remove only discrete classes of people.[10]

These are not legal procedures that become politicized but rather political acts given the aura of legality: 'I wish to say that the entire world knows that this is a political process. So we are not here speaking about legal procedures that evolve into political ones. This is a political process to begin with, and as far as what I would prefer, I would prefer the truth' (*Milosevic* (Transcripts), 30 January 2002: 352).

For Hannah Arendt, the point of the show trial is the performance of a 'spectacle with pre-arranged results' (Arendt, 1994: 266) or the obliteration, through compulsive staging, of the 'irreducible risk' (Kirchheimer, 1961: 1) that is the mark of the criminal trial (it is this risk that is misunderstood by those who describe war crimes initiatives as unsuccessful when they fail to result in convictions). In Australia, for example, the failure to secure convictions in the cases involving those accused of being former Nazis was a consequence of precisely this risk. The evidence was simply inadequate. In Australia, Goebbels's dictum was reversed: the man must go free. The opposite of this irreducible risk is embodied in Vishinsky's toast at dinner with the judges at Nuremberg where he announced: 'They will all hang' (Taylor, 1992: 211). Show trials, then, are not at the outer edges of legality but, rather, mark revolutionary departures from it. In the case of, what Orwell called, 'frame-up trials' (Orwell, 1970: 272) seeing is disbelieving (providing one sees using the sorts of instincts possessed by the young Alexander Solzhenitsyn, who said of the Moscow Trials: 'I was keenly interested in politics from the age of 10, even as a callow adolescent I did not believe Vishinsky and was staggered by the fraudulence of the famous trials' (Amis, 2002: 72)).[11]

Disagreement may exist over the precise meaning of show trials but, as I have indicated, the show trial plays a useful role for enthusiasts of war crimes trials. Whatever show trials may or may not be, war crimes and ordinary trials do not belong in that category. Following a lengthy indictment of Soviet-style show trials, Gary Bass states simply: 'The contrast with real legalism is stark' (Bass, 2000: 28). But, partly through the promptings of defence lawyers and defendants and partly because of the continuing salience of the victor's justice image, the spectre of the show trial continues to exert a powerful hold over war crimes trials, their supporters and their denigrators. There has been relatively little exploration, however, of the precise relationship between war crimes trials and show trials. In the second half of this chapter, I want to examine this relationship more closely. In particular, I continue my examinations of the relationship between law and politics by considering the experience of what I take to be the paradigmatic show trials, in the Soviet Union in the 1930s and in the Eastern Europe of the late 1940s and 1950s. These trials, described variously as 'betrayals of justice' (Shklar, 1964), 'charades' (Carmichael, 1976) and 'rituals of liquidation' (Leites and Bernaut, 1954), are posited, by most war crimes law advocates, as the opposite of the liberal legal tradition within which war crimes trials are situated. Enthusiasts of war crimes trials, then, have been pre-occupied with the question of show trials and have sought to sharply distinguish the Nuremberg tradition from the Vishinskyite tradition found in Moscow in the 1930s; true, there have been procedural irregularities and a pattern of victor's justice but war crimes trials, at least, are not show trials. Defendants may occasionally allude to show trials but, according to supporters of war crimes trials, these references are self-serving decoys pointing up the sharp distinctions between the Moscow tradition and the Nuremberg tradition.

These rhetorical clarifications and oppositions are another constituent element of the war crimes field, along with its didacticism and amnesia (chapter 4), its oscillations between its national and international tendencies (chapter 2), and its dual reckoning with collective guilt and individual responsibility (chapter 3). I argue here that while war crimes trials and show trials turn out to be highly variegated (I have attempted merely a distillation of their essential characteristics), they often share some structural similarities.[12] It is important, of course, not to view war crimes trials as show trials in the sense of being staged or scripted but nor must we accept them as models of natural justice. This chapter concludes that rather than dismissing war crimes trials as fatally politicized or, alternatively, enlisting them as beacons of liberal legalism, it might be more productive to approach them as spectacles in which the machinery and symbolism of the show trial is sometimes visible and in which the legitimation strategies and imperatives of the prosecuting state or community often are a key purpose or effect of the trial (see, too, chapter 4) (Shklar, 1964; Mégret, 2003).

2   Legality and deformity

The simultaneous emergence of two political phenomena is rarely accidental. The institutionalization of show trials and war crimes law occurred in the same period at the beginning of the twentieth century when political defeat was criminalized and enemies were transformed into criminals (the French Revolution can be viewed as a precursor here). At the international level, at least, what disappeared with this transformation was the notion of the duel between equivalent political adversaries, a contest with exclusively political consequences (Schmitt, 2003). The Treaty of Versailles, by assigning responsibility to the defeated enemy, and personal guilt to enemy leaders, accelerated the juridification of war or defeat and the turn to trial (see chapter 6 for a lengthier discussion of juridification). In the twentieth century, it became natural to assume that war's losers should be subject to criminal prosecution in a way that was clearly not the case in the nineteenth century or before, when death, amnesty or rehabilitation were more likely to be the favoured techniques. For example, as I have indicated previously, since coming to power in the UK, Prime Minister Tony Blair has presided over five wars involving the United Kingdom armed forces. In each case, there have been juridical consequences but in the case of Iraq (in 1998 and 2003), Sierra Leone and Kosovo, one of the results of war has been the indictment or trial of the individuals who opposed British intervention (the trial of Saddam Hussein, the indictment of Liberian and Sierra Leonean leaders in Freetown and the trial of President Milosevic in The Hague). It has now become routine, in other words, to view political adversaries as potential defendants.

Show trials, too, thrived in the 1920s, coinciding with the Versailles agreements, and reached a high point in the mid-1930s, anticipating the war crimes trials in 1945–9. Of course, there were nineteenth-century precursors in both cases (the trial of Wirz in the American Civil War for war crimes, the 'show' trial of Dreyfuss and the blood libel of Beilis), but there is little doubt that the early twentieth century saw a move to the judicial arena in dealing with fallen enemies both at home and in the aftermath of international conflict. In this sense, at least, war crimes trials and show trials belong to the same genre of responses to political or military success and are attempts to accomplish, alongside the physical destruction of an enemy, its moral, spiritual and juridical defeat.

War crimes trials and show trials influenced each other at another more basic level. For example, the Eastern European show trials adopted some of the nomenclature and procedure of the Nuremberg and Tokyo trials. In these trials, the defendants were accused of being rootless cosmopolitans, Titoists and *war criminals* (not an accusation levelled at any of the defendants in the 1930s trials) (Cotic, 1987: 122). In Prague, Geminder, one of the defendants, seemed to be gesturing back to Speer et al. and forward to Eichmann, when he admitted: 'Even though my activities were directed by Rudolf Slansky, that is no excuse for me' (Cotic: 131).

The show trials*influenced the Allies in their deliberations over the Nuremberg and Tokyo trials. The victorious powers were initially divided on the question of trials. Churchill, remembering the political embarrassment caused by the fiasco of the Leipzig Trials in 1921 as well as the volte face on the proposed trial of the Young Turks following the Armenian massacres, favoured a summary procedure for captured high-ranking Nazis and he asked his solicitor-general, Lord Simon, to draw up plans to have certain Nazis declared outlaws. At Teheran in 1943, Stalin proposed a toast to the summary execution of 50,000 of the German military and political elite. Churchill was appalled by the scale but not, initially at least, by the procedure. The Americans meanwhile were internally divided between the Morgenthau camp (favouring summary action) and the McCloy / Stimson camp (favouring judicial procedure) but eventually came round to the idea of trials (Beschloss, 2002). The Soviets also warmed to the idea of a major trial but they had contemplated something along the lines of the Moscow Trials. After all, by the time of Nuremberg, the Soviets had already tried and executed thousands of Germans on the Eastern front at Kharkov and elsewhere. By the time the Soviets reached Nuremberg, they were declaring the accused guilty (Nikitchenko) and toasting their imminent execution (Vishinsky). Vishinsky's presence alone made the 'show trials' imputation irresistible (he was, after all, Stalin's favourite prosecutor). Equally, there were strong voices on the Anglo-American side that worried about acquittals and were determined to secure a process that would guarantee certain 'outcomes' without giving 'undue weight to technical contentions and legalistic arguments'.[13] At one point, for example, Roosevelt warned that the disposition of the Nazi criminals 'should not be too judicial' (Marrus, 1997: 33).

There are other, perhaps superficial, similarities between war crimes trials and show trials. In both cases, the trial becomes a world 'event' or spectacle. The individuals involved feel themselves to be participating in a great political moment. In the 1949 Rajk trial in Hungary, for example, the prosecutor begins: 'The trial is of international importance' (Hodos, 1987: 59). This grandiosity is standard for war crimes trials, too. At Nuremberg, Robert Jackson opened the case by remarking: 'The real complaining party at your bar is Civilisation'.[14] In the Milosevic case, Carla Del Ponte began the Prosecution case by stating: 'Today, as never before, we see international justice in action'.[15] Gideon Hausner movingly invoked his six million fellow accusers in the Eichmann trial (unconsciously, no doubt, referring back to Vishinksy's comment at the beginning of the 'Wreckers' trial (Radek et al.) where he said: 'I do not stand alone . . .' (before listing the workers, the crippled, the communists who had suffered because of the alleged economic sabotage) (Kadri, 2005: 197). The participants in war crimes trials see themselves as immersed in matters of great political moment (while, of course, remaining above politics). Like the prosecutors in show trials, such trials are not simply matters of trial and conviction. Instead, they implicate larger political transformations and are efforts to influence and dictate these transformations. Not merely political or legal proceedings, they are world-historical trials.

Show trials, though, are marked by several properties whose resonance with war crimes trials I wish to explore in greater depth. First, show trials and procedural justice make very unhappy bedfellows. It is the defining trait of show trials that they betray a casual disregard for established rule of law norms. Second, show trials tend to be reactive juridical events formulated for a specific purpose and moment in time. Sometimes courts are established for the purpose of trying certain individuals, at other times existing courts extend or adapt their mandate or function to meet a particular exigency. In both cases, the show trial is an ad hoc, discretionary proceeding divorced from everyday judicial activity. Third, prosecutors, keen to secure convictions, tend to rely on concepts of conspiracy and 'membership of criminal organization' rather than on more straightforward attributions of personal liability. The more amorphous and encompassing the 'criminal enterprise', the better chance there is of capturing political enemies in its dragnet. Fourth, suspects do not emerge spontaneously through the accretion of evidence but are, instead, chosen for trial on the basis of their fit with the ideological requirements of the moment, and the broader aims of the conspiracy theory.

These deformities are all linked to a broader point, one I take up in the final section of this chapter. Show trials mark a philosophical commitment to two complementary ideas about war and crime. First, such trials erase the distinction between political error and criminal liability. Mistakes are transformed into crimes through judicial process. Second, and this is a closely linked point, show trials are juridical enactments of particular political realignments or historical transformations. 'We are objects of history' as Varenc Vagi conceded on his way to the gallows in Prague (Hodos, 1987: 91). The accused are guilty not because of what they have done but because of where they happen to stand when political forces are transformed. Major Dan Mori, the military lawyer defending David Hicks, one of the detainees at Guantanamo Bay, responded to Donald Rumsfeld's pre-trial statements that the Guantanamo Bay detainees were 'the worst of the worst' by saying that they were merely, at worst, the 'first of the worst'.[16] They, like show trial defendants, are unlucky but 'guilty' victims of circumstance. In show trials, the agency/structure distinction collapses. Or, to put it another way, there is only structure. Defendants are tossed around by objective historical forces over which they can have no control. These historical forces dictate questions of guilt or innocence.

2.1   Procedure

Procedurally, the classic show trials were deeply flawed, often surreal, exercises in phantom justice. Reading the personal accounts of the surviving defendants, one is struck by the grotesque nature of some of the proceedings. After months of torture, confession, retraction, threat and more torture, the accused were deemed ready to go on trial.[17] By the time the defendants arrived in court, they were broken men (the vast majority of defendants were men, though there were exceptions in Eastern Europe); their performances in court were exercises in robotic self-denunciation. Frequently, the accused were trained to recite verbatim testimony drafted in advance (Cotic, 1987: 66). The trials, in Moscow, were scripted by the Prosecutor in cahoots with Stalin (Rayfield, 2005: 306). In one case, the defendant was obliged to correct a mistake made by the Prosecutor who had accidentally missed a whole page of his submission (recalling Klaus Barbie's clarifications at Lyon on the meaning of crimes against humanity). In many cases, confessions were the only evidence available and any corroboration was available only from other confessions (Carmichael, 1976: 36). Defence lawyers merely repeated the Prosecution's defamations while judges followed instructions from the Party leadership. The whole process was described in some quarters as 'judicial murder'. By the end of the process, a number of inversions had been effected. In Prague, a son had called for the death sentence to be imposed on his father before committing suicide himself, wives denounced and divorced their husbands, and victims praised their murderers.[18]

War crimes trials are quite different from these show trials in a number of respects but they share with show trials some serious procedural deficiencies. This, indeed, has been the gravamen of the legalist objection to war crimes trials. In a procedural sense, it is not at all clear that war crimes trials have been the 'antithesis' of show trials. Nuremberg and Tokyo both were procedurally dubious. At neither trial was there a right to appeal to a higher court or appellate level. At Nuremberg, the defence was not furnished with evidence in the possession of the prosecution nor was the defence even made aware of the existence of some crucial documentation (Sereny, 1996: 578). Meanwhile, the accused at Nuremberg were tried and convicted on the basis of largely *ex post facto* laws either improvised for the trial itself (crimes against humanity) or imported from the United States (conspiracy). The constituent charters in both cases explicitly removed the standard procedural protections available to defendants in Western states. Article 13 of the Tokyo Charter, for example, stated that the Tribunal would not be bound by technical rules of evidence but would instead test evidence for its 'probative value' (this permitted the use of hearsay and unsworn statements at Tokyo (Minear, 1971: 118–24; Maga, 2001: 23)). At Tokyo, only one of the judges had any experience in international law (Pal), one had been a victim of those on trial (Jaranilla) and one had no knowledge of the official language of the trial (Zarayanov). In the end, it is alleged that the death sentence for some of the accused was passed on a 6 : 5 vote (Minear, 1971: 88).

In the past twenty years, there has been a convergence between the conduct of war crimes trials and common standards of procedural justice. Nonetheless, there is still a fair degree of novelty, flexibility and ad hocery (infra) in the system. The defendants in The Hague before the ICTY have found themselves subject to procedural innovations (concerning the anonymity and confidentiality of witnesses, for example) that have brought criticism from bodies such as the American Bar Association (Leigh, 1996). The spectre of ex post factoism hovers over the Iraq Trials, too, with the Statute giving the Court jurisdiction over crimes against humanity occurring as early as 1968 (long before some crimes against humanity had been properly defined) (Alvarez, 2004: 321). The Eichmann, Barbie, Milosevic and Nikolic trials were preceded by abductions or transfers of doubtful legality. Even the Trial Chamber conceded as much in its 'Decision on Preliminary Motions' (8 December 2001) in the Milosevic case. And in *Milosevic*, too, the Trial Chamber skated close to depriving the accused of his presumption of innocence in determining, at the jurisdictional phase, that the joinder of the three indictments (Kosovo, Bosnia and Croatia) was justified because of evidence of a common purpose to engage in a joint criminal enterprise (Gaparayi, 2004: 748).[19] This evidence included material that could be described as double hearsay.[20] Meanwhile, in the same case, a judge who had died in the middle of the proceedings was replaced by a new judge who had heard none of the preceding testimony. None of this adds up to a show trial. Milosevic was subjected to a form of justice, in some respects, far removed from that experienced by Radek or Bukharin. But, in the use of novel legal procedures and newly minted substantive laws, the trials held in The Hague reveal some uncomfortable parallels with the classic show trials.

2.2   Ad hocery

It is notorious that show trials are responses to political exigencies, or demonstrations of superior political power. But more than this, they are discretionary procedures – lying outside the normal routines of legal process – intended to eliminate, humiliate or create political opponents. The heavy hand of the political elite is everywhere in the demand for a trial of discredited leaders and political enemies. The same is often true of the international community's role in establishing tribunals for the prosecution of defeated enemies. The five major international war crimes institutions are all marked by a comparable deviation from normality. At Nuremberg, the Allies spent many months arguing and debating over whether war crimes trials would achieve the ends desired by the political masters (Beschloss, 2002). These were decisions to establish a new *ex post facto* machinery to punish defeated enemies, and were regarded as simply one of a number of possible mechanisms for eliminating these enemies (Bass, 2000: 150–72). The ephemeral nature of these procedures also mirrors the show trials. These are not hearings that have long or medium-term reverberations. There was no permanent show trial procedure after Moscow and, of course, one of the great disappointments of Nuremberg and Tokyo lay in their failure to deliver successor institutions. In the case of the Balkan trials, and those in Arusha of the Rwandan genocidaires, the courts are described explicitly as ad hoc tribunals. These were established by political decision at the highest level in New York (*Tadic* (Decision)). The challenges to the Court's constitutionality made in the Milosevic case, indeed, forced the tribunal to confront this ad hocery. In the 2001 Decision on Preliminary Motions, the Trial Chamber, in a piece of boot-strapping logic, held that the tribunal was a validly created body under the Security Council's 'peace and security' jurisdiction in Chapter VII of the Charter because the Council had expressly stated in Resolution 827 (establishing the Court) that it was acting to promote peace and reconciliation. The argument that the tribunal's ad hoc nature violated rule of law principles of fairness and equality was dismissed by the Chamber on the basis that the partial or selective nature of the tribunal was immaterial providing it had been 'established by law'.[21] Many of the show trials, too, had been 'established by law' but this hardly affords a convincing answer to the problem of selectivity. As Justice Douglas put it, describing the Tokyo Trial: 'It took its law from its creator . . . it did not therefore act as a judicial tribunal. It was solely an instrument of political power'.[22]

In the case of the ad hoc tribunals, the Security Council established courts with a specific mandate, and with limited territorial and temporal reach. These institutions were created to try a very local, specific, exceptional category of offenders. Territorially, the ICTY is restricted to the borders of the former Yugoslav state while the Rwanda tribunal has jurisdiction over Rwanda itself and neighbouring territories. The temporal range of each tribunal is also highly restrictive with the ICTY's coverage extending only as far back as January 1991 and Rwanda's covering only the period of the genocide itself in 1994.

Meanwhile, the courts have been subject to some degree of political interference. The ICTY Prosecutor has been called upon by the Council to investigate allegations of violence in specific cases (in 1998, the Council requested the Prosecutor to begin investigations into alleged crimes committed in Kosovo).[23] Even the ICC is likely to have much of its workload dictated by the willingness of the Security Council to refer matters to it under Article 13(b) of the Statute. Furthermore, the resolution giving the ICC jurisdiction over the Darfur crisis is not only ad hoc but also highly selective. Paragraph 6 expressly immunizes personnel from states (other than Sudan) not party to the ICC. This provision, the price paid for the US abstention, effectively deprives the Court of jurisdiction over any American servicemen who might serve in Sudan.

To conclude, show trials have been criticized for the provisional and ad hoc nature of the justice they dispense. Show trial mechanisms are created by political elites for specific purposes and are abandoned on the completion of the trials. The international war crimes machinery has been marked by similar tendencies. The Nuremberg and Tokyo trials left no institutional trace for fifty years. The ad hoc tribunals established by the Security Council have limited lifespans (the ICTY, for example, must complete all indictments by the end of 2008 and all trials by the end of 2010). Even the ICC, lauded as the world's first permanent war crimes court, will be subject to the vagaries of state inclinations and Security Council attentiveness.

2.3   Conspiracy

The choice of defendants in show trials very much depended on the nature of the offences to be tried. This was particularly the case where there were no recognizable offences. In Moscow and in Prague, by manufacturing a conspiracy, the prosecutors obviated the need to prove that the defendants had engaged in any identifiable acts. The defendants, then, were chosen for their match with the conspiracy or their imagined relationship to some vast, intangible network or organization of 'wreckers', imperialist spies or counter-revolutionaries. There was no need to establish anything as bourgeois as '*mens rea*' (Shklar, 1964: 204). This approach permitted recourse to a Kafkaesque world where proof of guilt could be found in a slavish adherence to the Bolshevik party line. Such apparent loyalty could be put down to double-dealing and the desire to preserve the integrity of the conspiracy (Leites and Bernaut, 1954: 205). Any behaviour at all could be explained in terms of conspiracy; as Squealer puts it (accounting for Snowball's bravery at the battle of Animal Farm): 'That was part of the arrangement' (Orwell, 1996: 70).

Once the conspiracy was asserted, it was possible for anyone to come within its embrace. Conspiracy is an idea about an idea. In such contexts, the need for any sort of evidence begins to disappear. Soon, all of political contestation came within the ambit of the conspiracy. Rivals and opponents of the dominant bloc were, by definition, conspirators. Eventually, many defendants at the trials began to concede their involvement in conspiracies they had been unaware of at the time of the supposed offence. In Prague, Otto Sling resisted this line initially, claiming that he knew nothing of the so-called conspiracy. The interrogators found this resistance absurd and pointless. After all: 'They had already crystallised the plan and objective of the grand conspiracy' (Cotic, 1987: 25). In a similar way, whole organizations or strata of society were labelled criminal. Membership of such organizations could also be used to signal that the individual himself was also criminal. This was a technique used in the Austro-Hungarian trial of Slavic rebels in 1908–16, and re-emerged again in the mid-century Eastern European show trials when, for example, previous membership in the International Brigades left individuals open to serious suspicion.

War crimes jurisprudence begins on this footing at Nuremberg where the proceedings are structured around the idea of conspiracy. Bernays, with the support of Stimson, had devised a plan whereby the whole German hierarchy would be charged with conspiring to launch an aggressive war and commit serious violations of the laws of war and crimes against humanity. Any individual who had become a member of a criminal organization engaged in this conspiracy became vulnerable to prosecution, and indeed, was presumed to be guilty of certain crimes.[24] This worked well enough at Nuremberg, albeit that it produced a skewed historical record, but it was discredited at Tokyo where political decisions largely unconnected to the war in the Far East, and dating back to 1928, were included as part of an all-encompassing conspiracy.[25]

Conspiracy, strictly speaking, has disappeared from the jurisprudence of war crimes (though it has reappeared in relation to charges brought against some Guantanamo detainees and remains a component of cases involving crimes against humanity at the domestic level (e.g. *Pinochet*)). In the contemporary scene, prosecutors have tended to favour concepts such as 'joint criminal enterprise' in order to capture the structural aspects of criminality in war. This theory of culpability, of course, is open to some of the same abuses that were seen at Tokyo and Nuremberg (Osiel, 2005). At the ICTY, joint criminal enterprise is a central feature of a number of the proceedings (including the three indictments issued against Milosevic).[26] This approach to conspiracy is more subtle than that seen at Nuremberg or the Moscow show trials, though unlike Nuremberg, where the IMT could at least ground its reasoning on the existence of conspiracy in the Charter, the Tribunal has had to develop the concept in the absence of any reference to it in its Statute. In *Milosevic*, there were shades of the Slansky trial in the Decision on the Motion for Joinder, where, before the Defence had led its evidence, the Tribunal found that there was a common purpose behind each of the criminal enterprises (paras. 20–1).

Joint criminal enterprise raises other problems, too. Like the conspiracy charges in show trials, the way in which participation in a criminal enterprise is defined ends up being over-inclusive. Too often, the existence of a conspiracy (involving, say, the creation of a new political entity through acts of ethnic cleansing) combined with a single act of persecution by an individual can be enough to implicate that individual in the overall enterprise or conspiracy. This form of joint criminal enterprise, known as extended joint criminal enterprise, can result in the accused being convicted for acts that these accused had no intention of committing (but were merely a 'foreseeable' consequence of the enterprise).[27] This (third) category of joint criminal enterprise was articulated first in *Tadic*, and marks a significant lowering of the culpability threshold. This is, what Mark Osiel has called, the 'elasticity' of joint criminal enterprise (Osiel, 2005: 1804). It was this elasticity that made conspiracy so appealing to show trial prosecutors, and it has its adherents in contemporary trial procedures, too. It exists alongside the 'vagueness' (Osiel, 2005: 1802–4) problem of conspiracy to produce over-broad and fictitious forms of collective responsibility. As two authors recently argued, joint criminal enterprise has the 'potential to lapse into [a] form of guilt by association' (Danner and Martinez, 2006). Prosecutors in contemporary war crimes trials show far greater restraint in using these forms than was the case in the show trials. Nonetheless, the structural similarities are pronounced. Bradley Smith, discussing debates among the Four Powers at Nuremberg, recalls the reaction of the Soviet and French delegates to the inclusion of conspiracy in the following terms: '. . . the Russians and French seemed unable to grasp the implications of the concept; when they finally did grasp it, they were genuinely shocked . . . the Soviets seemed to have shaken their heads in wonderment – a reaction, some cynics may believe, prompted by envy' (B. Smith, 1981, quoted in Danner and Martinez, 2006).

2.4   Selection of defendants

Much of the effort around the Moscow and Eastern European show trials centred on the choice of defendants. What role would they play in the ensuing theatre? Were they prominent enough to create a buzz around the trial or to serve as a warning to other potential deviators? Did they represent a cross section of the enemy's hierarchy? Was their elimination desirable? In the show trials, categories of potential defendants were created and individuals were then enveloped in those categories (Cotic, 1987: 70). In this way, the architects of show trials created classes of potential defendants and then worked on finding a representative sample from each of these classes. In this sense, at least, Shklar's famous definition does not quite capture what was occurring prior to the major show trials. The trials held in Eastern Europe were not organized for the purpose of removing political opponents but rather to create them (Kirchheimer, 1961: 1).

The point of the trial was the trial itself: its ramifications, its warnings and its effluxions of terror. The trials were initially ideas emanating from Moscow. Once the idea had taken a concrete form the search was on for possible players: judges, prosecutors, interrogators . . . and defendants. In Prague, investigations at first centred on fairly low-level communist apparatchiks. Then, under pressure from Moscow, President Gottwald, fearing for his own security, found someone he thought would be an ideal candidate for a major trial: Otto Sling, party secretary of Brno district. Sling, after torture, began to confess to involvement in a complex conspiracy. It was at this point that the name of Rudolf Slansky, Party General Secretary, began to emerge (Cotic, 1987: 26). The Soviet Advisers based in Prague believed they had found a figure of sufficient seniority to sustain a major show trial. The Czechs were initially bemused and wondered at the lack of evidence. But as one Soviet Adviser, soon to be purged himself, put it: 'We have been sent here to stage trials not to check whether the charges are true' (Cotic: 69).

High-profile communists were required for these trials: Slansky (Czechoslovakia), Rajk (Hungary), Kostov (Bulgaria) and Bukharin, Kamenev and Zinoviev (Moscow). The defendants had to be prominent enough to sustain charges of Titoism, imperialism and conspiracy (Karel Radek, the Soviet economic expert, was chosen for one of the Moscow Trials because he was 'famous' (Vaksburg, 1990: 85)). The indictment thus preceded the defendant. (This did not prevent Stalin from being upset at the coverage of the early show trials. He claimed that reporters had '. . . reduced everything to the level of personalities' (Rayfield, 2005: 272).)

There is an assumption that at Nuremberg the defendants simply presented themselves as candidates for trial. These twenty-two individuals who were tried at Nuremberg (one *in absentia*) were what the Moscow Declaration has described as major war criminals whose crimes had no fixed geographical location. But the accused did not simply emerge naturally through a process of identification. Instead, the Allies bickered among themselves about the ideal choice of defendants. The British Attorney-General made it clear that alleged culpability for particular crimes was not likely to be the primary concern: 'The test should be "Do we want this man for making a success of our trial?" If yes, we must have him' (Overy, 2002: 35). By the time the Allies did reach agreement, the category of major war criminals had become a patchwork of subcategories. For example, each of the armed services had to be represented (Raeder and Doenitz for the Navy, Göring for the Luftwaffe and Keitel and Jodl for the Wehrmacht), and a rather unseemly effort was made to find an industrialist who could be tried as part of the general effort to implicate the German economic elite. In the end, the Allies indicted Gustav Krupp, who, subsequently, was declared too old and too senile to strand trial. The various negotiations produced a list of twenty-four defendants but it is clear that these individuals were chosen for a variety of reasons sometimes tangential to their guilt or innocence. These were representative defendants (Minear, 1971: 104).[28] In discussions about conspiracy before Nuremberg, a British diplomat said: 'What is in my mind is getting a man like Ribbentrop or Ley . . .'[29] In the case of Nuremberg, there may have been acquittals (Schacht, Frick, Schirach), moments of embarrassment for the prosecution (Jackson and Göring at Nuremberg) and lengthy technical discussions, but the original war crimes trial shares with show trials the distinction of being directed at only one subcategory of violators within a particular society in which there are across-the-board breaches of that society's basic norms (in the case of Tokyo and Nuremberg these include the principles of distinction, proportionality, non-combatant immunity, the avoidance of unnecessary suffering). Allied breaches of war law (Katyn, Dresden, Nagasaki) were passed over and, indeed, lawyers for the accused were excluded from raising *tu quoque* as a possible defence.

Choosing defendants on the basis of political imperative has been a feature of the ICTY and ICTR trials, too.[30] For example, in the case of the ICTY, an attempt has been made to prosecute a representative sample of defendants from each of the warring factions in the former Yugoslavia. The Tribunal is engaged in an effort to indict individuals from the Bosnian Muslim side (e.g. Oric) and the Croatian side (e.g. Gotovina) in order to achieve some sort of balance (the majority of defendants remain Serbian).[31] This balance, though, comes at a cost. It may be that prosecutors have simply ended up disproportionately focusing on certain groups in order to satisfy the demands of the international community for 'legitimacy' (Jones, 2004: 493; Osiel, 2005: 1751–2). In addition, the Prosecutors have found themselves under pressure to ensure that the work of the Tribunal covered both insignificant paramilitary members (Tadic) and high-ranking members of the regular armed forces (the indictment of Mladic) as well as the political leadership of the Bosnian Serbs (Karadzic, Plasvic) and the Serbian state itself (Milosevic).[32]

The show trials in the Soviet sphere were intended as vindications of those who had prevailed in the political struggle. The Stalinist bloc had triumphed over Lenin's Old Bolsheviks; the price of defeat was trial, conviction and either lengthy jail terms or death. In many cases, defendants in show trials were chosen simply because it was expedient to have them removed from the political scene. In the 1930s, Stalin wished to 'eliminate potential enemies' or challengers such as those associated with the Trotsky bloc or the Kirov bloc or the Kamenev-Zinoviev group. This has been one of the aspirations, too, of war crimes advocates. For example, Payam Akhavan has argued that one of the purposes of the ICTY trials is the removal of political enemies from the post-war Balkan state (Akhavan, 2001), and, again, at Nuremberg, the Allies were keen to purge elements of the Nazi elite around whom a Nazi revival might convene. The selection of defendants in war crimes trials, as in show trials, can be (though this is not always the case) as much a matter of eliminating a representative sample of political enemies as it is about prosecuting the guilty.

3   Objective guilt and subjective innocence

Show trials are political spectacles. When Eisenhower described the Prague show trials as '. . . a mockery of civilised and humanitarian values . . . a political act', he missed the point that for the Stalinists, the trials were, of course, a political act (Cotic, 1987: 146). All behaviour *was* political and could be situated within the objective movement of social and economic forces. In a phrase both sinister and yet freighted with possibilities and meanings, Merleau-Ponty called these trials 'dramas of subjective innocence and objective treason' (Merleau-Ponty, 1969: 202). This paradoxical effect, I want to argue, is found in war crimes trials, too, and indeed, more generally (though I can only touch on this), in the way that, in current practice, war is justified through law. In dramas of objective guilt, mistakes or political misjudgements are converted into crimes. Subjective political action becomes objectively criminal. The obverse of this is that the objective movement of political and social forces results in a situation where individuals find themselves, in the absence of any subjective intent, on the wrong side of history. These effects have contemporary resonance. Because individuals can be guilty in the absence of personal intent or particular acts, they can also be subjected to precautionary action for the crimes they might commit in future (*pre-emption*) as well as becoming the object of repressive legalized violence simply because of the accidents of time and place (*collateral damage*).

Show trials are about the transformation of abstract political differences into easily intelligible common crimes (Hodos, 1987: xiii). It was not that the defendants' errors led them to commit crimes; their errors *were* crimes. Accordingly, belonging to the wrong faction, or merely predicting a counter-revolutionary outcome in some political struggle or visiting the wrong country at the wrong time, marked one down as a criminal suspect.[33]

This conversion of political acts into criminal categories will be familiar to those who have studied the history of war crimes. Of course, the Nazis and the Japanese did commit horrific crimes. But many of the defendants at Moscow and, to a lesser extent, in Eastern Europe were guilty of terrible crimes, too (the liquidation of the Kulaks, the massacre of peasants, enforced famine, mass deportation, the gulag and so on). Zinoviev and Kamenev supported Stalin through the early collectivizations and liquidations, Trotsky (who would have stood trial) ordered the killing of the Kronstadt sailors, and some of the discredited Eastern European leadership had authorized purges of their own. But these activities were not the subject of the trials. In neither the show trials nor the early war crimes trials was recognizably criminal behaviour the main subject of the prosecution case and the trials themselves. The central element both at Nuremberg and in Prague and Moscow was the effort to convert what had hitherto been viewed largely as political acts (aggression at the IMT, bloc membership in Prague) into common crimes, and not the prosecution of acts that had recognizable affinities (albeit that they were on a different scale) with common crimes (e.g. crimes against humanity or mass killing).

Vishinsky banned the word 'opposition' from the courtroom in one of the Moscow show trials. The use of this term implied for him a sort of equivalence between two rival belief systems. Neither Stalinist dictatorship nor the international community has much time for such rival ideologies. It was (and remains) simpler to view opposition as a crime against the social order; the drama of subjective innocence and objective guilt requires the transformation of friends into enemies, and enemies into criminals. Former Politburo members, International Brigade Associates and former comrades of Stalin: all metamorphosized from loyal party figures into enemies of the state, and then common criminals. Political affiliations or bloc allegiances became criminal acts.[34] In a later trial at Moscow, Vishinsky adopted a different tack. Instead of converting political acts into criminal deeds, he refused to accept that the crimes had ever been political. There was an effort to depoliticize the political trial; the defendant's behaviour could be described as a 'mere terroristic act' with no 'political platform' (Leites and Bernaut, 1954: 250; Carmichael, 1976: 85).

In the war crimes field, at its origins, there is a discussion of the relationship between crime and politics. In the Commission on Authorship of the

War at Versailles, for example, there was a debate about the nature of German transgressions. While the Versailles Treaty itself envisaged the prosecution and trial of the Kaiser for acts of aggression, the Commission's Majority Report revealed a measure of disquiet about this. For the Commission, an act of war such as the invasion of Belgium could be deplored but it remained a political decision rather than a criminal act. 'Public conscience reproves and history will condemn', the Commission stated, but no Court had the authority to prosecute such acts as crimes. A strong dissenting opinion from the American representatives applied this sort of reasoning to the category of crimes against humanity too, arguing that such acts could only be judged in 'another forum'.[35]

While this move from politics to crime was resisted at Versailles, it was embraced more fully at Nuremberg in relation to the crime of aggressive war and crimes against humanity. This transformation of the international order was expressed, theatrically, by Robert Ley, the Nazi Head of the Labour Front, and one of the twenty-four Nuremberg accused. Just prior to his suicide on 24 October 1945, Ley vented his outrage and indignation on the subject of war and crime: 'Stand us up against a wall and shoot us . . . well and good . . . you are victors. But why should I be brought before a Tribunal like a c . . . c . . . c. I can't even get the word out' (Sereny, 1996: 573). The word was 'criminal' and, after Nuremberg and Tokyo, the international legal order was to have some trouble getting the word out. But in 1945, the Allies were convinced that aggression was the supreme crime (whatever its status prior to the war, see chapter 6).

The prosecution of conspiracy, too, at least in some cases, involved the criminalization of ideas (the abominable Julius Streicher was executed for having published ideas (hugely atrocious ideas)). Carl Schmitt himself was investigated and questioned on the basis that, as an intellectual, his ideas might have contributed to the aggressive war undertaken by Hitler.[36] There is no doubt Schmitt would have agreed with Justice Pal who, at Tokyo, insisted: 'The historic causes of the war simply defy legal judgement' (Kopelman, 1991: 188). It was another of the dissenting judges at Tokyo, Bert Röling, who seemed to understand just what the trial was about. He conceded that crimes against humanity were not proper crimes under public international law (Minear, 1971: 53) but he accepted, too, that a new category of crime could be created after the fact for what were essentially political crimes, '. . . where the criminal is considered an enemy rather than a villain, and where the punishment emphasises the political measure rather than judicial retribution' (Röling, 1998: 48; Minear, 1971: 54).[37] This dual notion of politics as crime and ideas as action is shared to some extent, then, by the classic show trials and the early war crimes trials.

Two aspects of this bear elaboration. The first is that the usual requirements of Anglo-American legalism – proof, agency, corroboration – were deemed unnecessary in show trials. The personal motives and intent of the accused were irrelevant. They may have 'intended' to go into one room but they had ended up in another.[38] That was their crime. During the second Moscow show trial the following exchange occurs:

> Vishinsky: 'These actions of yours were deliberate?'
> Radek: 'Apart from sleeping, I have never in my life committed an undeliberate act.'
>
> (Carmichael, 1976: 99)

Radek understood that his intentions were beside the point. Whatever he did was a product of his membership of a particular class. These trials were triumphs of structure over intent; they advanced a strict liability theory of political criminality. Rajk, the star defendant in the Hungarian trials, captured this perfectly when he remarked during his trial: 'I fully agree with most of the statements of the Prosecution; I don't mean the secondary and in any case unimportant details, *but with the substance*' (my italics, Hodos, 1987: 62). Rajk understood that the trial was not about the detail of intent or proof of actus. In substance, he was an enemy. That was sufficient. This was all apiece with Stalin's morality: 'to place a stake incorrectly is to perish' (Leites and Bernaut, 1954: 27). And as Bukharin had put it at his trial: '. . . everything personal falls away . . .' (Leites and Bernaut: 50).[39] The defendants were objectively guilty whatever their intentions.

Many officials assumed that the Nazis were 'objectively guilty', too, prior to the Nuremberg Trial. The trial was intended only to confirm this pre-ordained guilt in a juridical spectacle. At the London Conference, the UK Government representatives noted that 'His Majesty's Government assumes that it is beyond question that Hitler and a number of arch-criminals must . . . suffer the penalty of death' (23 April 1945, Aide Memoire, His Majesty's Government, Minear, 1971: 18). Robert Jackson, too, conceded that there could be only one verdict (Minear: 18) though he resisted the Soviets on this point in public (Jackson Report, 1949: 433). General Nikitchenko, the Soviet Judge, believed the Germans were already guilty: 'We are dealing with chief war criminals who have already been convicted and whose conviction has already been announced by the Moscow and Crimea declarations' (Marrus, 1997: 104–5). The Nazis, to this extent, also were objects of history. Their guilt was objective in the sense of being advertised prior to trial by the victors but it was objective in another sense, too: it was a creature of the realignment of political forces. There was a mere six-year gap between the Nuremberg Trials and the Molotov-Ribbentrop Pact, something defendants like Speer were quick to point out during cross-examination by the Soviets. In the intervening period, though, the political milieu had shifted dramatically. What had been a matter of *realpolitik* in 1939 had, for one group at least, become criminal by 1945.

To take a contemporary example, Saddam Hussein's objective responsibility emerged only after his defeat in the 1990–1 Gulf War. Prior to that, he had used chemical weapons against the Iranians in 1982 and, more notoriously, against the Kurds at Halabja in 1988. No one in positions of authority in the West took much notice of these 'crimes'. After all, as Geoffrey Kemp, then Head of Near and Middle East Affairs at the State Department, said, 'he's our son of a bitch' (Darwish, 2003). A suppressed CIA Report indicates that Halabja was of enormous strategic significance, that the Iranians had used gas around this area, too, and that the attack was inspired by a desire to secure a military advantage. The victims at Halabja could be viewed as 'collateral damage', too (Pelletiere, 1992). Saddam's crimes had been transformed into necessities by the then existing political orientations of the hegemons. By 2006, these were necessities that had become crimes. In Koetsler's striking phrase: 'But who will be proved right? It will only be known later' (Koestler, 1946: 99).

The second aspect of this that I want to elaborate upon concerns the notion of 'error as crime'. This is precisely the equation that many realists have argued disfigures war crimes prosecutions. A. J. P. Taylor famously said that statesmen do not commit crimes, at worst they make mistakes. In April 2006, Lord Hoffman, subconsciously, adverted to this, in the House of Lords, when he said: 'All these defences [defences based on the notion that the commission of an offence may be justified or necessary if it is required to prevent a serious crime] thus depend upon the proposition that the war in Iraq was a crime as well as a mistake' (Hoffman J. in *R v. Jones*: para. 44). But according to Raymond Aron, adopting a Nietzschean formulation, all states are cold-hearted monsters pursuing state interests with no regard for 'international' law or some transcendent morality.[40] The difference between a criminal state and a respected hegemon was a matter of luck or intuition not morality. As Hermann Göring said in 1937: 'We will go down in history either as the world's greatest statesmen or its worst villains'. War crimes trials, like show trials, then, were a means by which history was objectified and political actors made the objects of history. The participants in such trials saw themselves as figures buffeted and defined by history. They happened to have found themselves in 'the wrong room', on the losing side in a political game. To be mistaken or to make the wrong choice was to commit a political crime, and political crimes could be converted into common crimes through techniques such as conspiracy. Tojo, himself, understood this and tried to resist it, to no avail, when he drew a distinction between 'policy guilt' and 'war-mongering guilt' (Maga, 2001: 45).

What the Stalinists and liberal advocates of war crimes trials have shared is the view that mistakes (while they can be understood as errors of judgement) are crimes (because they are committed by individuals on the wrong side of history).[41] In the case of show trials, there is a depersonalization of crime through the erasure of intent or subjectivity, and the consequent collapse of error and crime as categories. At Nuremberg structural guilt is traced through the conspiracy charges and aggression and crimes against humanity are converted from sovereign prerogatives into crimes that 'shocked the conscience of humankind'.

There are three contemporary incidences or effects of all this which seem relevant in any discussion of law, war and crime. First, in both show trials and war crimes trials, there is present the idea that individuals can be punished because they pose a danger to some new configuration of political forces or some contested notion of community. In the Moscow show trials, the defendants were sometimes accused of already existing political offences; at other times, a category of potential crimes was created (Cilga, 1940: 287; Leites and Bernaut, 1954: 287). Very often, too, the Prosecutors referred to vaguely defined terrorist or terroristic offences (this was a favourite of Vishinsky's). In the secret trials of Zinoviev and Kamenev in January 1935, each of the defendants was sentenced to terms of imprisonment for 'having had counterrevolutionary ideas that contributed to the murder' (Leites and Bernaut: 53). Imprisoning or interning people before they have committed a crime or in case they might commit a crime has a lengthy and not very respectable history. At Nuremberg, Göring differentiated between two categories of traitor: the person who had committed a criminal act and '. . . others . . . of whom one might expect such acts but who had not yet committed them'. All were to be taken into custody (Marrus, 1997: 111). This form of pre-emptive justice is found in some war crimes trials, too. At Tokyo, Röling, in discussing crimes against humanity and, in particular, the crime of aggression, likened them to '. . . political crimes where the decisive element is the danger rather than guilt' (Röling,

1999: 44; Minear, 1971: 54). This notion of pre-emption is now a trope of the war on terror in its international (pre-emptive self-defence, Iraq) and national (pre-emptive detention, Guantanamo Bay) modes. To put it rather provocatively, show trials and war crimes trials can be viewed as a form of preventative juridical violence. There is the same setting aside of existing legal rules (as with preventative war) in order to remove threats to the revolution (Moscow), national security (Guantanamo Bay), the international system (Iraq) or peace in Europe (Serbia).

Second, show trials are stark demonstrations of the disposability of human beings in the name of political projects. People are treated as means in the 'inexpiable struggle' that constitutes politics (Aron, quoted in Merleau-Ponty, 1969: xli). The victims of such trials – the wrongly accused enemy (of the people? of the international community?) – are victims of violence but the violence is necessary and revolutionary. The defendants in show trials are simply individuals who get in the way of large-scale political transformation. They are unlucky but as Lenin remarked, with typical brutality: 'When you chop trees, chips fly' (Cotic, 1987: 68). Defendants in war crimes trials are unlucky too. Mostly *their* lack of luck is not something to feel distressed about. Like many of the defendants in the show trials they were culpable individuals but they were unlucky compared to many similarly situated individuals. Most war criminals or aggressors, after all, are not prosecuted. And sometimes, even the participants in such trials concede that subjectively innocent people have been sacrificed in order to promote broader goals. Joseph Keenan, after the Tokyo Trials, compared the actions of Japanese defendants to '. . . that of American soldiers about to take a beachhead; that is the lives of morally and legally innocent men may be sacrificed in the achievement of the ultimate purpose' (Minear, 1971: 156–7). The victims are innocent victims, to be sure, judged by the standards of liberal legalism. But they are 'objectively guilty', like the inmates in Guantanamo Bay. The violence they are subjected to is said to be permissible and necessary because in accordance with progressive ends.

There are contemporary parallels with a third feature of show trials and war crimes trials, namely the shared appeal to intuition over legality. Often the objective guilt of individuals is a matter of commonsense or conscience rather than being subject to determination by the artificialities of technical law. Prosecutors at Moscow referred to the 'justice of the people', believing the rule of law itself to be sham. Kyrlenko, one of the Soviet Prosecutors, said: 'It is one of the most widespread sophistries of bourgeois science to maintain that the court . . . is an institution whose task it is to realise some sort of special justice above classes'.[42] There was no special justice, only the judgement of the proletariat. And this recalls, too, a Nazi Law of 28 June 1935 referring to the need to punish according to '. . . the sound perceptions of the people' (Minear: 17). Those who created the field of war crimes were not immune to this reasoning. As Robert Jackson put it: 'We can save ourselves from these pitfalls if our test of what is legally a crime gives recognition to those things which fundamentally outrage the conscience of the American people' (in Minear: 7). Modern international criminal law, for all its doctrinal sophistication and textual elaboration, finds its origins in the appeal to fundamental values or the 'conscience of mankind'. It, too, was the justice of the people.

4   Conclusion

Show trials represent the most fantastic deformation of legal procedure. The allegations forming the basis of the show trials involved the unlikeliest of conspiracies (in breath-taking indictments, individuals were described, all at once, as imperialists, fascists, Titoists and Trotskyists) and the evidence on which these conspiracies were grounded was largely fabricated (e.g. meetings were alleged to have taken place in hotels that had ceased to exist by the time of the alleged meetings). Procedurally, the show trials merely parodied legal procedure. For example, the Prague proceedings were subject to State Court on Matters of State Security, Regulation of 25 January 1950 stating: 'The Court must inform the Prosecutor in advance of the judgement it is about to hand down and get his opinion whether the judgement is correct . . . the Prosecutor's opinion is binding on the Court' (Cotic, 1987: 74). Dress rehearsals were conducted prior to these Czech trials and these rehearsals were taped so that if a defendant deviated from the script (in the way that Kostov had dared to in Sofia), the microphone was switched off and a tape would begin playing the defendant's pre-recorded responses.

  None of this is the case with war crimes trials. Yet, this chapter has argued against the complacent assumption that war crimes trials and liberal legalism are the antithesis of show trials. Indeed, there are sometimes striking resemblances. It is not that these forms are the same. The 'degree of risk' present in war crimes trials is, of course, much higher for the prosecuting state or entity (there are acquittals, there are uncomfortable revelations, there are dissenting judgments). Show trials, though, can tell us something important about the pursuit of international justice in the past half-century. The relationship between subjective innocence and objective guilt, a distinguishing mark of the show trial, informs both the early war crimes trials and the contemporary relations of law, war and crime.

Two views of the international order are in tension here. According to George Steiner, in *The Death of Tragedy*, tragedy is unknown to the Judaic tradition because there is always, in the end, reason and justice (Steiner, 1961).[43] Jerusalem or Jericho may fall or be destroyed but this is a just punishment leaving the prospect of rehabilitation and redemption. In the Judaic account of justice and punishment there is 'a marvellous continuity between thought and action' (Steiner: 7). Subjective behaviour determines outcome. In the standard legalist account of war crimes trials, there is a similar continuity between thought (conspiracy, intent), action (aggression, killing) and culpability (trial, imprisonment). War crimes law, simply, is the application of categories of legal reasoning to the problem of war. The defeated in war deserve defeat and the resulting punishments because they have done wrong.

Greek tragedy functions quite differently. Oedipus marries his mother and kills his father and yet seeks to do neither. He remains objectively responsible though he has neither willed nor understood his actions. And he must be punished. His fate, then, is Greek. Instead of a rational universe in which thought, action and consequence are in perfect alignment, there is a chaos of arbitrary death and pointless destruction overseen by capricious gods. Judgement is selective, and punishment, if it comes, is accidental and morally inexplicable. For sceptics, war crimes law is a field in which the arbitrary outweighs the rational, in which objective political forces determine punishment and in which judgement is ad hoc, unrepresentative and discretionary.

The war crimes field, then, is founded on a schism between Judaic judgement and Greek fatalism. In the Judaic version of the action / accountability axis, men are punished for a moral failure of some sort; they do wrong and are condemned before the tribunals of man or a reasoning God. In the Greek version, men are at the mercy of gods; they are unanchored to any rational universe. The continuity between thought and action dissipates to be replaced by 'an ironic abyss' (Steiner, 1961: 7).

6

Law's Hegemony
The Juridification of War

. . . the historic causes of the war simply defy legal judgement.

Justice Pal, Tokyo War Crimes Tribunal[1]

I honestly believe that every country ought to do what it wants to do . . . it is either proud of itself or less proud of itself.

Donald Rumsfeld[2]

. . . invasions have, since time immemorial, been a violation of international law . . .

Judgment, *United States v. von Weizsacker et al.*

An individual who, as leader or organiser, actively participates in or orders the planning, preparation, initiation or waging of aggression committed by a state shall be responsible for a crime of aggression.

Article 16, ILC Draft Code of Crimes

1   Law and war

War crimes trials belong to a wider genre of international politics I characterize as juridified diplomacy. Juridified diplomacy, as I have argued, involves the translation of political conflict into legal doctrine, and, occasionally, the resolution of these conflicts in legal institutions. The whole book has been about this tendency, and the various relationships embodied in it. In this chapter, I want to examine more directly the effects and claims of juridification. In the first part, I discuss some recent examples of law's hegemony over areas of international conflict before situating these examples of juridification in two wider tendencies: the first relating to the self-understandings and anxieties of those who practise and study international law, and the second linked to the juridification of politics in general. This prepares the ground for a second section, which considers a specific instance of juridification in which the problem of law and crime is sharpened or made most visible: the case of war.

Traditionally, war crimes trials were about war. This relationship, though, has slowly unravelled over the past half-century or more. At

Nuremberg, the IMT insisted on establishing a link between doing evil in war and the evil of war itself. Only those crimes against humanity committed in connection with the crime of crimes, the war of aggression, fell within the Tribunal's *de facto* jurisdiction. War crimes law was largely about criminal war. These categories were almost immediately unglued in the Control Council Law No. 10, which envisaged the prosecution of crimes against humanity lacking this direct link with the crime of aggression. The decoupling of war and crime continued in both customary international law, with crimes against humanity disengaged from war altogether (something confirmed in *dicta* in the *Tadic* decision), and in the various treaties declaring certain acts to be crimes independent of the existence of a state of armed conflict (e.g. the Genocide Convention (1948), the Torture Convention (1984) and the Apartheid Convention (1973)). Now, the problems of crime in war and war as crime are regarded as, necessarily, separable. The focus, as we shall see, in The Hague and in Rome, has been on crime in war. But international lawyers, having made war illegal (at San Francisco in the United Nations Charter) and breaches of the law *in* war criminal (in the Geneva Conventions and Protocols, and in the Rome Statute), have not relinquished the possibility of criminalizing war itself (and thereby reviving the original sin prosecuted at Nuremberg). This, surely, though, is the hard case for 'law, war and crime' because war-making is the ultimate sovereign prerogative (non-reviewable under domestic law in the UK (see e.g. *Chandler v. DPP, CND v. Prime Minister*)), and because war has long been viewed as an essentially political activity.[3] For these reasons, and others, the regulation and criminalization of war represents the culmination of the juridification project.

2   Juridification in general

In recent years, international criminal lawyers have proclaimed the arrival of a new order where impunity for war criminals is extinguished or swept aside by crusading domestic prosecutors (e.g. Garzón in Spain), by national courts (e.g. the House of Lords in *Pinochet*), by bold legislators (e.g. the Belgian war crimes legislation of 1993 and 1999, notwithstanding subsequent amendments), and by proliferating international (three) and hybrid (four by a conservative measure) tribunals. Who among progressive international lawyers can have failed to feel a frisson of delight as General Pinochet was sequestered in a country house with only Margaret Thatcher's best wishes for company (Beckett, 2002)? And if there was mild discomfort at the iconoclasm of Christopher Hitchens's mock indictment of Mother Teresa, his plea for a trial of Henry Kissinger garnered a great deal of support (Hitchens, 2001).

Alongside these initiatives in the international criminal law field, large areas of international social life, not primary topics of this book, are being subject to legal regulation. The international economic system increasingly is ordered by a network of private and public institutions (Wai, 2003). Disputes between nations concerning tariffs, or import controls and export subsidies, are decided by quasi-judicial bodies (a WTO Panel or the Appellate Body). Some scholars have begun to ask whether the economic system is constitutionalizing, i.e. becoming a legal order of a deeper and more intrusive nature (Cass, 2005). In the case of maritime law, disputes can now be resolved in Hamburg before a Law of the Sea Tribunal (ITLOS), and even the previously defunct Permanent Court of Arbitration has been revived in disputes between Eritrea and Ethiopia and in a case involving Hawaiian sovereignty. For many environmentalists, the system tentatively established in Rio and Kyoto would be immeasurably strengthened by a system of judicial oversight in which environmental disputes are settled by international courts (in 1993 the ICJ formed an environmental chamber specifically to deal with such cases).

Domestic courts, too, have widened incrementally their claims to regulate the 'international sphere'.[4] To take one example, associated with the subject matter of the book, the English courts are currently hearing a case, *Al Skeini*, involving the purported application of the European Convention on Human Rights and the UK Human Rights Act to the territory of southern Iraq. In this case, the applicants are seeking review of certain acts committed by UK soldiers against Iraqi detainees and civilians in Iraq. The English Court of Appeals (the case will be decided by the House of Lords at the beginning of 2007) held that the Human Rights Act *would* apply to cases where UK forces either had effective territorial control of the region in Iraq around Basra or, as in one case, were exercising a form of state-agent control in individual cases of detention. A domestic judicial organ is engaged, here, in a human rights review of conduct carried out during a military occupation overseas.

Two themes, at least, emerge from all this: the self-assertions of international law in one case and the juridification of politics on the other.[5] While this chapter concentrates on the latter, I want to begin, by way of introduction, by sketching some implications and antecedents of the former.

2.1   International law and national law

Situated within law faculties and part of the legal profession, international lawyers are caught between two impulses vis-à-vis other lawyers (Simpson, 1999). One is to claim a close affinity to domestic law, the other is to emphasize how interesting it is to work at some distance from conventional Austinian forms of legality. The first position finds expression in the mimetic efforts of some international lawyers. These vary in their style and ambition. Ambitious versions of this approach argue that international law bears a very close resemblance to national law in its institutional characteristics, in its textual concerns and in its interpretative dilemmas. Inevitably, this leads to a court-directed mode of professional practice. This can either be centred on the use made of international law by domestic courts (literal domestication) or on the way international law is performed by tribunals such as the International Court of Justice (domestication by analogy). Thus a whole cadre of international lawyers – sometimes also scholars of high standing – treat international law as a series of judicial opinions to be discussed, debated and disseminated. An international law conference or a conversation between such international lawyers would then be largely indistinguishable in tone and subject-matter from a similar conference or conversation among, say, property lawyers or tort lawyers. There would be the same gossipy familiarity with judicial personalities, the same doctrinal struggles and the same potential for insulation from social structure and political contestation. International law can then be studied and performed in forms identical to that of national law. Questions of enforcement and authority are largely sidelined as 'sociology' or 'theory'.

The second position involves making a radical break with the domestic analogy, and has tended to prevail among international lawyers who wanted to show that H. L. A. Hart was wrong to say that international law was a primitive or inchoate simulacrum of authentic law (Hart, 1961). The retort to this argument involved asserting that international law simply was different. Naturally, the more different it was the better able were international lawyers to explain why it did not meet the self-referencing standards of legality imposed by theorists of national or domestic law. The trend, until very recently, was to adopt a posture of sophisticated resignation when confronted by the law/non-law argument (in response to which Thomas Franck claimed international law was 'post-ontological' (Franck, 1995; cf. Franck, 2006)).

The attention paid to judicial institutions by the first group played into the hands of Hartians who could then argue that these courts and laws, while formally similar, were pale imitations of 'real' legal institutions. According to the second group this was the wrong way to go about defending the field. Instead, this group conceded that international law was quite distinct from national law and that the courts or treaties found in international law could not be equated with, and operated in a different way from, judicial institutions or contracts in domestic law. The emphasis, then, was on non-judicial forms of law: the practice of states, official statements by government representatives, the work of institutions, the persuasive effects of rule-making, the habit-forming effects of rule-following. Alongside these concerns was a tendency to de-emphasize the judicial, the textual and the retributive. International law had transcended these derivative styles and struck out on its own path (D'Amato, 1984/5; Franck, 1990).

All of this was entangled in a set of arguments international lawyers wanted to make in response to International Relations scholars, too, who questioned the enterprise of international law from the analytical perspective.[6] What was the point of studying these judicial forms if the material conditions of international politics dictated against their relevance? One answer to this seemed to lie in adopting a strong version of the first defence above in which legal institutions, and particularly judicial bodies, enforced international law in ways that were rather similar to the role played by such institutions domestically. A second answer concentrated on de-emphasizing the apparent parallels between domestic legal institutions and their international counterparts and, instead, insinuated international law into the structure of international relations by bringing out its persuasive and identity-forming functions (constructivists, e.g. Reus-Smit, 2004). International law could be consensual, customary, non-hierarchical *and* enforceable, albeit in a diffuse manner.

In the case of each 'defence', though, *criminal* law was an inauspicious model for understanding the project of public international law. For those stressing the domestic analogy, private or civil law was the appropriate model. States were contractually bound to each other, in the way individuals were in national legal orders. The courts and institutions (e.g. the International Court of Justice or the United Nations) operated as civil courts in which individual legal persons settled their differences as equals and in the absence of Leviathan. For those emphasizing the horizontal nature of international law, the absence of top-down enforcement was a virtue of the system. States could pursue their own ends only in the absence of the sort of overwhelming centralized power that seemed to be a requirement of a system of criminal justice. In any event, public international law precisely was an experiment in human relations that demonstrated the possibility of cooperation, collaboration and sanction in the absence of criminal repression. To this extent, traditional international law was more in tune with a professional *zeitgeist* that was beginning to turn from retributive to restorative justice.

Some lawyers, though, have turned their back on these conceptions of international law altogether. Richard Goldstone takes this view to its extreme and manages to consign international law's history to the dustbin when he says: 'It seems to me that if you don't have international tribunals, you might as well not have international law' (Scharf, 1997). This spasm of criminalization reflects trends in penal justice generally. Andrew Ashworth has argued that '. . . what we see increasingly is the tendency to assume that the only satisfactory way to respond to some sort of anti-social conduct is to create a new criminal offence'.[7] At the same time, though, international lawyers are embracing retribution in an era when commentators and practitioners working in, say, criminology or penology have seriously problematized the whole idea of prison-based criminal law (Roche, 2003; Snare, 1995). International criminal lawyers may have hitched themselves to a dead horse.

All of this makes the rise and rise of international criminal justice a decidedly mixed blessing for international lawyers. In claiming that the law of war crimes somehow completes international law by giving it teeth, by putting bad men in prison and by imitating domestic law's concreteness (discussed in Mégret, 2003), international lawyers may be undercutting a lifetime of professional commitment to a different sort of legal order. The success or failure of international law now seems more bound up with its capacity to secure convictions in criminal trials than in the everyday of diplomatic engagement or functional treaty-making. Even an event as fortuitous as the death of Milosevic now spells a period of remonstration against the inadequacies of the international legal order: able neither to secure convictions nor eternal life.

2.2   The juridification of politics

The second trend that accompanies the revival of international criminal law, and one in which this revival is thoroughly embedded, concerns the *juridification of politics* generally. The Belgian attempts to indict Sharon, Arafat, Castro and Tommy Francks, and the 1998 extradition proceedings instituted in the case of General Pinochet, have raised the possibility that the criminal law could be applied to people with whom we have sharp political disagreements.[8] This has its latter-day antecedents in American political life where it seems natural to think in terms of impeaching the President rather than going to the bother of defeating him at the polls. Whether one is against Bush or Clinton, there is a temptation to criminalize the conduct of the President rather than merely deplore it. This approach peaked during debates about the war in Iraq. Many opponents of the war initially thought of it as something they were against (strategically or morally). This was followed by a displacement of the political by the legal. Suddenly, it was not enough to be against the war, one had to declare it illegal. But declaring it illegal seemed to have a natural consequence: President Bush and Prime Minister Blair were criminals and ought to be sent to The Hague to face justice. So, anti-war posters often announced that the war was immoral, illegal and *criminal*: bad policy = jailed world leaders. Around the time of the approach to the war I was often asked in the media why, if the war was illegal, the ICC was not issuing indictments against Bush and Blair. There was an understandable conflation of illegality with criminality (I will discuss this in greater detail in the next section). Of course, I declared, it was inconceivable that Blair would have to appear in court to justify his actions. Wasn't it? But a few months later there he was in front of Lord Hutton (albeit not in a criminal trial) explaining the Government's justifications for going to war to an inquiry into the BBC's reporting of the Iraq War.

For a while, then, it seemed that juridification would choose its victims with great impartiality; Saddam Hussein would go on trial because he possessed weapons of mass destruction, Bush and Blair because he did not have them. On 29 May 2003, the BBC flagship radio programme, *Today*, carried a report by one of its journalists, Andrew Gilligan, contending that the Blair Government and, in particular, its press officer, Alistair Campbell, had 'sexed up' an intelligence document on the threat posed by the Baath regime. Particular attention was given to the question of whether the Government had demanded the insertion of, or had inserted, or had encouraged the insertion of, a claim that Iraq could use weapons of mass destruction in forty-five minutes. The report led to a vicious dispute between the BBC and the Government, and culminated in the revelation that Dr David Kelly, an Arms Control Expert at the MOD, had been Gilligan's source for the story. Kelly endured a brief but torrid time in the public eye, including an abject appearance at the Foreign Affairs Committee of the House of Commons, before being found dead in a wood near his home in Cambridgeshire. Kelly's fate set in train the events that led to the Government establishing, in July 2003, an inquiry under the steward-ship of Law Lord Brian Hutton, with the intention of investigating '. . . the circumstances surrounding the death of Dr Kelly'.

But what were these circumstances? Or, more problematically, what was the permitted ambit of reviewable circumstances? At one extreme was the view that this was simply a glorified Coroner's Report into the causes of Dr Kelly's death. All else was extraneous (Murray, 2004). The terms of reference certainly made an effort to concentrate Hutton's mind in this regard describing a number of issues that did not fall within the judicial remit (para. 9). But for many of those queuing outside the Royal Courts of Justice, this was an inquiry into the war itself. Lord Hutton's job, in the eyes of the anti-war coalitions, and in the fears of the Government itself, was to put Her Majesty's Government on trial and convict it of bad, dis-honest, illegal and perhaps, even, *criminal* acts.

In the end, Lord Hutton told the nation that Dr Kelly had committed suicide (no one seriously believed he had not) and admonished the BBC so severely that both the Chairman of the Board of Governors, Gavyn Davies, and the Director-General, Greg Dyke, resigned. The Blair Govern-ment meanwhile was reprimanded gently for having released Kelly's name without warning Kelly himself and for the misdemeanour of having exer-cised a 'subconscious' influence on the Joint Intelligence Committee's intelligence warnings.[9]

But the Hutton Report did not still the desire for judgement. How could it? Juridification attempts closure but the ambit of judicial inquiry is usually too narrowly construed to achieve it. Hutton concentrated his intellect on an important but, perhaps, not all-important matter: did the Prime Minis-ter lie? This question was not properly differentiated in the public mind from the larger query: did Iraq have usable weapons of mass destruction and, therefore, was the war justifiable or even lawful? In the end, juridifica-tion produced something rather technical and obscure. Amidst a rash of high-table admissions (from David Kay declaring that no weapons of mass destruction would be found ('we were mistaken') to Paul Wolfowitz describing the hunt for such weapons as a pretext), Lord Hutton brought down his report declaring that the Blair Government had made an inno-cent mistake.

Only days after Hutton handed down his report, President Bush acceded to demands that *he* set up an inquiry into the intelligence received leading to the intervention in Iraq. Shortly after that, Blair entrusted a senior civil servant, Robin Butler, to do the same job for the UK. The very inquiries described earlier as 'impossible' (Murray, 2004) were convened.

What do these processes tell us about (international) politics? Do they replace politics altogether? When George Bush announced the US Inquiry he assured the nation that he wanted to know the full facts about what had happened (as if he was a judge being asked to chair a Royal Commission into the behaviour of some other branch of government). The Inquiry was to report after the November 2004 elections because Bush did not want to 'politicize' the inquiry (*Melbourne Age*, 8 February 2004). This is a revealing phrase because at one level juridified diplomacy is precisely that: depoliticized politics. A judicial inquiry is an attempt to rise above politics or, at the very least, denude politics of controversy. Yet, this displacement cannot achieve such a result. Even in domestic political life, some areas of dispute are incapable of judicial or quasi-judicial resolution. Depoliticization is impossible because, in some circumstances, there is only politics.

Juridification, particularly through the criminal law, seems to promise completion for international law by placing at the centre of the field a project that most strongly resembles national law at its most emblematic. In the case of international (and domestic) politics, juridification promises the depoliticization of issues involving deep-seated political differences. Often, though not always, these procedures prove to be disappointing precisely because law cannot entirely displace such differences. War is the difficult case because decisions to go to war are the essence of international political life and national political conflict. For these reasons, the criminalization of war, partly because it is associated with the criminalization of politics (chapter 5), has been one of the most fraught projects in the modern history of international law and relations.

3   The juridification of war

In 1914, following the murder of Archduke Ferdinand, the Austro-Hungarian Empire issued an ultimatum to Serbia. The terms and conditions of the ultimatum were such as to make a Serbian capitulation highly improbable. The world thus began its drift to war. All this is familiar enough. What is less well known is that Serbia responded to the Austro-Hungarian communication with a suggestion that the differences between the two countries be resolved by the Permanent Court of Arbitration in The Hague. In retrospect this seems like a quixotic gesture to a hopeless formalism. Instead of the Great War, there might have been a lengthy Permanent Court of Arbitration judgment (Simpson, 2000).[10] But perhaps the Serbian effort looks less absurd viewed in the light of a century of juridification (and, indeed, one of its successor governments sued NATO in 2000 for having bombed its territory in 1999). I want to conclude this chapter by examining a specific genus of juridification: the juridification of war, and a specific case of the juridification of war: the criminalization of war.

Ten years after the trial of Rudolf Slansky, the defendant (executed at the end of his trial in 1953) was partially rehabilitated. Slansky was exonerated of having committed common crimes (for example, among the plethora of indictments he faced, he had been accused of murder) but he remained guilty of political and ideological errors (Hodos, 1987: 163). This decision effected a reversal of the trial's original purpose, which was to 'transform abstract political-ideological differences into easily intelligible common crimes' (Hodos: xiii). The decision seemed to resurrect a liberal separation of crime and politics. It has long been a central part of the liberal law project that the legal order ought to remain neutral among competing political preferences. The political choices to which an individual commits and the orientation a person adopts towards the system are, ideally, irrelevant to questions of criminal culpability. Of course, this conception of law has been rocked by successive critiques (by Law and Society scholars, by Marxists and in critical legal studies scholarship). Criminologists, too, have argued that the criminal law is a mechanism by which a political society protects itself from deviant behaviour or consolidates its own normative claims. As the Chinese proverb puts it, crime is a creation of the criminal law (Allott, 2002). What domestic societies have criminalized, among other forms of behaviour, is war. There is a war on war, or a criminalization of violent opposition to society.

International society has struggled to establish this idea of itself as a society to be protected from the outside. Prior to the twentieth century, what modern international law understood as crimes against humanity or genocide were simply acts of murder, rape, or assault committed on a mass scale at the national level or vile acts of war committed during armed conflict. In the latter case, punishment came in the form of action at the national level (if it came at all). In cases where the criminal law was applied, it was applied by national courts, since only states were capable of repressing such crimes. Lacking a self-understanding as a society, wars against 'international society' remained inconceivable. But, unlike war crimes or genocide, inter-state war could not be criminalized at the national level because warring states did not belong to each other's societies. The whole idea of sovereign immunity or 'act of state' arises from this fact. States were barred from prosecuting or suing each other's official representatives (including heads of state) in their own domestic courts because of this.

In the nineteenth century, war was conceived of as an essentially political act. Lawyers played little role in deciding whether wars were advisable or legitimate. There was certainly no sense in which wars could be viewed as criminal. As Lord Bingham put it in *R v. Jones*, 'It may, I think, be doubtful whether such wars [discussing wars of aggression] were recognised in customary international law as a crime when the 20th Century began' (para. 12). This was an era in which Machiavelli, Cardinal Richelieu and von Clausewitz dominated strategic thinking about war and peace. Quincy Wright, in a survey of the pre-twentieth-century position regarded war as '. . . an event, the origin of which is outside of international law' (Wright, 1925).

Versailles, then, revolutionized war and crime, and laid the ground for a criminalization of war at Nuremberg. Chapter 7, 'Law's Origins', traces the transformation of the international order in the twentieth century from one in which states are treated as equals, with this equal status remaining unchanged by war or hostility, to one in which distinctions are drawn between states on the basis of their conformity to certain models of good government or their alignment with particular political projects. This change had important consequences for the way in which war itself was understood. Previously viewed as a form of combat at the inter-state level with the combatants subject to certain rules of the game and accorded reciprocal status, war in the twentieth century, sometimes, became a matter of police action on the part of the 'international community' aimed at dissident states within international society (Schmitt, 2003). For Schmitt, the modern history of international law begins at Versailles. The criminalization of Germany represented the moment when the international community's rise to self-consciousness coincided with the punitive treatment of its enemies. The Allies combined the self-righteous anger of the French and British with the zealous constitutionalism of the Americans to produce a settlement which treated Germany not just as a defeated adversary but a criminal state. This, in turn, prefigured the development of a distinctively twentieth-century conception of international society. The creation of an international community required the identification of groups and states outside this community and, ideally, representing a threat to that community. The use of armed force by such states became 'aggression' rather than war. This, in turn, required a juridical effort to distinguish war from aggression. For those opposing the aggressors, 'pest control' had displaced war.

Schmitt's account has its attractions, and I develop it further in the final chapter, but here I want to suggest that it gives insufficient attention to the level of opposition to the 'criminalization of war' project within international society and among international lawyers. I argue that yet another constituent relationship in international criminal law is formed around the tension between the project to criminalize war and a counter-project that denies the applicability of criminal categories to decisions about war and peace. There is a tension between the hegemonic tendencies of law (its inclination to juridify all aspects of social life, including war) and a pragmatic strain in both law and politics that emphasizes the limits of the law.

The post-Versailles landmarks in the criminalization of war are found at Nuremberg, Tokyo, at the United Nations in the 1950s, 1970s and 1990s, and in the negotiations surrounding the inclusion of aggression as a crime in the ICC Statute at Rome in 1998. In this section, I juxtapose against these efforts the claims of those who believe evaluations and assessments of war belong outside the juridical sphere. These critics of the criminalization project can be divided into two camps (these are further subdivided later in the chapter): political realists (who believe decisions about war and peace are a matter of strategic judgement and misjudgement) and legalists (including those who wanted to maintain the strict distinction between the *ius ad bellum* and the *ius in bello*).

This opposition between juridifying war and limiting law is present from the outset in the deliberations of the Commission on Authorship of the War established by the Versailles Peace Conference to investigate the question of who was responsible for the Great War. The tension is there in the relationship between the findings of the Commission and the intentions of its backers, and in the relationship between the Treaty of Versailles itself and the Commission Report. The Treaty of Versailles in Articles 227–230 established preliminary responsibility for the war. Article 227 introduced for the first time in history the idea that an individual leader could be held accountable for the decision to go to war. The Kaiser was to be prosecuted for 'violations of international morality and the sanctity of treaties'. This clause, which did not appear in the US–German version of the Treaty, was included because the Allies had instilled in their citizens a strong sense that the Kaiser was personally responsible for the war. A great deal of propaganda disseminated throughout the war personalized the conflict: Article 227 made good on this personalization. However, the Commission on Authorship of the War, the first expert gathering on the question of individual responsibility for war, was not minded to accept this view of armed conflict (the Commission considered crimes against humanity and war crimes, too, but the focus here is on the crime of aggression).

The Commission established to determine 'authorship' of the war in fact rejected the whole idea that wars could be authored. According to the Majority, aggression was simply not an act capable of judicial determination. Indeed, it was not an 'act' at all but instead a consequence of social, political and economic forces beyond the ken of any court or commission.[11] The question of authorship was a matter for historians and statesmen, and not for courts (who were likely to be consumed by the question for several years).

In any event the 'peacemakers' (Macmillan, 2001) went ahead with plans to convene trials. These plans were undone by the Kaiser absconding to the Netherlands, and by the Allies' lack of territorial leverage over the defeated Germans (this is a history recounted in chapter 2). The interwar years, though, were marked by a series of further attempts to criminalize war. The League of Nations Draft Treaty of Mutual Assistance in 1923 declared aggressive war a crime as did The Geneva Protocol of 1924 (stating that wars of aggression violated the solidarity of the international community). The League's Assembly used the term 'crime' to characterize aggressive war in the preamble to a resolution prohibiting wars of aggression. These were very much in the manner of reform proposals from the margins, however. At the centre, the status of war was shifting not in the direction of the criminalization of aggression but towards making war illegal or, at least, subject to forms of collective security. The League of Nations Covenant placed some limits on its exercise; aggressive wars were to be met by coalitions of force deployed under the terms of the Covenant. The Kellogg-Briand Pact (1928) meanwhile prohibited recourse to war as an aspect of foreign policy but did not refer to the *crime* of aggression. Indeed, Kellogg-Briand was so couched with reservations and ambiguities that it is unclear what sort of war could possibly fall foul of the Pact. The United Kingdom, in a Note of 18 July 1928, warned that the Treaty could have no effect on British action in its Empire. Meanwhile, Mr Kellogg, the US Secretary of State himself, reminded the Senate that his Treaty had placed no restrictions on the right of self-defence (a right that was self-judging and applicable outside US sovereign territory) (Pal, 1955: 241).

None of this (*pace* Schmitt) added up to the criminalization of war. Indeed, critics of the Nuremberg and Tokyo War Crimes Trials remarked that there was a distinct lack of precedents for the crimes against peace tried in the destroyed German and Japanese cities (Minear, 1971; Maogoto, 2004). Nevertheless, under the IMT Charter and, in the reasoning of the Tribunal itself, aggression was regarded as the 'crime of crimes'; the crime containing the 'accumulated evil of the whole' (Arendt, 1994). It was, as Robert Jackson put it, 'the crime which comprehends all other lesser crimes' (Röling, 1998: 11). The war had been conducted abominably by the German state. There was no shortage of 'standard' war crimes, for example, the massacre of foreign civilian populations, the shooting of POWs and the use of slave labour. Crimes against humanity were introduced to cover the atrocities committed against Germans themselves (in particular, of course, German Jews). But all of this, in the Tribunal's eyes, was largely a product of one over-arching scheme to wage a war of aggression. The jurisdictional requirements articulated in Article 6 meant that convictions for crimes against humanity could only be secured if these crimes were committed in connection with the war of aggression or war crimes. Robert Jackson conceded that this requirement was included in order to avoid scrutiny of Allied practices either in the colonies or in the southern states of the United States. The crime of aggression, then, was utterly central to the case at Nuremberg (as it was at Tokyo).

But Nuremberg arrived at a moment that was not particularly propitious to the concept of aggression as crime. The discussions at San Francisco had established a system under which engagement in illegal wars would be met by overwhelming force from a community-authorized coalition of states. There was no reference to the idea that criminality would attach itself to such breaches of international peace and security. Indeed, it was made plain in the Charter that the Security Council was to have absolute primacy in dealing with such threats (including, under Article 39, acts of aggression). This was a nod to a realist sensibility that had lost some faith in legalistic solutions to problems of international order (Simpson, 2000). Writers like E. H. Carr and Hans Morgenthau were thoroughly disaffected by what they viewed as the misguided utopianism of interwar proposals for treaties abolishing war or institutions that sought to tame human inclinations. It was simply naive, they believed, to assume that diplomacy could be subject to legal control. In Shakespeare's *Richard III*, while Richard dissembles and plots and prepares his bloody denouements, King Edward is congratulating himself on a good day's work bringing the many rivals within the court together in a compact. 'You peers continue this united league . . . I have made my friends at peace on earth' (II. i). Richard himself ('determined to prove a villain') exploits this faith in compacts and leagues. When he comes upon the gathering of princes and dukes, he begins: 'A blessed labour, my most sovereign lord. Among this princely heap . . .'. It is clear from his contemptuous tone that he intends to profit from this peace treaty (he does). The criminalization project seemed similarly doomed from the perspective of the post-war realists. Neville Chamberlain, with a subsequently unacknowledged prudence, may have been buying time at Munich but his agreement with Hitler, promising 'peace in our time', became emblematic of law's failures in this regard. Making war a crime would not end wars, it would merely ensure that war's aggressors could work under cover of law and war's losers would fight to a bitter end (Hankey, 1950: 24).

Robert Jackson and his associates forged ahead at Nuremberg regardless but this realist tendency inhibited the development of the permanent war crimes court he sought as well as the genuinely new sensibility in international relations and law he seemed to believe was necessary. At Tokyo, the tension between the juridifiers and the constraining realists was played out within the Tribunal itself. On one hand there was the zealous abolitionism of Chief Prosecutor Keenan; on the other hand, there were three significant dissenting judgments from Justices Bernard of France, Pal of India and Röling of the Netherlands.

For Keenan, and, presumably, General MacArthur, the Tribunal's chief architect, the distinction between good and bad wars or between publicly authorized wars and unauthorized wars was central to the trial project. This distinction certainly changed the status of the adversaries but did it have any implications for the status of military personnel engaged in such wars? Keenan implied that in some cases the distinction between crimes of war and war as crime should be erased altogether. This was one of two famous efforts to effect this sort of shift (the other occurred during the 'war on terror' after 2001). In each case, there was enormous resistance from the legal and military establishments.

At Tokyo, Keenan suggested that all Japanese soldiers who had fought in the war in the Far East could be indicted for crimes against peace (Maugham, 1951: 18–39). According to him, to fight in an illegal war was to fight illegally (Dinstein and Tabory, 1996: 19). The Japanese had embarked on an aggressive war and '... since the war was illegal, all natural and normal results flowing from the original act are also illegal' (Pritchard, 1998: 425). Chief Justice Webb agreed with Keenan. The logical conclusion of the aggressive war doctrine was that 'a soldier or civilian who opposed war but after it began decided it should be carried on . . . was guilty of waging aggressive war' (Pritchard, 1998: 7). The majority rejected this approach arguing that it defied the whole structure of an international law of war based on a distinction between *ius ad bellum* and *ius in bello*.

After the attack on the Twin Towers, and the war on Afghanistan, lawyers in the US Justice Department embarked on a similar effort in relation to Taliban (and al-Qaeda) forces. In the Gonzales Memo, the Chief Legal Counsel to the White House argued that the illegality of the war conducted by the Taliban (it was a failed state and it was engaged in terrorist activities) meant that Taliban personnel (detained at Guantanamo Bay) could be deprived of their rights under the Geneva Conventions. Again, the legal and military establishments cavilled at such changes to the existing structures of international law. In each case, the criminalization of certain types of war ('aggressive' war, 'terrorist' war) threatened to undo prior legal commitments while intensifying the juridification of war.

Keenan was much less successful than Gonzales and the Justice Department lawyers but the rejection of this reading of the law of war and force was only one of the problems he encountered before a surprisingly independent bench at Tokyo. Justice Pal's dissenting judgment included an indictment of the criminalization of war, and recalled both the American dissent at Versailles as well as prefiguring, albeit more stridently, doubts expressed (by Americans and others) during the Rome negotiations for an International Criminal Court. For Pal, the decision to prosecute the defeated Japanese for the crime of aggression exposed the trial as irremediably political. Pal argued that it was defeat rather than aggression that was criminalized, that aggression was a political act falling outside the ambit of legality, and that the lack of precedents in this case meant that the Japanese were being tried for committing acts that were not criminal at the time of commission (a clear violation of the non-retroactivity rule in Western jurisprudence).

Pal's most important insight though was to reveal international law as a project for stabilizing and securing existing power distributions within international society. For him, the criminalization of aggression was simply a way of freezing the status quo. The criminal repression of territorial change was meant to ensure that the frontiers created by the original sin of colonial maldistribution would remain fixed by the legitimating force of an international rule of law. The deepening juridification of war was intended to remove armed struggle from the repertoire of anti-colonial, anti-Western political movements and states. Japan had demonstrated to the colonized peoples of Asia that the European powers were no longer militarily invincible. True, they had replaced one form of colonialism with another but it seemed arbitrary to Pal that Japanese colonialism should be subject to criminal sanctions while European aggression over the past four centuries should be implicitly endorsed; the prosecution of the Japanese was an act of imperial hypocrisy.[12] In this, he anticipated the little-publicized justifications offered by the Iraqi state when it invaded Kuwait and claimed that it was simply undoing arbitrarily drawn imperial boundaries between Kuwait and Iraq that had been imposed by colonial administrators seeking to fragment Iraq.

Recalling the American delegation at Versailles, Pal maintained that '. . . the historic causes of the war simply defy legal judgement' (Pal, 1953). Wars, unlike acts of murder, but like most momentous political decisions, do not fit readily into a legal matrix. It is not at all clear, according to Pal, what is responsible for a particular act of war: Economic depression? An alienated underclass? The scarcity of some prized good such as land or oil? Even if one was to identify a specific socio-economic or political cause, the question of then attributing individual criminal responsibility remained highly problematic. Quincy Wright, writing in 1925, argued that wars were more akin to diseases: 'In so far as wars cannot be attributed to acts of responsible beings, it is nonsense to call them illegal' (Wright, 1925; Minear, 1971: 59; Pal, 1953: 33). In short, according to Pal, the personalization of responsibility for war was likely to be arbitrary, counter-intuitive and dictated by the accidents of history.

Of course, the courts at Nuremberg and Tokyo relied neither on precedents nor a judgment about ultimate causes of the war for the criminalization of aggression. Instead, they posited the existence of an international society whose existence and fundamental mores had been threatened by Japanese and German 'aggression'. Robert Jackson, after conceding that the Germans had breached no treaties with the United States, nonetheless claimed that the Nazi war was a war of aggression: '. . . an illegitimate attack on the international peace and order' (London Conference at 383–4). The Tokyo court, too, seemed to concede the lack of precedents for its judgment, saying that there was no need to consider whether there was conspiracy to wage war in violation of specific treaties and assurances (i.e. law) because '. . . the conspiracy to wage war was already criminal in the highest degree'.

This creative solution to the absence of precedents created a separate problem though, and it was one that Bert Röling took up in his dialogues with Antonio Cassese some decades after his dissenting judgment at Tokyo (Röling, 1993). Röling was uncomfortable with the charge of aggression levelled against the Japanese. The criminalization of aggression required a conception of international society against which this aggression was directed. According to Röling, in 1945, such a society did not exist. The sense of shared moral purpose, cultural affinity and political direction necessary to the criminalization of sovereign behaviour was absent (chapter 7).[13] There were neither existing precedents nor a moral or social consensus that would have rendered precedents unnecessary (this did not stop Röling from supporting convictions in some cases).

The paradox in all this, then, is that while Nuremberg and Tokyo may have been 'landmarks dwarfing the surrounding scene' (McCormack and Simpson, 1997), they were also moments of ambiguity for the criminalization of aggression and the juridification of war. The defendants at Nuremberg had exploited an Achilles' heel in the Allied case: the Soviet invasion of Poland in 1939 and the Molotov-Ribbentrop Pact. Speer asked the Soviet Prosecutors whether Russian diplomats had read *Mein Kampf*, and if they had, why they had entered into a treaty with Hitler (chapter 4). Soon, the Prosecutors were avoiding matters that might embarrass the Soviets. It was well known to the Prosecutors at Tokyo, too, (and something Roosevelt had agonized over (Minear, 1971)), that though Japan was being charged with aggression towards the Soviet Union, it was the Soviets who, by declaring war on Japan in 1941, had breached the non-aggression treaty between the two countries (Minear: 97).

These embarrassments are inevitable: the crime of aggression has the potential to cause discomfort for any state while the sovereign prerogative to make war remains fundamental to the system. At Nuremberg, the Tribunal avoided this problem by developing the crime of aggression in a way that made it highly specific to the Nazi State. The conspiracy charges were one way in which this was done. The crime of aggression was reworked into a norm applicable to states captured by a vicious cabal of conspirators intent on regional or global domination. This had the virtue of being tailored to the Nazi case (though even here the fit was not perfect) but the vice of being inapplicable to ordinary cases in which force was employed in the international system. At Tokyo, meanwhile, the project involving the prosecution of leaders who embark on illegal wars was bruised by the scathing dissenting judgments and by the imperfections of the Military Tribunal's final judgment (e.g. its belaboured and unconvincing efforts to convict Japanese leaders for political decisions made in the 1920s).

All of the above (the realist objections, the awkward double-standards, the problem of international society, the specificity and contingency of the charges laid against the Japanese and Germans) explains why, in relation to aggression at least, the Nuremberg Principles endorsed by the United Nations General Assembly in 1946 proved to be a far from definitive sign of the future development of international law.[14]

Of the three core crimes (war crimes, crimes against humanity and the crime of aggression) prosecuted at Nuremberg, the law of war crimes developed apace in military manuals, in the Geneva Conventions of 1949 and in much domestic legislation (e.g. the UK Geneva Conventions Act), and the category 'crimes against humanity' inspired a series of treaties ranging from the Genocide Convention in 1948 through to the Torture Convention and beyond. The crime of aggression, on the other hand, may have contained 'the accumulated evil of the whole', but it fell into the doldrums after Nuremberg and Tokyo. The General Assembly requested the International Law Commission to draft a Code of Crimes against the Peace and Security of Mankind in the 1950s but there was no agreement about how to define the crime of aggression. The Assembly itself defined aggression in 1974 but this document did not have the status of law.[15] All of this led one eminent commentator to complain: 'The die had been cast in favour of politicization of aggression rather than juridicisation' (Bassiouni, 1997: 9).

The most serious blow to the juridification project came at the high-point of the development of the law of war crimes generally. In the 1990s, with the field in its pomp, tribunality was very much the policy choice *du jour*. The response to atrocities committed in Bosnia was the establishment of ineffectual 'safe havens', and some limited and prematurely truncated air-strikes directed at Serb targets. When these strategies failed, the international community turned to war crimes tribunals. The ICTY was decreed into existence by a chastened Security Council in 1993, and the Council followed this with a similar measure (following an even more feckless initial response (Dallaire, 2004)), after the Rwandan genocide of 1994). Meanwhile, the hybrid tribunals, discussed in chapter 2, began to proliferate (in Sierra Leone, in Cambodia and in East Timor). But what was most remarkable about all this was that the 'crime of crimes' was missing from the ICTY Statute (and then, more explicably, from the various hybrid tribunals). It may be that the drafters of the Statute believed the wars in the Balkans were largely internal armed conflicts to which the crime of aggression was an irrelevance (if so, the inclusion of grave breaches of the Geneva Conventions, applicable at the time of the Statute's adoption only to international armed conflict, was a curious move). More likely, the Secretary-General and the Council believed either that aggression no longer had sufficient contemporary standing as a crime or that its inclusion would have, as James O'Brien argued in the *American Journal of International Law*, 'involved the tribunal squarely in the political issues surrounding the conflict' (O'Brien, 1993).

Coinciding with this renewed institution-building vigour in the field of war crimes trials, three important ILC Draft Conventions were undergoing development. These, at least, seemed to promise the rehabilitation of the crime of aggression and the juridification of war. Alongside the continuing development of the ILC Draft Statute for an International Criminal Court, there were also Draft Articles on State Responsibility (1996) and a Draft Code of Crimes Against the Peace and Security of Mankind (1996). In each case, the crime of aggression played a relatively prominent role. The ILC Draft Statute (Article 20) included the crime of aggression as one of the core crimes over which the ICC would have jurisdiction; the Draft Code of Crimes (Article 16) provided that: 'An individual who, as leader or organizer, actively participates in or orders the planning, preparation, initiation or waging of aggression committed by a State shall be responsible for a crime of aggression'; and the ILC's 1996 Draft Articles on State Responsibility enumerated, in Article 19, a list of acts, including aggression, for which a state would be held criminally liable. Ten years later all that had changed. The Rome Statute in Article 5(2) expressly excluded aggression from the Court's jurisdiction until such time as 'a provision is adopted defining the crime and setting out the conditions under which the Court may exercise jurisdiction under it'. Meanwhile, the Draft Code had been quietly dropped from the international agenda, and the ILC's Articles on State Responsibility were adopted in 2001 but without reference to the crime of aggression.

These uncertainties typify a field in which a constitutive relationship is that between the criminalization of aggression and the imperative to shear off crimes against peace into another field altogether, for example politics, history or conscience. I want to conclude this chapter by, first, delineating the political projects that, today, make up the 'question of aggression as a crime' and then sketching some final caveats to the juridification project.

The criminalization project has lost some of its verve since the failure to settle on a single definition or procedural context at Rome. Nevertheless, there are significant interests that continue to agitate for the revival of crimes against peace as a category within international law. This can account for the, perhaps, illusory, quest at the various prepcoms held since the Rome Conference for a definitive answer to the problem of aggression.[16] There are completists who believe that the criminalization of aggression will make international criminal law whole (see section 2, above). For them, it makes little sense that war crimes or crimes against humanity are part of an institutional structure when the original or supreme crime is missing. Some of this is nostalgia for Nuremberg (Persico, 1995; Ferencz, 1980: xii); some of it is part of a historical mission to make universal what was applied selectively at Nuremberg and Tokyo (the German and Japanese delegations were keen supporters of the crime of aggression at Rome).

Prominent NGOs, meanwhile, are enthusiastic about criminalizing aggression because it promises to be a powerful irritant in ongoing campaigns to embarrass overextending Great Powers in a highly interventionist era in international relations.[17] Crimes against peace can also be useful in the pursuit of particular political ends. This was particularly noticeable in efforts to portray President Bush and Prime Minister Blair as aggressors or criminals during and after the war in Iraq. The Great Powers themselves, of course, support the criminalization project, in the abstract. It is, after all, important to be on the side of those who wish to abolish 'unjustifiable' wars (it is also necessary that this project never come to fruition for reasons I will discuss shortly).[18] Finally, there are lawyers who point to a body of declarations, resolutions and jurisprudence that appears to establish the criminal status of aggression. This paper trail running from Nuremberg through to the 1974 Declaration on Aggression seems to point in only one direction: the holy grail of a workable definition, institutional superstructure and body of jurisdictional norms for the crime of aggression. The failure of the Rome delegates to include aggression must have been mystifying in this context.

But this resistance is less puzzling when one considers the opposition to the crime of aggression. This appeared at the Rome negotiations in a number of different guises. There were jurisdictional arguments about who should possess competence over aggressive wars, substantive arguments about whether aggression required an 'armed attack', and about what sort of justifications might act to legitimize a use of force, and more prudential arguments about whether aggression belonged in the Statute at all (given its political nature and its potential to disrupt the work of the Court).

Crimes against peace are controversial precisely because the use of force in international relations remains a sovereign prerogative that sovereigns are understandably unwilling to entirely disavow and because of the structurally decentralized and morally heterogeneous nature of international society. This is why, ranged against the enthusiasts, is a formidable group of non-believers. This group can be divided into four: *sovereigntists* (who know a clear definition will only constrain states from using force in their own interests); *new imperialists* (who want to use force to advance universalizing political programmes and know that criminalizing force will limit their capacity to do so); *anti-imperialists* (who worry that the criminalization of aggression is simply a mechanism for punishing resistance to new imperial projects) and *legalists* (who worry that the structure of international society and the opposition to criminalizing aggression produced by that structure have resulted in an absence of the sort of precedents and clear definitions necessary to establish a crime of aggression).

Briefly, *sovereigntists* argue that neither law not institutions have any place in the decisions of nation-states when matters of core security are at sake. Dean Acheson, former United States Secretary of State, adopted a variant of precisely this argument when he said, during the Cuban Missile Crisis, that: 'The power, position and prestige of the United States had been challenged by another state; *and the law does not deal with such questions of ultimate power* – power that comes close to the sources of sovereignty' (Acheson, 1963).

Whole attitudes of mind and bodies of thought are dedicated to this view that parts of the international order are anarchic or without law. This perspective has found widespread support in the media since 11 September. It is a view apparently prevalent, also, within the Bush Administration. The UK House of Commons Select Committee reported on their investigations in the United States in the following terms: 'The impression we obtained from those with whom we discussed the question was that, instead of establishing first whether military action would be legal, the US would act first and then use international law to defend its action retrospectively if it were possible to do so.'[19]

Michael Glennon reports that Madeline Albright, on being told by the then UK Foreign Minister Robin Cook that Foreign Office British lawyers were finding it hard to justify war in Kosovo, replied: 'Get new lawyers' (Glennon, 2001: 178). According to this view, states are entitled to make their own judgements and mistakes in matters that go to the heart of state sovereignty. To criminalize the use of force in such circumstances merely offers the prospect of unenforceable law or the criminalization of defeat (rather than aggression). When Mark Kendall-Smith refused to serve in the war on Iraq in 2004, he was court-martialled and sent to prison. The Judge Advocate in that case, Jack Bayliss, told Kendall-Smith that he had seriously misunderstood the crime of aggression (it applied only to high-ranking officials) and that, anyway, his job was to carry out the policy of Government not evaluate that policy for conformity with international law.[20]

Crimes against peace were formulated to punish, after the fact, the imperial designs of the Japanese in East Asia and the Germans in Europe and Africa. But other imperial projects were expressly excluded from the ambit of the tribunals at Tokyo and Nuremberg. Soviet territorial expansion in Central Asia and Eastern Europe, and European Empire in Asia and Africa were not subject to scrutiny. *New imperialists* are disturbed not by the selectivity of this but by the whole idea of criminalizing force which they find jejune and unsatisfactory. The category 'crimes against peace' has the potential to seriously imperil international society by seeking to criminalize the use of military force by key members of the international elite: 'A nation ought to do what it wants to do' (Rumsfeld, 2004).

It is explicit in the new projections of the Bush Administration and the Blair Government that force must be used to pursue international order and justice. The US Government's 2002 *National Security Strategy* defends the rights of the United States to use pre-emptive force to confront its enemy, and the Prime Minister, in a 2004 speech to his Sedgefield constituency, called for the dismantling of the Westphalian system of international law prohibiting unauthorized force, in order that a muscular humanitarianism could be pursued.[21] Robert Kaplan, a leading realist thinker in this imperial tradition, has named this a 'pagan ethos': one unconstrained by commitments to non-intervention or law or morality or the predilections of the Security Council (as many such commentators pointed out before the Iraq War, if war was necessary, how would the disapproval of the Cameroon make it unnecessary?). The essence of leadership is the capacity to adapt to changing conditions and engage in flexible war-making. As John Gray puts it: '. . . this connection between peace and the possible use of force [is] a permanent feature of the human affairs' (Gray, 2006). If Blair is right, and force will be necessary to end humanitarian catastrophe or prevent genocide or restore order (and in the absence of Security Council authorizations or agreement on new laws of humanitarian intervention or universal compliance with the Non-Proliferation Treaty, NPT), then that force will have to be aggressive force (if, say, the 1974 Declaration is to be the basis for an understanding of aggression).[22] If Kaplan is right, and the world is about to enter an anarchical phase, then force to protect economic interests or gain control of degraded resources will be an inevitable feature of this phase (Kaplan, 1994). Attempts to criminalize aggression will begin to look increasingly forlorn in this context. Either these definitions will be rejected as too expansive (therefore permitting the projection of almost limitless imperial force) or too utopian (thereby restricting the projection of this force). Richard Perle and David Frum are blunt proponents of the latter view: '. . . the UN must endorse our "inherent" right to defend ourselves against new threats . . . if not, we should formally reject the UN's authority over our war on terror' (Frum and Perle, 2003: 271).

Anti-imperialists, meanwhile, come to the same conclusion for opposite reasons. Justice Pal's jeremiads in Tokyo suggest that a juridical distinction between aggressive wars and legitimate wars will simply become a projection of Great Power preferences. During the negotiations at Rome, there were those who feared the inclusion of aggression might be bought only at the high price of giving the Security Council primary jurisdiction over the crime. Indeed, the original ILC Draft in 1994 did precisely this. Article 23 provided that the ICC would have jurisdiction over a *crime* of aggression only where the Security Council had already determined the existence of an *act* of aggression. This was consonant with the Charter but anti-imperialists worried that it would also mean that crimes against peace would be applied to 'other people'.

No wonder, then, that even those who had begun to assume aggression would be included as a core crime, eventually came to believe that the problems of definition, the sharp disagreements over jurisdiction, the lack of precedents and the anarchic structure of international relations meant that jurisdiction over crimes of aggression would have to be deferred. This was the outcome articulated in Article 5(2). The conclusion some *legalists* reached was that the crime of aggression was no longer and perhaps never had been 'a firmly established rule of international law'.[23]

The existence of these four sets of criticisms does not mean aggression will disappear from the international scene. Its repression through criminal law remains a central ambition in at least one conception of war and crime. And there are periodic reminders of its importance. When the Deputy Legal Adviser to the UK Foreign Office, Elizabeth Wilmshurst, resigned in protest at the Iraq War, she declared that the war would be not just a breach of Article 2(4) imposing civil liability on transgressors (there was widespread support for that position) but an act of aggression (a much more controversial assertion). In the original 7 March Secret Advice from the Attorney-General to Blair on the legality of the war in Iraq (Goldsmith, 2006), the UK's chief legal officer suggested that a domestic case might be brought against the Prime Minister given that aggression was a crime under international law and therefore UK domestic law (para. 34). The Iraqi Special Tribunal has included a curiously parochial version of the crime in its Statute. And as I write this book, two important legal decisions have been handed down, each referring to crimes against peace. Lord Bingham's opinion in *R v. Jones* begins in ringing terms: 'The immense, perhaps unprecedented, suffering of many people in many countries during the twentieth century had at least one positive result: that it prompted a strong international determination to prevent and prohibit the waging of aggressive war.'[24] And in the *Democratic Republic of Congo v. Uganda*, the DRC's submission describes Ugandan activities in DRC as 'acts of armed aggression' (Decision, para. 1, para. 23).

Yet, for all the potential applicability of the crime of aggression to these cases, neither court finds the crime to be relevant to its findings.[25] In both cases, there is a reluctance to juridify this aspect of political life. In *R v. Jones*, Bingham held that aggression is not a crime under UK domestic law (he worries about the possibility that the tacit assimilation of the crime into domestic law (through 'incorporation' by the Court) would 'draw the courts into an area which, in the past, they have entered, if at all, with reluctance and the utmost circumspection' (para. 30)). The waging of war *may* be criminal, the Court states, but it also falls squarely within the political discretion of an executive exercising its prerogative powers.[26] In *DRC v. Uganda*, the majority judgment, and one of the separate opinions, agonize over the justiciability of the question of force at issue in the case. In the end, the Court finds that Uganda has breached the *ius ad bellum* but it makes no finding at all about whether an act of aggression has occurred. Even in the case of the findings on the use of force alone, the Court's views are framed by the realization that force is a highly charged socio-political matter not a single episode of aberrant unilateralism (something that Justice Pal had emphasized in his dissent at Tokyo (Pal, 1953: 558)). Judge Kooijmans, in his Separate Opinion in *DRC v. Uganda*, introduces his opinion with the following quote: 'To explain the intervention of one State into the affairs of another is rarely simple or uncontroversial . . . Moreover, the results are likely to be tentative, partial, and complex, and therefore less than totally satisfying. One is more likely to end with a "thick description" of a complex episode than a "scientific" explanation of a discrete social event.'[27]

4   Some final caveats

The foregoing discussion of the crime of aggression suggests that the juridification of international relations has its limits. Of course, the case for juridification has been powerfully argued. Indeed, there are compelling reasons to charge individuals with crimes against humanity or war crimes or torture. The Pinochet and Nuremberg precedents are important ones, for all their failings, and the sight of a former oppressor defending himself in court brings with it a cathartic sense of justice being, if not done, at least attempted. Yet, this chapter has shown, too, that the juridification of war through the criminalization of aggression has been a hugely controversial and chequered project. I want to end by canvassing three reasons why this controversy exists, and why the idea of individual responsibility for war ought to give us pause.

First, the juridification of war has been fixated on questions of individual agency. This is hardly surprising. The criminal law is an exercise in abstracting motivation from situation, in decontextualizing events, and in substituting individual culpability for social or political responsibility.[28] Indeed, a standard defence ploy in war crimes trials involves displacing personal guilt with systemic violence or malfunction. The Milosevic Trial was organized partly around this opposition with Milosevic himself emphasizing the structural and social catalysts of the war, and the prosecution working diligently to convict Milosevic and *not* the Serbian state (chapter 3). War crimes trials describe a world of bad men doing evil deeds. The problem is the man: 'no man, no problem' (to paraphrase Stalin). In the middle of 2005, I switched on the news to hear that Osama bin Laden had issued another vicious threat against civilians in the West. The speech was apocalyptic, personal and retributive. President Bush's response was eerily symmetrical. Both of them envisaged a world in which the removal of individual enemies would clear the ground for new political projects. It may be a little bracing to collapse Bush, bin Laden and the war crimes project but each has on occasion displayed a disregard for history, for context and for politics.[29] This, of course, was the gravamen of the objections to crimes against peace made by the American delegation at Versailles, and by Justice Pal at Tokyo. It remains a potent and salutary critique.

Second, juridification, in rendering atrocity or war through law, may create equivalences that do injustice to the lived experience of human populations or rely on 'idiot rules' (Franck, 1990) that are unresponsive to the nature of war or the character of particular wars (Koskenniemi, 1999; Douglas, 2001). The criminalization of aggression also might be too blunt a mechanism for dealing with the problem of force in international relations. The definitions in the 1974 Declaration on Aggression or the ILC's 1996 Draft Code could potentially encompass interventions ranging from the Iraqi invasion of Kuwait in 1991 to the Vietnamese intervention in Cambodia (Kampuchea) in 1979 through to the NATO bombing of Kosovo and Serbia in 1999. The sorts of 'idiot rules' elaborated in these definitions seem over-inclusive judged against, say, the response of international lawyers to these acts (many found the intervention in Kosovo to be 'legitimate', but the Iraq War 'criminal'). More nuanced rules, of course, may be unworkable.

Third, and finally, crimes against peace supplant prudential, strategic and moral judgement by drawing bright lines between acceptable and unacceptable behaviour. If decisions about war and peace are complex and compromised, then the criminalization of aggression promises a sort of anti-politics where responsible and responsive decision-making is suspended in favour of the mechanical application of legal categories: Was there a cross-border element? Did the attack constitute 'armed force'? And this anti-politics has a more sinister aspect. The problem with crimes against peace is that in the absence of clear standards and/or shared values in international society, there is a tendency to criminalize our enemies *because* they are our enemies. Once a state has been described as an aggressor then all sorts of judgements can be suspended. Negotiation, diplomacy, the economic calculations of realism, the classic Westphalian assumptions about the equality of nations, and the sense that 'it must always be kept in mind that after a war we have sooner or later to live with our enemies in amity' (Hankey, 1950), all give way to the imperatives of punishment and retribution.

In the end, the rhetoric of aggressive war will be utilized for precisely these ends but as a legal category it is more likely that aggression will be consigned to the category of a 'crime to come' because it can neither be defined and applied universally (it would embrace the actions of the Great Powers, it would require a thick description of which international law is incapable) nor removed altogether from the international agenda (it is mandatory to describe certain outlier states and their leaders as 'aggressors').

7

Law's Origins
Pirates

1 Infinite justice

The spectres of perpetual war and infinite justice preside over the contemporary world. This current incarnation of perpetual war, as well as dissolving the distinctions between war and peace, has promised permanent enmity. For the Great Powers, there is to be no negotiation, no diplomacy and no compromise with today's adversaries. Instead, there is to be an endless justice, sometimes requiring indictment and prosecution but, mostly, fought using executive power and, sometimes capricious, military violence. In chapter 6, I considered the criminalization of war: a project dedicated to converting enemies into criminals (putatively, a move from politics (and war) to law). This chapter turns to the war on terror: a war on a figure who is neither a criminal (entitled to the protection of the criminal law, subject to war crimes trials) nor an enemy (afforded certain protections under the law of war). In the case of the war on terror, then, we have a transition from law back to politics (and war).[1]

In this chapter, I argue that a central figure in this war on terror is the 'enemy of mankind'. The original enemy of mankind is the pirate: an originating presence who is, at the same time, a harbinger of law's fate, a construct of war and peace, and an object of both legal regulation and unregulated violence. Piracy inaugurates international criminal law (pirates are the first enemies of mankind) and the pirate figure is reinvented in order to renew (or radically transform) the idea of international community that underpins this legal order (terrorists are the latest enemies of mankind). Paradoxically, though, the re-emergence of the pirate-terrorist, essential to the remaking of international community through the war on terror, also threatens that community's prior legal commitments (frequently the treatment of the pirate-terrorist is unconstrained by law).

In section 2, 'Enemies of mankind', I discuss how, in law's doctrinal fictions, the pirate's defining characteristic is the universal hostility he is said to inspire rather than, as two influential alternatives suggest, in either the private motivations lying behind his behaviour or the *locus* of his acts (e.g. on the high seas). I consider here the different legal traditions inspired by the pirate figure (universal jurisdiction, individual accountability in international law, and the law of war crimes). I describe how the pirate is treated as the forerunner to the contemporary pirate-terrorist – denied legal rights and cast beyond civilized conflict, he is neither defendant nor warrior. I argue that this turn (back) to piracy is apiece with the contemporary quest for moral clarity in international society, and the sharp differentiations between good and evil currently grounding certain conceptions of this society (e.g. *United States National Security Strategy*, 2002).

This project to convert enemies into pirates, though, has been a fraught one. In contemporary commentary and criticism, alternative conceptions of the pirate figure have pressed against this effort. For example, the pirate-terrorist has been posited as a prisoner of war (entitled to the protections of the Geneva Conventions), as a detainee (entitled to the protection of the International Covenant on Civil and Political Rights), as a criminal suspect (entitled to fair trial guarantees), and, of course, as a former friend (the effort to situate bin Laden's activities in the context of the Cold War) or heroic figure (the pirate-terrorist as anti-colonial champion).

This pirate, discussed in section 3, is a figure of ambiguity; at different junctures he is glamorous, transgressive, dangerous, a former ally and a possible adversary. The inability to settle on a stable legal definition of the pirate-terrorist can be explained, partly, by this overarching opposition between the pirate elaborated in this section (liminal, ambiguous, alternately friend and enemy, 'freedom-fighter') on one hand, and the law's more conventional renderings of the pirate figure as an evil outsider on the other hand (section 2). Piracy is perpetually threatening to collapse into insurgency or rebellion or privateering. What we end up with is a figure who is sharply demarcated in much of the field's judicial and doctrinal work as an enemy of mankind, and fluid and ambiguous in our politics and in some of our legal practice as enemy, ally, proxy, privateer and combatant (legal and illegal). It is this opposition that informs the current debates about the definition of terrorists and illegal combatants (and the discomfort expressed around these categories). This opposition, too, goes some way to explaining an apparent contradiction between the moralizing certainties around the subject of pirates, and the intense debate about their character or identity.

The chapter ends (in section 4. 'Enemies of Empire') by arguing that pirates are not enemies of mankind but enemies of empire (i.e. adversaries of particular political projects often masquerading as the 'international community'). Pirates, like (some) war criminals, are figures who find themselves on the 'wrong' side of existing political configurations (chapter 5). Rather than viewing them as the 'worst of the worst', they can be best understood as subject to the often highly discretionary legal and political violence of the hegemons. In the end, the pirate-outlaw is the enemy, not of mankind, but of particular men with particular political projects. This explains the ambiguities surrounding pirates (their association with rebellion, dissent, oppositional politics) and the hegemonic desire to see them eliminated as outlaws (particular projects naturally wish to represent themselves as universal, and their enemies as 'villains of the world' (Rediker, 2004)).

2 Enemies of mankind

Piracy is regularly invoked as the first international crime,[2] or the first offence to give rise to universal jurisdiction (Randall, 1988: 792) or the precursor to contemporary offences against the dignity of mankind.[3] Pirates, on this view, are the original terrorists (Halberstam, 1988: 269). They disrupted international commerce, they were an irritant to Empire, they acted in pursuit of disqualified ends (greed, anarchy), they were *res nullius* (having allegiance to no state) and they behaved abominably, showing no regard at all for the 'laws of war' or the principles of maritime civility or the *ius ad bellum*.[4] Neutrals, enemies and friends all belonged to an elaborate patchwork of other-regarding norms. The treatment to be afforded to such legal persons very much depended on the context in which they were found. With piracy, the matter was simpler. These were enemies of all men – the identity of the pirate was bound up with the idea of universal antipathy.[5] One could have mixed feelings about the French or about revolutionaries, but general agreement prevailed in relation to these ocean-going plunderers. It was simply a case of naming them and eliminating them.[6] The pirate band, too, was outlaw. Sometimes whole peoples were assigned this status, for example the Cretans during the period of Roman dominance in the Mediterranean. Later in the development of international law, the pirate state, defying the mores of international intercourse, inherited this status. It, too, was ostracized, forfeiting its legal powers and immunities, and becoming an enemy of mankind.

This enemy of mankind trope, employed so vigorously in relation to pirates, proved highly adaptable and influential in the development of international (criminal) law. The whole idea of making individual human beings the beneficiaries (human rights law) or subjects (war crimes law) of international law is influenced by the treatment of pirates. In most international treatises of the nineteenth century, for example, pirates are the only non-state actors to feature. Individual responsibility begins with piracy. Pirates were unusual: they were outside the international order (they defined what it meant to be outside the order) and yet were also unique in being the only natural persons subject to that legal order's direct control. Diplomats, soldiers and aliens, for example, were subject to forms of legal protection or punishment but their legal personality was subordinate to or derived from the personality of the state. An injury to an alien under the law of state responsibility or diplomatic protection was an injury to the state of nationality. Under this classical conception, diplomats, heads of states and aliens were limbs of the state and not freestanding independent persons. Similarly, breaches of the laws of war by soldiers were punishable at the local level by states exercising normal territorial jurisdiction and military discipline; any responsibility at the international level was owed by the state of the soldier's nationality (or allegiance) to the state injured by the war crime. In these cases, individual harm or deviance was assimilated to interstate relations.

The regulation of piracy, on the other hand, required a recognition that individuals had personality in international law. This idea took root in the twentieth century in the form of individual responsibility for breaches of international criminal law and in the form of human rights claimable against the state. Thus, the state found itself answerable to individuals within its jurisdiction and state officials found themselves, after Nuremberg, subject to norms of international law. The origins of this development are acknowledged throughout the jurisprudence of war crimes. The war criminal, like the pirate, is characterized as an enemy of mankind – 'hostis humani generis' – operating outside the bounds of law and outside the jurisdiction of national law (e.g. *Eichmann*). He is engaged in *a form* of killing or plundering that is unacceptable. War criminals thus became the successors to pirates (see a critical discussion in Kontorovich, 2004). They threatened international society because the particular form of violence they indulged in was a departure from legitimate violence. This, in turn, gave rise to a new class of enemies subject to universal jurisdiction (e.g. Geneva Convention IV, Article 149).

This idea of universal jurisdiction, too, is central to an understanding of piracy. The law of piracy detached criminal jurisdiction and enforcement from territorial sovereignty by providing for a form of extra-territorial jurisdiction. Because pirates were enemies of mankind, states, unusually, could apply their laws regularly outside sovereign or colonial territory. Piracy was itself extraterritorial so forms of jurisdiction and enforcement were created that were also extraterritorial. The freedom of the seas advanced by Grotius in his famous debate with John Seldon was a freedom enjoyed by pirates, too, because the freedom of the seas established a zone in which states, no matter how powerful, were prohibited from exercising full sovereign power, say, by acquiring sovereignty over the oceans. The International Law of the Sea imposed this restraint on state action. But though the high seas were beyond regular state sovereign control, they were also the locus of an extraordinary extension of one of the attributes of that sovereignty in the name of taking universal jurisdiction over pirates. States were not bound by territorial limitations in this regard.[7]

Customary international law, now codified in the 1982 UN Convention on the Law of the Sea (UNCLOS), provides for universal criminal jurisdiction as a way of reconciling freedom with constraint. Article 105 of the Convention permits states to take jurisdiction and seize pirate ships on the high seas or outside the territory of sovereign states. Indeed, Article 100 provides that states have a duty to suppress terrorism in the high seas 'or in other places outside the jurisdiction of any state'. And states may bring pirates before their national courts (Article 105). So, though the high seas are beyond sovereignty in one sense, in another sense sovereigns (and only sovereigns) – as Article 107 makes clear only 'authorized' vessels may seize and apprehend pirate vessels – enjoy extraordinary extra-territorial rights there.

Piracy, beyond sovereignty in one sense, provokes an extension of it in another. The law of piracy, then, inhabits a zone precisely balanced between international and domestic space, and between the imperatives of cosmopolitanism (extra-territorial jurisdiction over piracy is an early version of universal jurisdiction over 'crimes against humanity') and the requirements of sovereignty (this jurisdiction was exercised by sovereigns for the protection of sovereigns, i.e. it was a form of extra-territorial jurisdiction over 'crimes against states or empires'). The law of piracy, as with international criminal justice in general, is hybrid (see chapter 2). It provides an origin for the development of international criminal justice and post-sovereign universalism but it is structured around the extended powers and competencies of the sovereign.[8]

This extension of sovereign power has, of course, migrated to other areas of regulation. In *Filartiga*, a US federal case arising out of torture in Chile, a judge in a US court, in deciding whether to allow the exercise of universal (civil) jurisdiction under the Alien Tort Claims Act, noted that:

'The torturer has become – like the pirate and slave-trader before him – hostis humani generis, an enemy of all mankind' (*Filartiga*: 890).

But how is it that international criminal law came to represent pirates as enemies of mankind? And, importantly, how does this analogy (applied to torturers and war crimes) work in relation to pirate-terrorists?

The popular image of the pirate is of a corsair attacking vulnerable ships on the high seas or a Captain Hook figure existing beyond the civilized world but preying on it at its weakest points; like Hans Eworth's painting of Suleyman the Turk (hanging at Tate Britain), the pirate represents a figure of 'fear and fascination'. This corresponds to some portrayals of piracy in law. King James defined piracy as 'depredations committed on the seas by certain lewd and ill-disposed persons' (Ormerod, 1921: 1), and the English (and Scots) common law refined this to include '. . . acts of robbery on the high seas' (*Republic of Bolivia*: 785), a specific genus of robbery taking place both on the high seas and in territorial waters (*Cameron v. HM Advocate*), 'the use of force with the intention of committing plunder' (*Athens Maritime*), and robbery frustrated or otherwise on the high seas (*In Re Piracy Jure Gentium*). These are over-inclusive definitions encompassing, for example, a snatched handbag on an ocean-liner or a bottle of whisky stolen from the shop on a cross-channel ferry. Most international law definitions focus, therefore, on the presence of a second vessel and a private motive or purpose. UNCLOS defines piracy as an illegal act of '. . . violence or detention, or any act of depredation committed for private ends by the crew or the passengers of a private ship . . .'.[9]

What, though, are private motives? Many definitions associate private motives with mercenary intent.[10] This squares with the everyday image of pirates threatening the integrity of the high seas trade by seeking out ships laden with gold and plundering them. These, too, seem to be the 'private ends' envisaged by the drafters of UNCLOS. But while in many cases, private acts are assimilated to selfish motives or an intent to plunder, the definitions become more complex in some commentary and jurisprudence. In one set of definitions, the emphasis is on the absence of authorization rather than the motives of the individuals involved (Brierly, 1928: 154; Oppenheim, 1955: 608). In one case, the failure to act within the laws of warfare or the law on the use of force becomes a defining feature of piracy (*In Re Piracy Jure Gentium*: 598). This idea is found, too, in Justice Story's opinion in *US v. Brig Malek Adhel* (Halberstam, 1988: 274) where piracy is defined as an absence of public authority, including a 'lawless appetite for mischief' or 'plunder *lucri casa* . . . not commissioned and engaged in lawful warfare'. Here, pirates are akin to illegal combatants.

The emphasis is on the absence of authorization rather than the presence of pecuniary motives on the part of the individuals involved (Brierly, 1928). In this way, the sailor in the act of mutiny is reduced to the status of pirate. According to this view, the pirate is not marked by his or her plundering psychology but rather by the absence of public authority. It is very much a question of who they are as well as what they do.

States and state actors cannot, under this conventional definition, commit acts of piracy (except when they mutiny and cease to be publicly authorized) but nor, seemingly, can private actors acting for public or political ends (e.g. recognized insurgents or belligerents) commit acts of piracy. This latter distinction between private and public ends was explored in detail in a case called *Republic of Bolivia v. Indemnity Mutual Marine Assurance*. Here, an English court had to determine the status of a group of rebels operating on the Bolivian-Brazilian border. The case required consideration of some exclusions in an insurance policy in the aftermath of losses incurred after an attack on the insured shipping by Bolivian rebels representing the 'Free Republic of Acre'. Acts of piracy were indemnified but acts of rebellion were not. The key definition in the insurance schedule referred to piracy as 'plunder for private gain . . . not for a public, political end'. The court held that despite the presence of some private motives these motives were not enough to deprive the Bolivian insurgents of the privilege of public action. The activities of the El Acre 'privateers' were essentially political. These rebels were dedicated to the overthrow of a particular state authority in a particular place. Theirs was not plunder for personal greed and gain, but plunder for political change in a single place.

This representative case (notwithstanding that it is an English case about a specific insurance policy) suggests that neither private greed nor the absence of proper authority is the controlling feature of what it means to be a pirate. In *Republic of Bolivia*, the distinguishing mark of the pirate is his lack of politics. He is not the enemy of one sovereign but rather an irritant to all. Pirates are not 'our' enemies, with that term's implication of political contestation, but rather the enemies of all. The El Acre rebels were enemies of one particular state not of all states. So, though the activities of the El Acre insurgents may have been, in form, almost exactly that of pirates, their plunder had a public purpose. It was lawless but only in relation to the laws and sovereign authority of Bolivia. Theirs was behaviour lacking the '. . . spirit and intention of universal hostility'. In 1937, the Conventions signed at Nyon and Geneva established that attacks during the Spanish Civil War on merchant vessels unattached to the belligerents were to be 'justly treated as acts of piracy'.[11] These attacks were beyond the pale of humanity because they were aimed at no one in particular. As the defence lawyer in *Republic of Bolivia* put it, pirates are 'criminals at war with society generally'. Such groups are enemies of mankind because they are not enemies of only one particular sovereign.

But this raises an important question about groups who are neither insurgents nor plunderers. Is the political actor whose actions are indiscriminate but public, political and non-pecuniary, for example, a pirate? In particular, are terrorists 'enemies of mankind'?

There has been an effort among some international lawyers to categorize Al-Qaeda, or the PLO (at the time of the *Achille Lauro* affair) as pirates (Halberstam, 1988; Reisman, 2001). There is a problem, though, with the attempt to analogize terrorists with pirates. Notwithstanding the inevitable parallels between some terrorists and the conventional imagery associated with piracy, terrorists, most often, *are* acting for political ends. Recent writing has attempted to get round this problem by arguing that organizations such as Al-Qaeda are pirate bands acting for *disqualified* political ends. Specific political agendas such as those pursued by the insurgents in *Republic of Bolivia* or the rebels in the *Santa* incident (where naval officers took control of a Portuguese vessel in an act of rebellion in 1960 against the Salazar regime (Green, 1961: 496)) remove the resulting activities from the pirate category whereas an organization (or state) at war with the international community is configured, like the pirate, as existing outside the realm of politics, acting in the name of inhumanity. Private greed accompanied by violence (and therefore piracy) is apolitical but so, too, are political projects directed against 'everyone'. This sort of political project is converted into an act of private madness directed at international society generally; a League of Nations committee concluded in 1926 that for the purposes of piracy, 'private ends' could encompass 'anarchistic vengeful motivations'. The contrast, then, is between international terrorism (enemies of all civilized people) and the activities of the El Acre rebel (or the Basque separatist?) who is as the court put it: 'Not only not the enemy of the human race but he is the enemy of a particular state' (and therefore not a pirate (*Republic of Bolivia*: 4)).

In the Ambrose Light case, the court held that insurgents could be exempted from the category of pirates only if they were *recognized* insurgents.[12] In a discussion of the *Santa Maria* case, Leslie Green has argued that the actions of the Portuguese rebels could not be piracy because the men were acting for public ends, and public ends directed towards only the Salazar Government. For him recognized insurgents, and insurgents directing their insurgency to a single enemy, were part of the international system already and therefore could not be enemies of that order. An ILC Report, too, in 1955 stated that warships could never qualify as pirates because 'universal public enmity, could only exist where the political element was lacking'.[13] Where the political element was present, sheer malice could be deemed to have supplied the necessary 'private' element (at 41).

The hijackers who flew passenger airliners into the Twin Towers were not acting in a private capacity for private gain but nor were they, according to this view, acting against one state. Instead, they were malicious enemies of all men. Theirs was a private war with mankind. In the war on terror, then, it is not the quality of the act that is decisive but rather the personality of the actor. Is *this* terrorist an enemy of mankind (and of all states), or simply an enemy of one state? Michael Reisman has pursued this line in distinguishing previous crimes of terrorism (by, for example, the IRA or Basque separatists) from the attack on the Twin Towers. The activities of the IRA were directed at particular political ends whereas, according to Reisman, the terrorist attack on the United States was an 'aggression' against the 'values of the system of world public order'. As a result of the attack, 'all peoples who value freedom and human rights' have been forced into a war of self-defence (Reisman: 833). Thus the attack on the United States was not simply a hideous breach of international law and an attack on a particular set of values (say, capitalism or US foreign policy in the Middle East), but an assault on international society aimed at the destruction of that society by those outside it. The key attribute of piracy-terrorism is an animus against the whole world.[14]

Malvina Halberstam has made a similar distinction in contrasting the *Santa Maria* incident with the hijacking of the *Achille Lauro*. In the latter case, the Palestinian Liberation Front seized a cruise ship en route to Port Said and held the passengers hostage before killing Leon Klinghoffer, a Jewish-American guest on the ship. There is little doubt that such acts (often described as 'terrorism') fall foul of various conventions on international law, but these conventions circumscribe the jurisdiction of states and do not depend on characterizations of the wrongdoers as 'enemies of mankind'.[15] This is an important distinction in terms of both jurisdiction and enforcement because, arguably, any state can seize a pirate ship (Halberstam, 1988: 272). Most international lawyers take the view that insurgents who capture a ship are free from interference or interception as pirates providing they do not prey on foreign shipping or neutrals onboard (Brownlie, 1998: 228). The Harvard Research in International Law Commentary excludes in its definition of piracy, wrongful attacks for political ends whether sponsored by states or undertaken by belligerents or 'unrecognised revolutionary bands'.[16] The essence of piracy, for Halberstam, though, is not the presence of 'two ships' or 'private ends' or 'unauthorised force' or 'plunder' or 'non-political motives' but instead the existence of a hostility against the whole world (and the absence of any state with an obligation to the pirates). This test, for her, is satisfied in the case of the *Achille Lauro* (terror directed at the US, Israel and Italy as representatives of the international community) and not in the case of the *Santa Maria* (rebellion directed against the state of Portugal).[17] According to this sort of argument, the activities of pirate-terrorists like al-Qaeda – malicious and declaring a hostility towards the world at large – reach beyond a reasonable conception of the political (theirs is not a political programme directed against one sovereign). The response to such pirates need not, in turn, be constrained by the legal order that underpins reasonable political intercourse. In the case of terrorism, the conflation of certain forms of terror with the idea of piracy results in a universal jurisdiction over pirate-terrorists (anyone can try them) combined with their increasing vulnerability to unilateral, discretionary political action (pirates could simply be executed without trial in the seventeenth century). In the words of Judge Moore, in the Lotus case, the pirate is to be treated as: 'outlaw, as the enemy of mankind . . . whom any nation may in the interest of all capture and punish'.[18]

Piracy, then, is very specifically related to the relationship between the political and the legal that runs through this text. Large parts of this book have been about different forms of judicialization, or the move from politics to law. But, in a reversal of this trajectory, the conversion of criminals or enemies into pirates marks a move from law back to politics or war. The field of law, war and crime, then, is constituted, partly, by an opposition between the criminal law (producing trial and conviction, or, occasionally, acquittal (chapters 2, 3 and 4)), and the repression of piracy and outlawry (provoking combinations of discretionary violence, law, immunity and licence (chapters 5, 6 and 7)). This movement between law and politics is also a movement between the use of judicial processes (though always political) to punish enemies on one hand (law, criminality), and resort to non-judicial methods (though often grounded in legal forms) to remove these enemies from the political scene, on the other (war, piracy).

An example of this idea of piracy as a political alternative to law can be seen in the debates about what to do with the Nazi State and its leaders after the end of the Second World War. In 1943, as the Allies began to contemplate war crimes trials, there was resistance among those of a more punitive inclination. Anthony Eden took the position, shared by Churchill, that Nazi guilt fell outside the framework of law (Overy, 2002: 7). He was in favour of summary execution or political action, arguing that there was simply no international law capable of confronting the sort of evil seen in the 1930s and 1940s. The United Kingdom made this argument at the Inter-Allied Information Committee: 'His Majesty's Government are deeply impressed with the dangers and difficulties of [a trial]. And they think that executive action without trial is the preferred course'.[19] But, of course, this was not quite political action. Summary execution, after all, required some legal authority. The Lord Chancellor, Lord Simon, suggested that Nazi fugitives be treated like the outlaws of medieval Britain. This pseudo-legal procedure permitted any citizen to kill an outlaw declared such by the Grand Jury: '. . . the Sheriff did not try the outlaw or bring him before any court for trial; he merely hanged him' (Overy, 2002: 4).

This idea of outlawry was taking hold, too, among prominent academics. Georg Schwarzenberger shared the Eden view that the Nazis fell outside the ambit of decent international law. In his book *International Law and Totalitarian Lawlessness*, he called for the Nazi State to be designated an outlaw regime or pirate state, one that could no longer avail itself of the protections of international law, and one in relation to whom the term neutrality could have no meaning (Schwarzenberger, 1943). Henry Morgenthau, Roosevelt's Treasury Secretary, meanwhile, was busy working on a plan that would combine the two ideas of state piracy (a pastoralized Germany) and individual outlawry (summary execution for a number of high-ranking Nazis) in one overarching scheme for an emasculated post-war Germany (Bass, 2000: 166; Beschloss, 2002).

In Iraq, today, this accommodation of the legal and the political is present in the way enemies are conceptualized. Three months after the invasion of Iraq by US/UK-led forces in March 2003, Iraqis and allied troops began to uncover mass graves: sites of atrocities committed by the Iraqi regime. The relatives of victims called for some form of punishment of those responsible. One relative spoke bluntly: 'Either the people who did this must be brought to court or we should ask for the authority to kill them' (McCarthy, 2003: 1).[20] The 'people who did this' were at once criminals and pirates.

In contemporary international society, the idea of piracy has enjoyed a renaissance on a number of fronts. Of course, there is the revival of old-fashioned mercenary-piracy itself in the South-East Asian shipping lanes and enclaves, and elsewhere.[21] As I completed this chapter, the headline news in many newspapers and on radio bulletins concerned an attack by pirates on a British cruise ship off the coast of Somalia (O'Neill, 2005). The *London Evening Standard*, meanwhile, at the end of 2005, sought to frighten London commuters with the headline: 'Pirates attack cross-channel ferry' (in fact, the ferry, rather than plying a trade between Dover and Calais, had been on its way to the UK from South Korea after repairs).

On a broader level, the pirate state is a readily identifiable figure in the practices of the international community and in the rhetoric of the Great Powers.[22] As I discussed earlier, arguments are being made for placing terrorist suspects in a parallel legal regime and having them subject to universal jurisdiction or relatively unfettered enforcement action (Halberstam, 1988). This is reflected, too, in the linguistic and jurisprudential formulations of the Bush Administration. Recalling Anthony Eden's language, Donald Rumsfeld has called the Guantanamo Bay detainees the 'worst of the worst', and Paul Bremer, the former head of the Coalition Provisional Authority in Iraq, described Shia cleric Muqtada al-Sadr as 'an outlaw'.[23] Afghanistan was characterized as a 'failed state' in the infamous Gonzales 'Torture Memo' (advice given by US Attorney-General to the President purporting to deprive captured Taliban fighters of the right to Geneva Convention protections normally accorded to POWs).[24]

Much of this rhetorical and jurisprudential energy is exercised with a fundamental question about the nature of international society. That question is at the centre of this book's concerns. How ought we to understand the identity of enemies, now, and in history? To describe an adversary (say, the state of Afghanistan or the Taliban or Osama bin Laden) as 'criminal' might be a useful rhetorical ploy (creating the impression of an enemy to be destroyed and without mercy). President Bush's deployment of the mythic imagery of the Wild West is intended to produce this effect. The chief characteristic of the Wild West was that it was a wild and lawless place made lawful by the moral zealousness of the frontier colonists, and the imposition of a rough, discretionary law and order directed by the Sheriff at clearly defined enemies; criminals were smoked out dead (as pirates) or alive (as criminals). The use of this language seemed to be a way of positing a form of (legalized) retribution as an alternative to trial.

But in liberal legal traditions criminals are tried and convicted not killed or liquidated by Special Forces. Inevitably, then, in characterizing bin

Laden as 'criminal', US officials were signalling or bringing into play two contradictory images: the image of lawlessness and vigilantism on one hand and the image of trial and conviction on the other. The President might think that calling bin Laden a criminal means that he must be killed more ruthlessly than if he were just an enemy; after all, since we accord honour and respect to our enemies, (international) criminals should be denied that respect. Amongst international lawyers (and not just international lawyers), though, it means that bin Laden should be prosecuted and tried before a court offering him the privileges and immunities of criminal suspects (after all, he is no longer an enemy to be killed but a criminal to be defended in court).

What is being conjured into existence is a figure, or identity, who sits outside these two categories: not quite an enemy entitled, after all, to certain protections under the Geneva Conventions and Protocols, nor quite a criminal entitled to due process and civil rights (nor of course a friend). The illegal combatant, the terrorist and the Islamic 'fanatic' all seem to fall between these stools. If a criminal is at war with a particular society, and an enemy is at war with a particular state, then we might suggest that this new (or revivified) character is at war with everyone or with international society or the international community. He is 'the enemy of mankind' and in invoking this term, we inevitably call up another figure, that of the pirate.

3 The ambiguities of piracy

The pirate figure, then, is central to an understanding of the mechanics of modern international society, and the reinvention of international law through the law of war crimes, and, latterly, in the war on terror. But an examination of the pirate through history also explains why the field of war crimes law, the war on terror and the very idea of international community have produced so much dissension; the identity of the pirate has itself long been subject to disagreement, indecision and conflict.

The ongoing attempts at the international level to define enemies of mankind, most notably in the case of terrorists or aggressors, have met with failure precisely because these definitions always have the potential to become self-definitions (the definers, too, wish to engage in forms of terrorism (Falluja) or aggression (the invasion of Grenada), and because the pirate has always been a figure of extraordinary ambiguity.

This return to piracy comes with some baggage, then. The failure to achieve the requisite level of certainty (about illegal combatants or about terrorists) can be traced back to piracy's origins. Were pirates enemies of mankind? Were they acting in their private capacity or with an animus against the world? Were they the 'evil of the evil'? The historical record suggests that this was not always the case.

Alongside the notion of the pirate as an enemy of mankind, there is, in the cultural life of the West, a tradition in which pirates occupy a borderland between respectability and deviance. In Thucydides' *History of the Peloponnesian Wars*, there is a passage in which piracy is discussed: 'For in early times, the Hellenes . . . were tempted to turn pirates . . . indeed this came to be their main source of livelihood, no disgrace being yet attached to such an achievement, but even some glory . . . Old poets ask – 'Are they pirates?' as if those who are asked the question would have no idea of disclaiming the imputation (Thucydides, 1996: 1.5).

The literary figure of the pirate, too, is quite often sympathetic, sometimes transgressive, rebellious, communitarian and often opaque (think Daniel Defoe or Robert Louis Stevenson). Frederic, the apprentice pirate in the Gilbert and Sullivan opera *The Pirates of Penzance* would have been an apprentice pilot but for a mistake made by his nursemaid. He loves the pirate band he has joined but at the end of his apprenticeship, he regrets that duty will require him to kill them all as enemies of the Crown. The other pirates, meanwhile, are revealed first as 'orphans' and then as 'noblemen'. The identity of the pirates is at all times in question.[25] In Brecht's song 'Pirate Jenny', a cleaner on board ship is, unknown to the crew who treat her badly, a pirate sympathizer and spy ('you'll never guess to who you're talking?'). How could this mere cleaner be a pirate, how could this *woman* be a pirate?

Pirate society, meanwhile, has been mythologized as a socialistic brotherhood: an alternative society. Pirates were a threat to the economic interests of major powers but they also questioned the whole idea of the state. Pirates had learned to live outside the law and beyond sovereignty. Though they may have wished to render the state powerless, they did not yearn for the power of the state. In this way, they provided an example of an alternative sovereignty, a non-territorial sovereignty. Pirates were a substantive threat (they preyed on merchant shipping) but they were also a formal threat (they posited an alternative to statism) (Rediker, 2004). Pirates offered ideological opposition by living a counter-life (Byron contributed greatly to this view of piracy) (Rediker, 2004: 16–17).

This story is further complicated by the fact that pirates often *were* part of the ruling elite or, at least, in the pay of this elite. Privateers, were state-sponsored pirates, immune from exercises of universal jurisdiction and entitled to a degree of respect under the rules of engagement operating on the high seas. Even when pirates were unlicensed, the law was applied very selectively. In sixteenth-century England, pirates were sometimes hanged, but not all of them could be disposed of in this way because, with the uniform application of nominal anti-piracy laws, 'the south coast of England would have been virtually depopulated and the Spanish Armada would have met with little opposition' (Mitchell, 1976: 12).

The status of the pirate band, too, is fluid. Frederic may feel obliged to kill his comrades in the pirate community. After all, he thinks, they will forever be pirates, beyond reform. On the other hand they are his friends. Sometimes pirates become states (or friends). Again, in the Peloponnesian Wars, there are the pirate bands who successfully carve out a zone of power or jurisdiction on the high seas before engaging in land appropriations. It is these pirates that turn out to be the forerunner to the city state and, eventually, the sovereign state. Sovereigns, against whom enemies of mankind are often juxtaposed, turn out to be the descendants of these same enemies. Thucydides describes a transition from a pirate class to a more static, civilized life usually adopted by the most successful pirates or by those colonizers who had expelled the pirates. The pirates, then, begin as romantic heroes, a respectable job for a young Hellene. At some point, these pirates ceased to be respectable. This occurs at the very point when their power becomes a threat to the state (or the state system). But this is the point, too, at which pirates are on the cusp of becoming respectable citizens of Mediterranean society. Some state systems, then, find their violent foundations in the successes of piracy.

Then there is the case of the state that becomes a pirate – a responsible polity transformed by internal trauma or excessive hegemonic ambition. The history of piracy is dotted with examples of states that pursue their economic and political interests through piracy. These pirate states may be forerunners of the contemporary outlaw states: partly demonized, partly tolerated. Illyria, for example, was regarded as a 'predatory state' by the Romans (Ormerod, 1921: 19). The most obvious contemporary example of the state assigned pirate status is that of Nazi Germany. Towards the end of the war, many state officials were talking of Germany as a state 'hijacked' by a small group of co-conspirators.[26]

Often, too, pirates, far from being enemies of mankind, were barely pirates at all. Sometimes they were licensed as privateers, sometimes they were acting more informally at the behest of respectable sovereigns and sometimes they were recognized persons under international law. Indeed, the whole distinction between pirates and a multiplicity of other agents was often very obscure. Certainly, the pirate was not at all times criminal. Piracy was often a mode of production supported by the Great Powers and Empires and there is great uncertainty surrounding the legitimacy of piracy in, say, the ancient Mediterranean where it was, at various times, regarded as a form of production, a cheap way of getting slaves to market and a method of harassing competitors.

This uncertainty surrounding piracy is reflected in the transformation, through association with the Great Powers, of the Barbary pirates from pirate to quasi-sovereign. Here the pirate becomes a confident, land-based actor capable of generating acts of recognition on the parts of others. The Barbary states in Tunis and Algiers, for example, acquired such recognition after years of piracy, and the US began paying tribute to the Barbary pirates at the turn of the eighteenth century (Braithwaite and Drahos, 2000: 419). There is a transformation from private greed to public respectability (all the while engaging in the *actus* of piracy). As one writer on piracy puts it: 'At different stages of their history, most of the maritime peoples have belonged to first one class, then another'.[27]

The privateer, of course, lies precisely at this crossroads between legitimate 'war' and illegitimate 'crime'. Privateers were essentially licensed pirates. Their depredations were directed at a particular adversary and their booty was sanctioned by Prize Courts (sometimes specifically established for this purpose). There was often controversy over the status and acceptability of privateering. During debates concerning the Admiralty Jurisdiction of the newly created United States there were those who believed that privateering against the British had to be encouraged, and that any form of jurisdiction that permitted 'adventurers' to receive 'the rewards of their success and bravery' was to be warmly welcomed.[28] In the United Kingdom, too, the High Court of Admiralty issued licences to pirates so that they could become privateers (Gosse, 1928; Braithwaite and Drahos, 2000). Everyone was using pirates and decrying their existence.

4   Enemies of Empire

Ultimately, pirates are usefully protean: they fight proxy wars, they attack rivals and they become fellow-sovereigns. Most of all, though, pirates as enemies of mankind are vital in the mobilization of political and legal resources around the idea of 'mankind' itself. This book has been about war crimes and implicit throughout is the idea of an international community punishing breaches of that community's most sacred norms. I want to conclude by suggesting that mankind punishes war crimes and piracy but, at the same time, relies on these outsiders for its existence as a 'community'.

Bert Röling, the Dutch judge at the Tokyo War Crimes Trials, in his interview with Antonio Cassese, worried that the notion of piracy could not extend to war crimes or terrorism precisely because of the lack of solidarity in the international system; or because the 'international community' did not exist; or because the project of modernizing international law had not gone far enough (Röling, 1991: 97). Perhaps, though, the pirate category is precisely how international community is made. It might be argued that the presence of mere 'enemies', in the Geneva Convention sense of the word (enemy personnel entitled to certain protections under the laws of war), is evidence of a lack of community, and the continued presence of legitimate ideological or political disputation and conflict, or pluralism. In order to *construct* international community, adversaries must be transmuted into pirates. Enemies become outlaws, criminals become pirates. *Our* enemies become enemies of mankind. Pirates, then, are enemies of particular political projects that happen to have been universalized, e.g. Empire, globalization, Christianity, America.[29] When the particular is universalized, particular enemies must become enemies of mankind. Here, we adjust Blackstone's dictum that 'every community' has a right to punish pirates by quoting Otto Kirchheimer: 'every regime has its foes or in due course creates them' (Blackstone's *Commentaries*: 71; Kontorovich, 2004: 190; Kirchheimer, 1961: 1). In this sense at least, piracy might also be characterized as international law's future. The concept of piracy, applied widely enough, anticipates a future deepening or homogenization (forced or otherwise) of international society.

All of this recalls Carl Schmitt's distinction between foes and enemies (Schmitt, 1996). The revival of piracy (initially, the pirate state at the end of the Great War) signals, for him, the beginning of an international order marked by police action rather than war. In this order, the international community fights humanitarian wars or policing actions against outlaws and pirates. Old wars, between equal sovereigns, are abolished. The pirate, then, is symptomatic of the passing of a tradition in warfare from equal combat to police enforcement or, in Schmitt's chilling phrase, 'pest control'. The transformation of the Iraqi resistance from military adversaries to terrorist brigands is an example of this. Almost at every instance towards the end of the first phase of the 2003 invasion, whenever the US Army met serious resistance, this opposition was instantly rendered as piracy or terror. This is the second story of new wars, alongside the idea of them as predominantly internal and chaotic affairs (Kaldor, 1999). When the US and its allies fight wars, these wars will be wars against pirates or terror or disorder – never the old-style war between two states with conflicting political projects or territorial ambitions. Pirate states will be subject to territorial intrusion as part of an enforcement action on the part of the legally empowered Great Powers acting in a policing capacity: not the 'war between' but the 'war against'. These will not be wars between sovereigns but enforcement actions against some transcendent evil (sometimes represented by a particular sovereign). In the occupation phase, a similar process occurs. There can be no legitimate resistance (implying the possibility of politics and disagreement) only the pathology of counter-imperialist piracy.

This is all part of a wider move away from what had been a central feature of the modernization of international law, namely the effort to distinguish between different categories of identity, for example neutrals/non-neutrals, combatants/non-combatants, war/peace, pirates/enemies and so on (it was also a feature of this modernization that the identity of sovereignty itself was fixed as neither good nor bad but simply sovereign). Now, a counter-trend appears to have emerged in which more and more actors are assimilated to piracy as these various distinctions are eroded. This has occurred, for example, in the marginalization of neutrality and in the shift in risk from combatants to non-combatants during humanitarian wars or, as I have already noted, in the way in which members of the Iraqi resistance were repositioned as 'terrorists' even as the initial stage of the war was being fought or in the way in which pirate states are contrasted with decent sovereigns.[30]

If the problem of international law is a problem of social solidarity then piracy may appear to be its saving grace. The completion of international law, for some, would be marked by the final consummation of the 'international community', marking a change from the pluralistic, competitive society in which international law seeks to ameliorate the effects of war and difference to the idea of international law as a sort of moral community defined in part by the presence of outsiders. But, in the 'war on terror' these outsiders are configured as *beyond* international law, too. These are not enemies of society whose elimination or incarceration confirms the majesty of law, but rather radically estranged outlaws whose lack of legal protection becomes a feeling of international law.[31] The 'war on terror', as I have indicated, has called into existence a figure not readily locatable within our conventional understandings of legal personality in wartime. He is neither (war) criminal nor enemy (nor friend), though always potentially one of them, but is instead a pirate figure subject to expansive projections of state or elite violence, and sometimes cast beyond the law into what the English Court of Appeals in *Abbasi*, a case about the detention of British nationals at Guantanamo Bay, called 'a legal black hole'.

The trend towards the moralizing clarities of good and evil in the international system returns us, though, to our ambiguous foundations in the regulation of piracy. If the pirate is our foundational figure here, the original enemy of mankind to whom all other adversaries are to be assimilated, then it is little wonder that categories are blurring as we recover this figure. This is because the return of the pirate is a return to ambiguity, and because the identity and identification of pirates have always raised difficult questions about war and peace, about sovereigns and non-sovereigns, and about policing and warfare. Pirates, conceived as enemies of mankind, turn out instead to be merely humankind in its plural guises.

But Empire (and community) need piracy.[32] This contains a literal truth: pirates (transformed into privateers) are agents of imperial ambition and, at the same time, objects of it. Osama bin Laden, after all, was once 'licensed' as one of 'our' terrorists just as the High Court of Admiralty issued licences to pirates in order that they become privateers. But at a deeper level, the existence of 'enemies of mankind' (whether pirates or war criminals, and whatever ambiguity surrounds their identity) is one way of ensuring the continued purchase of 'mankind' as a category capable of pursuing international justice or waging perpetual war.

8

Law's Fate

'Law, war and crime' is a big subject that was once a small subject. The first war crimes trial in the modern era is thought to have been that of Major Wirz (during the American Civil War), a Swiss national prosecuted under a legal code developed by a German who had fought in the Napoleonic wars (Franz Lieber). The first trial for crimes against humanity occurred at Nuremberg in 1945, and the first serious, if abortive, attempt to criminalize war took place at Versailles in 1919. The subject of this book did not exist until the middle of the twentieth century; the intersection of law, war and crime is a novelty of our age.

I have approached this new field *as a field* with a view to divining its presiding doctrines, its perplexities and its underlying structure. I have elaborated on a number of relationships within the field that seem important if not defining. These relationships have revolved around questions of law and politics, of space and place, of subject, of promise and anxiety, and of violence and legality.

The success of this field means that it seems natural now to think in terms of international war crimes trials and schemes for cosmopolitan, retributive justice. Amnesties, impunities, political action and so forth have tended to justify themselves as departures from the juridical norm. Law and crime are now central to our understandings of how war should be judged. And we understand, too, that war must be judged, and that we are capable of judgement. This is the modernist project of law made global.

Behind this fury of judging, though, is a less visible orientation, an ancient sense that we are at the same time incapable of judgement: that judgement is still to come, or that humanity's predicament is defined by the desire to judge and the deferral of justice.

This returns us to a question that has informed large parts of this text. Is war a product of human design or an accident of history? The whole notion of justice in war and just war assumes the former. Wars are nasty, sanguinary and poisonous but they are redeemable through the justness of the (victor's) cause and the justness of the (vanquished's) punishment.

The forces of democracy, decency or God will prevail in the end because of the justice they embody and the justice they apply. This modern war, then, is also an ancient war: a war of good and evil, a war of pest control or collective punishment, a war that is no longer war but merely police action or community self-assertion or religious purification. This is the war of the Old Testament or the medieval doctrine of just war. It is enjoying a period of ascendancy.

Judging by accounts of recent wars, they are rarely experienced this way by those that fight them. From *All Quiet on the Western Front* to *Jarhead*, soldiers have equivocal experiences in which the good do evil and the killing sometimes can feel arbitrary and without purpose. This accords with some structural explanations of war in which the cause of war is understood as a competition for resources or a tragic mistake or preening vanity or national compulsion.

George Steiner contrasts Old Testament wars with the Peloponnesian Wars. In Thucydides, as in Homer, there is no justice (why does Troy fall never to rise again?), only wars in which men, driven by 'obscure fatalities and misjudgements . . . go out to destroy one another in a kind of fury without hatred' (p. 6).

What sort of wars are we now waging? And how should we respond to them? With law? Or with fatalism and irony?

Notes

Preface

1 Security Council Resolution 1593, 31 March 2005.
2 At least one notable paradox of this contemporary scene was the coincidence that has produced on one hand a legalist high-point in the creation of the international criminal court with its aspirations to tame lawlessness in the international order, give teeth to the laws of war and enforce human rights observance, and on the other a renewed existential crisis for international law provoked by the internment of Taliban and al-Qaeda detainees in Guantanamo Bay, the prosecution of an unlawful war against Iraq and the maltreatment of Iraqi detainees at Bagram and Abu Ghraib.
3 The five cases are Sierra Leone (the Special Court for Sierra Leone), Iraq twice (the Iraqi Special Tribunal), Kosovo (the trial of Milosevic at the ICTY) and Afghanistan (the proposed trials of Guantanamo Bay detainees before US Military Commissions).
4 See *Prosecutor v. Kayishema and Ruzindana*, ICTR 95-1; ICTR 96-10 (Appeals Chamber), 1 June 2001, para. 63–71; *Prosecutor v. Tadic*, IT-94-1 (Appeals Chamber) (Judgement), 15 July 1999, para. 48 (henceforth *Tadic* (Judgement)).
5 The International Criminal Tribunal for the Former Yugoslavia costs approximately $90 million a year.

Chapter 1 Law's Politics

1 The first epigraph is from *Milosevic* (Transcripts), Opening Statement, 12 February 2002, at 6; the second is from *Milosevic* (Transcripts) (Interlocutory Appeal Hearing) 30 January 2002, at 351.
2 See Schmitt, 1996.
3 Throughout the text, the term 'war crimes law' is used as a shorthand for the body of rules, principles, norms and institutions that seeks to regulate the conduct of war (and, in some cases, 'peace'). It encompasses customary crimes such as crimes against humanity, treaty crimes such as torture, and embryonic offences (e.g. the crime of aggression). The usage here refers to more than war crimes (i.e. narrowly understood as grave breaches of the Geneva Conventions and serious violations of the laws of war). I use this term war crimes law or the law of war crimes interchangeably with international criminal law (though as a term of art the latter includes also e.g. the law on extradition or mutual assistance in criminal matters (e.g. the work of Interpol)).
4 *United States of America v. Alstötter et al.* ('The Justice Case') (1948). This trial is the subject of the Spencer Tracy film *Judgment at Nuremberg* (1961).
5 *Attorney-General of the Government of Israel v. Eichmann* (1961); *Prosecutor v. Akayesu* (1998).
6 A phrase used by the Chief Prosecutor at Tokyo, Joseph Keenan, Maga (2001): 1.
7 However, to advertise war crimes trials as political trials would undermine the project of maintaining their detachment from politics. The more legalistic, universalist,

disinterested they are the more detached from politics and the less pragmatic they appear. On the other hand the more pragmatic they appear the more like show trials they become.

8 *Milosevic* (Transcripts), 30 January 2002: 352.

9 *Tadic* (Decision on the Defence Motion for Interlocutory Appeal on Jurisdiction) (1995) at paras. 9–48 (henceforth, *Tadic* (Decision)).

10 As the Defence Motion of 19 November 1945 in the Nuremberg Trials put it: 'The Judges have been appointed exclusively by the States which were one party in this war' (Marrus, 1997: 120).

11 *Prosecutor v. Delalic*, IT-96-21, Trial Chamber Judgement at http://www.un.org/icty/celebici/trialc2/judgement/index.htm; *Prosecutor v. Oric*, IT-03-68 (Amended) Indictment at http://www.un.org/icty/indictment/english/ori-3ai050630e.htm.

12 *The Guardian*, 13 August 2003: 20.

13 Notwithstanding the fact that three of these situations were referred to the Court by the state subsequently under investigation.

14 War Crimes (Amendment) Act 1988 (Australia) s.5; War Crimes Act 1991 (c.13) (UK) s.2.

15 For a discussion of some of the problems associated with the ICTY in particular see M. Scharf and A. Kang, 'Errors and Missteps', *Cornell International Law Journal* 38 (3) (2005): 911–48.

16 *War Crimes: Report of the War Crimes Inquiry* (Cm 744, 1989) at 5.43. In *Polyukhovich v. The Commonwealth of Australia* (1991), 172 CLR 501, Justice Deane articulated the most typical response to this problem: 'The *ex post facto* creation of war crimes may be seen as justifiable in a way that is not possible with other *ex post facto* criminal laws . . . The wrongful nature of the conduct ought to have been apparent to those who engaged in it even if, because of the circumstances in which the conduct took place, there was no offence against domestic law', at 643.

17 Though even for Goldstone, politics, with its difficult choices and shabby compromises, still has to be negotiated. In an early passage in the book, Goldstone asks Henk Heslinga to assist in an investigation into the South African Third Force. Heslinga, we are told, had been a member of Koevoet, 'a notorious unit that had operated against SWAPO' in Namibia. When Heselinga reveals this to Goldstone, Goldstone is 'impressed with [his] candour' and tells him to remain with the Commission.

18 For a discussion of vengeance see Rich Cohen, *The Avengers* (New York: Knopf, 2000) pp. 197–203.

19 The Court went on to say '[t]he question whether the war-related claims of foreign nationals were extinguished . . . is one that concerns the United States only with respect to her foreign relations, the authority for which is demonstrably committed . . . to the political branches', at 12.

20 One indication of this expansion is found in the slow retreat of sovereign immunity in international law and in national law. In England, the *Pinochet* judgment dissolved the absolute immunities of former Heads of State (when those immunities had been implicitly 'waived' by international treaty obligations), the *Jones v. Saudi Arabia* judgment at the Court of Appeals refused to grant immunity to Saudi officials accused of torturing UK citizens in Saudi Arabia (though this holding was reversed on appeal to the House of Lords) and a decision in the Charles Taylor case before the Sierra Leone Special Court found that incumbent Heads of State would not be immune from the jurisdiction of a mixed tribunal (at least when that tribunal was predominantly 'international').

21 Indeed, our fascination with and sense of righteousness about crimes against humanity may obscure the degradation and marginalization of other liberal traditions, e.g. hospitality to benighted strangers or the redistribution of wealth.

22 Stating: '[. . .] the Accused will not be allowed to make any public appearance or in any way get involved in any public political activity. The Accused will however be allowed to take up administrative or organisational activities in his capacity of President of the Alliance for the Future of Kosovo'.

23 See for decision and background, *Prosecutor v. Haradinaj*, IT-04–84 (Decision on Modified Provisional Release), March 10 2006 at http://www.un.org/icty/haradinaj/appeal/decisione/060310/index.htm.

Chapter 2 Law's Place

1 'PM backs Saddam Trial in Iraq', *Daily Mail*, 15 September 2003.

2 *Melbourne Age*, 6 April 2006: 12.

3 This debate is now being played out in Sudan too with the Sudanese Minister of Justice Mohammed Ali al-Mardi recently declaring: 'Our judiciary is capable of handling all the cases and Sudan is serious, desirous and capable of trying any of those who committed crimes' (*Sudan Times*, 15 December 2005).

4 Decisions will be made only if there is a supermajority of judges in favour. This leaves scope for any one of the international judges to prevent convictions she believes to be unfair or unfounded. See United Nations Assistance to the Khmer Rouge Trials (UNAKRT) (2006) at http://www.unakrt-online.org/.

5 The Central African Republic Ministry of Justice has declared its own legal system to be incapable of trying former premier Ange-Félix Patassé (*Reuters*, 26 April 2006).

6 Rome Statute, Article 16: 'No investigation or prosecution may be commenced or proceeded with under this Statute for a period of 12 months after the Security Council, in a resolution adopted under Chapter VII of the Charter of the United Nations, has requested the Court to that effect; that request may be renewed by the Council under the same conditions.' See, too, Security Council Resolution 1422, 12 July 2002 (a further resolution was passed in 2003 but a 2004 draft resolution had insufficient support in the Council).

7 Cavell's execution was sensational, and Alfred Zimmerman, the German Secretary of Foreign Affairs, was forced to make a public statement defending the killing. His statement offers an early pseudo-feminist reading of international criminal law to justify the execution: 'No criminal code in the world – least of all the laws of war – makes such a distinction; and the feminine sex has but one preference, according to legal usages, namely, that women in a delicate condition may not be executed. Otherwise man and woman are equal before the law, and only the degree of guilt makes a difference in the sentence for the crime and its consequences' (Horne, 1923).

8 The Wirz trial after the American Civil War is a possible exception.

9 The Court did not exclude the possibility of a DRC court hearing the Yerodia case (or, indeed, an international court acting under Security Council authority).

10 See too Judgment on the Guatemala Genocide Case, Judgment No. 327/2003 (25 February 2003): '[T]oday there is significant support in doctrine for the idea that no State may unilaterally establish order through criminal law, against everyone and the entire world, without there being some point of connection that legitimizes the extraterritorial extension of its jurisdiction', at www.derechos.org/nizkor/guatemala/doc/stsgtm.html.

11 As of January 2006, there have been no examples of the latter at trial.

12 Historically, civil wars had not been regarded as part of international criminal law (Ratner, 1998).

13 The tension among the British political classes over UK prosecutions of soldiers accused of having committed war crimes in Iraq is perhaps an exception to this.

14 There were breaches of international humanitarian law and there was control by a foreign power over paramilitaries operating within Bosnia. See *Tadic* (Decision).

15 Efforts have been made to criminalize international mercenarism and large-scale cross-border environmental crime. See ILC Draft Code of Crimes (1996).
16 *R v. Sawoniuk* [2000] 2 Cr App R, 220.
17 There are a number of general criticisms of cosmopolitanism (though these are not the primary focus here). The communitarian critique (e.g. Walzer, 1994) has focused on this lack of embeddedness in the cosmopolitan project. The community of human beings, or the *civitas humanis*, is simply too thin to sustain a rich, progressive theory of global life. Worse, still, as Costas Douzinas has argued, the human rights movement (cosmopolitanism's closest living relative) atrophies when it embraces the pragmatic, the institutional, the international, the bureaucratic and the diplomatic, and repudiates the ethical, the utopian and the local (Douzinas, 2000). Another retort to the cosmopolitan idealism is found in the idea that human rights and justice have to be fought for where they are breached; at the local and the national level (Alvarez, 1999).
18 If there were precursors to *Eichmann* at the IMT proceedings they were found in the testimony of the three Holocaust survivors, and in Hartley Shawcross's closing statement for the prosecution. In the end, Nuremberg was not about the Holocaust but was a project designed to anchor Nazi atrocities to international legal norms. In this, it was somewhat successful but, as a pedagogic tool, its successes came to be realized retrospectively.
19 In a recent Appeal before the Tribunal, the Appeal Court considered the principle of *lex mitior* (the principle that a convicted felon will benefit from any change in law prior to sentence); the Court rejected the appeal on the basis that the change in law occurred in Serbia and that Serbian law did not form part of the law of the ICTY. See *Prosecutor v. Deronjic*, IT-02-61-A at http://www.un.org/icty/deronjic/appeal/judgement/der-aj050720.pdf, para. 97.
20 Article 180, para. 2, of the BiH Criminal Code provides for command responsibility in the same form as Article 7(3) of the ICTY Statute.

Chapter 3 Law's Subjects

1 IMT, Judgment, *American Journal of International Law* 41 (1947): 172 at 221.
2 *Prosecutor v. Tihomir Blaskic*, IT-95-14-T, 3 March 2000. See, too, ILC Draft Articles, Second Reading (1999).
3 ILC Articles on State Responsibility (2001).
4 This resolves itself as (at least) four models of criminality. The first is the responsibility of individuals *qua* individuals. Here I refer to the trial of soldiers who commit extraordinary crimes of war without any authority from their superiors. Second, is the liability of officials who commit crimes on behalf of the state. Here the collective and the individual become mixed. The third model is organizational criminality of the sort seen at Nuremberg, and the fourth model is state crime (a fifth model might attribute some responsibility to the very structure of international society itself).
5 This was the case even in the laws of war. Violations of this law were a matter of interstate responsibility, e.g. Article 91 of Hague IV (1907) states: 'A Party to the conflict which violates the provisions . . . shall, as the case demands, be liable to pay compensation'. This includes compensation for individuals. See, too, C. Greenwood, 'International Humanitarian Law' in F. Karlshoven (ed.), *The Centennial of the First Peace Conference* (London: Kluwer Law, 2000).
6 Such 'moral communities' were standard fare in the writings of early publicists like Suarez and Vitoria.
7 This provision has been recommended for removal in the *World Summit Report* (2005).
8 *Agence France Presse*, 'Death rate of Iraq mothers triples, UN survey finds', 4 November 2003 (according to the study the number rose from 117 cases of maternal death per

100,000 live births in 1989 to 310 in 2002); S. Zaidi and Mary C. Smith Fawzi, 'Health of Baghdadi children', *The Lancet*, 2 December 1995: 356.

9 E.g. the UN Commission on Human Rights (now replaced by a Human Rights Council) adopted Basic Principles and Guidelines on the Right to a Remedy and Reparations for Victims of Gross Violations (UN Docs. E/CN.4/RES/2005/35).

10 Even Security Council Resolutions began to name individual violators of international law. This began with Osama bin Laden but there are now many individuals named in similar resolutions: e.g. SC Resolution 1521 (2003).

11 Though it is not clear whether this provision refers only to state civil liability or whether 'responsibility' here can encompass forms of criminal responsibility.

12 *Prosecutor v. Jelisic*, IT-95-10 (Appeals Chamber), 5 July 2001 at para. 49.

13 There is nothing in the Genocide Convention itself to exclude the possibility of individual action. The Convention, after all, in the case of murder, refers only to the requirement that the accused has killed members of the group with an intent to destroy it in whole or in part. There is no requirement that the killings be in any way substantial. Courts, though, have tended to understand genocide in precisely this way, e.g. the court in *Krstic* noted that 'the destruction in part must be of a substantial nature so as to affect the entirety' (para. 10).

14 Stimson et al. 'Memorandum for the President', 1945, in Marrus, 1997.

15 See *Milosevic, Rule 98b bis Decision* at para. 288ff.

Chapter 4 Law's Promise

1 The quote is from an Iraqi who carries with the him a list of those Baathists present at the Hilla massacres in 1991.

2 Australia, Parliamentary Debates, HR, Vol. 158, 23 Nov–Dec 1987, 35th Print, 1st Sess., 7th Period, Speaker, Mr Reith, War Crimes Amendment Bill (1987), 26 Nov 1987 at 2735 ('If we are to learn from the lessons of those times we must ensure that justice, which is the corner-stone of our democracy, is not tainted').

3 See Persian Gulf: The Question of War Crimes, 1991: Hearings before the Committee on Foreign Relations, 102d Cong., 1st Sess., 17–20 (1991) (statement by Professor Anthony D'Amato). For further examples of this pedagogic rhetoric see Reid, 1994: 6.

4 *Prosecutor v. Drazen Erdemovic*, IT-96-22-T, 29 November 1996, Sentencing Judgment at para. 65.

5 E. Ward and M. Hieman, 'Iraqi Run Tribunal is Major Progress towards Rule of Law System', *Christian Science Monitor*, 19 July, 2005 at http://www.csmonitor.com/2005/0719/p09s02-coop.html: 'The Iraqi Special Tribunal is poised to strengthen the atrophied Iraqi judicial system. Since Hussein's fall, its judges, prosecutors, and counsel have been instructed by international experts in human rights law, evidence collection and management, and courtroom administration. This education, and the actual experience of the trials, will be invaluable in raising the standards of Iraq's bench and bar.'

6 ICTY Press Release, 11 July 2005, CVO/MOW/988e.

7 ICTY Press Release, 23 June 2005, at CT/MOW/981e.

8 There may be a sense, too, in which genocides always seem to take place the day before yesterday. By the time we verify their existence through the testimony of survivors or the study of aerial photography, it already seems too late. Nevertheless, the trial is a re-enactment of history with a (usually) more satisfactory ending.

9 For a discussion see Gubar (2003).

10 Hannah Arendt/Karl Jaspers, *Correspondence, 1926–1969*, p. 54 quoted in Osiel, 2000: 128.

11 The Court speaks at one point of the need to exclude foreign material and yet also permit an exhaustive account of the Holocaust. See *In re Eichmann*, 18–19.

12 Douglas, *contra* Arendt, sees *Eichmann* as a triumph, but is bitterly critical of the *Demjanjuk* proceedings and worries about the equivocal effects of *Zundel*. Nor does Douglas deny that the didactic aims of a trial can come into conflict with its judicial function. These tensions themselves are part of what it means to make law and history. The Eichmann trial, then, produces occasions of discomfort for the bench but these moments are not failures of law or didacticism but rather successes for the trial's dual purpose. Legal proceedings can, of course, simply 'teach' (these are 'show' trials, chapter 5) and, equally, they can avoid history (witness the IMT's contortions around the subject of the Holocaust, see section 6). Douglas distinguishes, also, the ways in which history is recounted or interpolated in successive trials, from the documentary form preferred at the IMT to the testimonial histories heard at Jerusalem during the Eichmann trial and then to the statements of the professional historians who occupied centre stage during the Zundel trial.

13 Israeli Military Spokesman quoted in 'Israeli outcry forces army to act against soldiers', *The Guardian*, Friday, 3 August 2001, p. 15.

14 Shakespeare, *The Winter's Tale* (III. ii).

15 Gerard Henderson, 'The cause is still a just one', *Melbourne Age*, 11 May 2004, p. 11.

16 Trotsky's Citizens' Tribunal (designed to refute the charges made at the Moscow show trials) met in the Blue House owned by Frida Kahlo between 10 April and 17 April 1937.

17 Carla Del Ponte, Opening Statement, *Milosevic* (Transcripts), 12 February 2002: 3.

18 Letter of Resignation (a Minute dated 18 March 2003 from Elizabeth Wilmshurst (Deputy Legal Adviser) to Michael Wood (Legal Adviser)).

19 'It is very true that the memory of the Holocaust shakes every Jew to the depths of his being, but once this case has been brought before us it is our duty to subdue even these emotions as we sit in judgment' (*Eichmann*: 17).

20 General Comment No. 41 at para. 16 (2004).

21 This figure is an estimate taken from Z. Brzezinski, *Out of Control: Global Turmoil on the Eve of the 21st Century* (New York: Touchstone, 1993).

Chapter 5 Law's Anxieties

1 J. Steele, '"I am the president of Iraq. I do not recognise this court"', *The Guardian*, 20 October 2005, p. 1.

2 Quoted in Julian Mortenson, *A Week at the Trial of Slobodan Milosevic* (2005) at www.slate. com/id/2126142.

3 Henry Kissinger said, of the Iran-Iraq War: 'It's a pity they can't both lose'. In fact, the United States would have been happier to see the Iranians defeated by a still largely pro-Western Saddam.

4 In the end, Saddam was represented by Iraqi lawyers (two of whom were assassinated) and a former US Attorney-General, Ramsay Clark.

5 Certain Criminal Proceedings in France (*Republic of Congo v. France*), Provisional Measures Hearings, Submissions of Jacques Vergès, Transcript CR 2003/20, 28 April 2003, paras. 1–5.

6 *Milosevic* (Appeal Hearing) at 351. In his Opening Statement, Milosevic also said: 'They are not satisfied with the crime committed over Yugoslavia and the settling of accounts with Serbia because of their defeat in both world wars. They want to proclaim us the culprits, who were the victims of their aggression, and me, with the help of this tribunal, to bring me before Nuremberg to reverse the roles', Transcripts, 14 February 2002, at 268. For a discussion of this victor's justice at Nuremberg itself, see Gilbert, 1995: 4, 'The victor will always be the judge, and the vanquished the accused'. (I thank Vladimir Petrovic for bringing this to my attention.)

7 Hess, *Final Statement*, 31 August 1946 in Marrus, 1997: 220–1.

8 Lord Campbell of Alloway, *Hansard*, 14 July 2005, Col. 1222 at http://www.publications. parliament.uk/.

9 In Moscow Trial No. 1, 1936, 19–24 August, there were 16 defendants, 15 of whom publicly confessed. Moscow Trial No. 2, 1937, 23–30 Jan, featured Karl Radek, a Comintern economics expert. There were 17 defendants (8 Jews), 11 of whom were executed (Klinghoffer and Klinghoffer, 2002).

10 Some recent legislation related to the war on terror may end up working in this way, too. Section 13 of The Terrorism Act 2006 (UK) (on the glorification of terrorism) states: '. . . indirect encouragement comprises the making of a statement describing terrorism in such a way that the listener should infer that he should emulate it' at http://www. publications.parliament.uk/pa/ld200506/ldbills/069/06069.1-5.html#jE002. The Act was prompted by the July 2005 bombings in London and there seems little doubt that the drafters of the Bill contemplate its application to Islamic preachers and not university lecturers. Indeed, the Prime Minister has already said that it would be used to outlaw the sorts of placards seen in London following the publication of the Danish cartoons ridiculing the prophet Mohammed (BBC News, 15 February 2005).

11 Many, many others were more credulous than the famous Russian writer. Show trials, it might be argued, are obviously more fraudulent than the average war crimes trial. However, it was not the case that this fraudulence was obvious to observers at the time. According to Orwell: 'Opinion on the Moscow sabotage trials, for instance, was divided' (Orwell, 1970). Beatrice Webb, the founder of the London School of Economics, too, believed that the trials were genuine, and the *New Statesman*, though anxious about the procedural irregularities, felt that the trials had exposed acts of sabotage (Amis, 2002: 21). The French poet Paul Eluard remarked: 'I am too busy defending the innocent who proclaim their innocence, to have any time left to defend the guilty who proclaim their guilt' quoted in S. Žižek, 'The Empty Wheelbarrow', *The Guardian*, 19 February 2005, p. 23. Amis seems to believe this was largely a myopia of the Left but the US Ambassador to Moscow at the time, Joseph Davies, informed his government that there was 'proof beyond reasonable doubt to justify the verdict of guilty' (Rayfield, 2005: 311). Trotsky commented, dryly: '. . . if Goebbels had admitted he was an agent of the Pope, he would have astonished the world less than Yagoda's [the head of the NKVD under Stalin and Beria's predecessor] indictment as the agent of Trotsky' (Rayfield: 278). In fact, the world was not particularly astonished.

12 There were other trials of course that have been labelled show trials both in the Soviet Union (e.g. the Provincial show trials in 1937) and outside the Soviet Union (from the use of legal procedure during the Terror in France to the various Nazi show trials beginning with the Reichstag Fire Trial). On the Provincial show trials see Ellman (2001: 1221–33).

13 Stimson et al., 'Memorandum for the President', 1945, in Marrus, 1997. See, too, Henry Morgenthau (quoted in Bass, 2000): 'If we force these military tribunals to follow the technical procedures and customs of an American court, such as the Supreme Court . . . I greatly fear that notorious criminals will be permitted to delay or avoid punishment by reliance on technical legal rules' (p. 172).

14 Robert Jackson, Opening Statement for the Prosecution at http://www.law.umkc.edu/ faculty/projects/ftrials/nuremberg/Jackson.html#The%20Lawless%20Road% 20to%20Power.

15 *Milosevic* (Transcripts), 12 February 2002: 2. The theatrical elements of each are often noted, also. The Prague Trials were thoroughly rehearsed and special courtrooms adapted from a Trade Union Hall in order to accommodate the audience. The Shakhty (Engineers) trial in 1928 was held in the Hall of Columns in Moscow (a hall with theatre

equipment installed). Meanwhile, the Eichmann trial was held in a theatre and the initial choice for the forthcoming Cambodian Trials was the Chaktomak Theatre in central Phnom Penh.

16 Michael Dan Mori, Speech at University of Melbourne, 18 April 2006.

17 Perhaps the most notorious 'threat' was contained in a piece of legislation, Stalin's Decree of April 7, 1935, which made children of 12 and above subject to the death penalty. This acted as a covert warning to many of the defendants in the Moscow Trials.

18 See e.g. E. Loebl, *My Mind on Trial* (New York and London: Harcourt Brace Jovanovich, 1976), J. Slanska, *Report on My Husband* (London: Hutchinson, 1969) and Artur London, *L'Aveu (The Confession)*, (Ballantine, 1971).

19 Meanwhile, the war on terror is being pursued using legal forms not dissimilar to some of those emblematic of show trials, and present at times in war crimes trials. At Prague in 1952, and at Nuremberg in 1945, the defendants were not permitted to meet with their (court-appointed) lawyers in the absence of security officers.

20 For an example of double hearsay see the evidence utilized in the Milosevic case, e.g. 'B-179 heard in Bubanj Potok conversations between Milan Prodanic and Jovica Stanisic that the Accused had to be informed about everything that was being done' (Motion for Acquittal para. 285).

21 *Milosevic* (Decision), at para. 8.

22 *338 US Rep.* 215 (27 January 1949).

23 Security Council Resolution 1160 (1998), para. 17.

24 The presumption of guilt was partly rejected at the Control Council hearings after Nuremberg where the Courts were inclined to consider the individual guilt of the accused.

25 Count One of the charges at Tokyo read: 'All the accused . . . participated . . . in the formulation or execution of a common plan or conspiracy and are responsible for all acts performed by any person in execution of such a plan' (at 47).

26 E.g. *Tadic* (Judgement) at paras. 195–226; *Prosecutor v. Vasilejvic*, IT-98–32-T (2004) at http://www.un.org/icty/vasiljevic/appeal/judgement/val-aj040225e.pdf; *Prosecutor v. Simic*, IT-95-9-T (Trial Chamber Judgement) (2003) at http://www.un.org/icty/simic/trialc3/judgement/sim-tj031017e.pdf.

27 *Tadic* (Judgement) at paras. 195–226.

28 Sometimes it was important that a particular representative should not be charged. At Tokyo, the major political decision turned on the question of trying the Emperor. He was not charged (something, Chief Justice Webb and Justice Bernard found difficult to accept (Minear, 1971: 117)).

29 London Conference at 301.

30 Of course, this is not a practice unique to international criminal tribunals. Prosecutors in domestic courts are involved routinely in decisions about whether to proceed or whom to proceed against. Plea-bargaining is common, individuals are given protection in exchange for evidence, Prosecution agencies always need to make decisions about the allocation of resources.

31 This has not worked terribly well. A vast majority of Serbs continue to believe that only fellow Serbs are being tried by the Tribunal (Rangelov, 2004).

32 Sometimes it is alleged that this political pressure operates at the domestic level to shape local prosecution strategies, too. In the debate in the House of Lords over the decision to investigate Trooper Williams for alleged war crimes arising out of Operation Telic in southern Iraq (Hansard, 14 July 2005, Col. 1219 at http://www.publications.parliament.uk/), one peer argued that the investigation had been undertaken for political motives: 'On 24 March, the Adjutant-General wrote to CGS and CIC Land, copying his letter to the Brigadier, to inform them that he intended to write to the Director of Army Legal

Services to ask him to draw the case to the attention of the Attorney-General for the purpose of having resort to the jurisdiction. In that letter, the reason given was: "With current legal, political and ginger group interest in the deaths of Iraqi civilians during Operation Telic: our investigation and subsequent failure to offer for prosecution could become a cause celebre for pressure groups, and a significant threat to the military justice system." '

33 By merely expressing an apprehension about a particular outcome, one was deemed to have willed that outcome (Leites and Bernaut, 1954: 179, 153).

34 There were rare occasions when defendants were accused of simple murder. Kamenev and Zinoviev were charged with the murder of Leningrad party boss Kirov. It was a charge of murder, too, that shattered Rudolf Slansky during his interrogation and trial. He continued to hold on to the distinction between objective criminality and personal responsibility, between his mistakes and the crime of murder. The distinction between the two was revived in the mid-sixties when Slansky was partially rehabilitated, exonerated in the case of the common crimes of murder but not from his political or ideological errors (Hodos, 1987: 163). In the original trial the complicity or culpability of the accused was political and moral, and therefore criminal (Hodos describing the Prosecutor's Opening Statement in Prague at 59).

35 In the end, a precursor to the crime of aggression was included in the Treaty of Versailles at Article 227 but this had little effect on the eventual outcome. A combination of the Kaiser's exile in Holland and a rising sensitivity to the requirements of German rehabilitation meant that neither crimes of aggression nor crimes against humanity would be prosecuted at Leipzig.

36 For a discussion see M. Schmoekel, 'Review of Carl Schmitt: *Antworten in Nürnberg*', *European Journal of International Law* 13 (2) (2002): 550.

37 In trying to prove that Milosevic was guilty of leading a joint criminal enterprise there has been an inevitable tendency to assimilate a series of political acts to mass criminality. For example, in the Motion for Acquittal hearing in 2004, the Court pronounced itself satisfied of the prima facie case against Milosevic on the basis that he had, after all, been the leader of the Serbs. One witness confirmed that the people of Knin saw him as 'the protector of the Serbs' (para. 249).

38 Lenin had said of Bukharin: 'he went to one room and found himself in another . . .' (Leites and Bernaut, 1954: 153), Speech at 8th Soviet Congress, 30 December 1920.

39 In fact, there was an attempt to establish both subjective guilt and objective responsibility (p. 205). This is why the interrogators were so insistent that the defendants write confessions they themselves were convinced by. It was not enough to be forced into making false confessions about one's subjective behaviour, the interrogations were aimed at getting the defendants to understand their objective position in history and the guilt that arose from this.

40 'A state? What is that? Well! open now your ears to me, for now I will speak to you about the death of peoples. State is the name of the coldest of all cold monsters. Coldly it lies; and this lie slips from its mouth: "I, the state, am the people"' (F. Nietzsche, *Thus Spake Zarathustra*, Wordsworth Editions, 1997: 1.11).

41 No doubt liberal advocates of war crimes trials will take umbrage at the conflation of themselves with Stalinists. The point to note here is that liberal advocacy (whatever the intentions) has produced a highly skewed set of mechanisms for dispensing justice in which whole groups continue to be immunized while others are the relentless focus of war crimes investigations.

42 Kyrlenko himself was executed after a trial lasting twenty minutes (Amis, 2002).

43 This view of Judaic thought may seem counter-intuitive and idiosyncratic to contemporary readers. *Jewish* irony and despair, after all, have become cultural types. Equally, the

amorality of Greek tragedy probably is overstated by Steiner. The Greeks possessed a morality, albeit one radically different from our own (I thank an anonymous referee for this latter point).

Chapter 6 Law's Hegemony

1 Dissenting Judgment, in Kopelman, 1991: 94.
2 Roundtable with European Journalists, 6 February 2004 at http://www.defenselink.mil/transcripts/2004/tr20040206-0431.html.
3 *Chandler v. DPP* [1964] (AC) 763, 791, 796; *CND v. Prime Minister* [2002] EWHC 2777 (Admin) [2003] 3 LRC 335, paras. 38, 40.
4 See e.g. the assertion of universal jurisdiction in the Scilingo case in Spain (for a discussion see Richard Wilson, 'Argentine Military Officers Face Trial in Spanish Courts', *ASIL Insights*, December, 2003). See, too, Guatemala Genocide Case, 42 I.L.M. 686 (2003); Peruvian Genocide Case, 42 I.L.M. 1200 (2003).
5 In the case of Iraq, this juridification took three forms: Judicial Proceeding, Inquiry and Expertise. The focus here is on court-based mechanisms (both in domestic cases (*CND v. Prime Minister, Doe v. Bush*) and in international matters (the Legality of Force case at the World Court concerning the legality of the Kosovo intervention)). Inquiry was the method present in at least three cases following the war: the Hutton Inquiry into Dr Kelly's death (C. Gearty, 'A Misreading of the Law', *London Review of Books*, 19 February 1994); the Butler Inquiry into intelligence surrounding the war; and the US Commission of Inquiry into the same. The question of expertise is taken up in Craven et al. (2004) (here a group of international law scholars reflect on the role they played in opposing war through the law developed at San Francisco and discuss the reaction from colleagues and other experts concerning the appropriate relation between law and politics, and between study and activism).
6 Public international law, then, ended up occupying a borderland that was defined by the defences it mounted against two sets of arguments which asserted that international law was unenforceable as law and descriptively implausible as analysis. These defences were complicated by the ambivalent attitude of many IR scholars to international law's status. Law was at once intensely glamorous (treaty-conferences, trials, cases in The Hague) and explicitly marginal. When it was glamorous it was marginal, when it came in from the margins (to do sociology or explanation) it became a poor man's international relations and lost its glamour (Simpson, 1999).
7 Ashworth, 'Introduction' in Snare, 1995: iii. On the other hand, international criminal law remains embryonic when contrasted with the typical Western legal order. At the moment, the risks of over-criminalization remain small (I thank Rob Cryer for this insight).
8 I do not mean to suggest here that the indictments contained allegations lacking substance.
9 Jonathan Freedland ('If it went to the West End they'd call it Whitewash', *The Guardian*, 29 January 2004) has argued that Hutton disregarded all evidence implicating the Government in anything more serious (e.g. Kelly's statement to BBC journalist Susan Watts that the forty-five-minute claim had 'got out of all proportion' or Alistair Campbell's diary entries outlining the demands he had made to change the intelligence dossier).
10 See Legality of Force Case, ICJ Reps, 2004 (case brought by the Serbian Government against NATO members at the International Court of Justice claiming that the air attack against Serbia was illegal in international law). See, too, *New York Times*, 30 April 1999, A1; 'Yugoslavia seeks a legal order to halt NATO bombing', *New York Times*, 12 May 1999, A14. The latter report claims that NATO has 'mocked' Yugoslavia's claim. For a scholarly analysis see Bruno Simma, *European Journal of International Law* 10 (1) (1999): 1–22.

11 A similar unease is expressed by the ICJ in *DRC v. Uganda* (2005) when, prior to making findings on the illegal use of force, it acknowledges 'the complex and tragic situation which has long prevailed in the Great Lakes region' (para. 26). This unease is central to the Separate Opinion of Judge Kooijmans in the same case: 'Is it possible to extract from this tangled web [of history] one element, to isolate it, to subject it to legal analysis . . . ?' (Separate Opinion, para. 11).

12 The Japanese leadership was being tried for acts of pre-emptive self-defence (Pal) that were regarded as much more acceptable by the Western powers in subsequent decades. In 1973, the United States had warned that it would regard any attempt to cut off oil supplies in the Middle East as an act of war (the Japanese justified their 'aggression' in terms of economic self-defence) and in 2002 the US National Security Strategy developed a theory of pre-emption that was not dissimilar to the Japanese justification for its invasion of, say, the Philippines. This pre-emption doctrine has survived the 2006 NSS (Kadri, 2006).

13 The US, UK and France all agreed with Röling at different times during discussions around Nuremberg. See Minear (1971: 48–9).

14 G.A. Resolution 95(I), 11 December 1946.

15 G.A. Resolution 3314, 14 December 1974. See, too, Declaration on Friendly Relations 1970 (G.A. Resn 2625); G.A. Resolution 2131, 21 December 1965.

16 PCNICC/2002/2/Add. 2 (24 July 2002).

17 Having said that, The Coalition for an International Criminal Court was agnostic on this issue prior to the Rome negotiations.

18 See e.g. the attenuated definition of 'aggression' included in the Iraqi Special Tribunal Statute.

19 Select Committee on Foreign Affairs, Foreign Policy Aspects of the War against Terrorism, HC 384 at para. 221.

20 The reasoning in the case appears contradictory. Bayliss J. is reported to have ruled that the legality of the invasion was irrelevant. But he makes legality absolutely central in stating: 'Legal Opinion may be divided as to the correctness or otherwise of the advice given by the attorney-general. But when such advice has been given, members of the armed forces cannot go behind it'. Richard Norton-Taylor, 'RAF Doctor jailed for refusing to go to Iraq', *Guardian Weekly*, 21–7 April 2006, p. 8.

21 Robert Cooper, one of Blair's former advisers, has said: 'The challenge to the postmodern world [the successful states] is to get used to the idea of double-standards. Among ourselves, we operate on the basis of laws and open cooperative security. But when dealing with more old fashioned kinds of states outside the postmodern continent of Europe, we need to revert to the rougher methods of an earlier era – force, pre-emptive attack, deception, whatever is necessary to deal with those who still live in the 19th century world of "every state for itself".' 'The Postmodern State' in *Reordering the World*, ed. Mark Leonard (London: Foreign Policy Centre, 2002).

22 Notwithstanding the failed attempts to get agreement on a doctrine of humanitarian intervention or the subordination of sovereignty to the law prohibiting genocide. See *Report of Secretary-General's High Level Panel* (2004).

23 *R v. Jones (Margaret)* [2005] QB 259.

24 *R v. Jones* [2006] UKHL 16 per Bingham J. at para. 1.

25 Lord Bingham, delivering the lead opinion in *R v. Jones*, concludes his examination of international law by saying: '. . . the core elements of the crime of aggression have been understood, at least since 1945, with sufficient clarity to permit the lawful trial (and, on conviction, punishment) of those accused of this most serious crime. It is unhistorical to suppose that the elements of the crime were clear in 1945 but have since become in any way obscure' (para. 19). In fact, the core elements were not very clear in 1945 and have

become less so since then. In 1945, a highly specialized criminal trial was established for the purpose of trying defeated enemies. The lack of precedential value has become clear in the light of a sixty-year period in which there have been no prosecutions of crimes against peace, a vigorous debate about the existence of the crime, and deep ideological disagreements about the compatibility of the international system and the criminalization of aggression. Lord Hoffman, in *R v. Jones*, is in '. . . no doubt that [aggression] is a recognised crime in international law' but he can point to only the Nuremberg Judgment and Article 5 of the Rome Statute (*postponing* the exercise of jurisdiction) as support for this proposition.

26 It may also be a crime (under the Treason Act 1351), for example, to oppose such a war by 'giving aid and comfort' to enemies.

27 *DRC v. Congo*, Judge Kooijmans, Separate Opinion at 1 (quoting John P. Clark, *Journal of Modern African Studies* 39 (2001): 262).

28 This has implications for human rights generally. The human rights movement is being pulled in two directions from its institutional, pragmatic, gradualist, incrementalist middle ground. One is towards structure: the WTO, linking human rights and trade, rethinking poverty and so on. The other is towards agency and the 'evil men' view of history; this is the international war crimes wing of the human rights project.

29 Each (and here the human rights movement is implicated, again) seeks also to undermine sovereignty. To hear Richard Haass speak of suspending the sovereignty of outlaw states, or making that sovereignty conditional on certain behaviour, is to witness a former Bush official appropriate the language of the war crimes and human rights movements.

Chapter 7 Law's Origins

1 Conversely, just as the criminalization of aggression meets with resistance from those who see war as a quintessentially political activity beyond or outside law, so, too, the war on terror is resisted by those who refuse to concede that enemies can be configured as extra-legal persons to be eliminated without judicial oversight or detained without trial.

2 For one of the earliest recognitions of international crimes as crimes under English law, see 15 *Ric* II c.3.

3 See e.g. Kaufman J. in *Filartiga v. Pena-Irala*, 630 F. 2d. 876 (2d Cir. 1980) at 890.

4 On the idea of pirates as *res nullius* see G. Schwarzenberger, 'The Problem of an International Criminal Law', *Current Legal Problems* 3 (1950): 269; on piracy and empire see Schmitt (2003: 65).

5 See e.g. *Filartiga*; *Prosecutor v. Furundzija*, IT-95-17, Judgment (10 Dec 1998); *Eichmann*.

6 See Oppenheim, 1955, sec. 278; *Texas v. Johnson* 491 US 397, 422 (1989) per Renqhuist (noting that the British had summarily hanged pirates).

7 For two versions of this see *In Re Piracy Jure Gentium*, para. 1 (discussing piracy as a crime giving rise to universal jurisdiction and piracy as an offence over which states may legislate extra-territorially).

8 At the same time, paradoxically, the response to piracy both extended state power (extra-territorial jurisdiction, supra) and offered a challenge to statism (by introducing the idea of enemies of mankind against whom the machinery of the international community could be mobilized in a way that became a threat to sovereignty too).

9 United Nations Convention on the Law of the Sea (1982) and United Nations Convention on the High Seas (1958). There is some controversy about whether the actus of piracy needs to be combined with private motives or ends (cf. Gooding, 1987, with Constantinople, 1986).

10 Indeed, mercenaries themselves were largely regarded as pirates in the pay of states or guerrilla groups (e.g. in Angola in 1977).

11 Nyon Agreement 181 LNTS at 135, 137.

12 *US v. Ambrose Light*, 25 Fed. 408, 412–13 (S.D.N.Y. 1885).

13 ILC Rapporteur's Report to the GA [1955] 1 Y.B. Int'L L Commission at 55.

14 This, too, may be the reasoning behind the Third US Restatement on Foreign Relations Law which provides that states may take jurisdiction over matters of international concern 'such as piracy, slave trade, attacks on or hijacking of aircraft, genocide, war crimes, and, perhaps, *certain acts of terrorism*' (sec. 404).

15 See, e.g., Montreal Convention 1971, 24 UST 564.

16 'Comment to the Draft Convention on Piracy', *American Journal of International Law* 26 (Supp.) (1932): 749, 750.

17 Hezbollah and Hamas, for example, consider themselves to be at war with Israel and not the US (far less humanity or the international community) (Hiro, 2003).

18 *The S. S. Lotus (France v. Turkey)*, P.C.I.J., Ser. A., No. 9 (1927) at 70 (Moore, J., dissenting).

19 Inter-Allied Information Committee, 'United Kingdom Aide-Memoire', St James Declaration, 27 April 1945 at 4. See, too, S. I. Rosenman, *Working with Roosevelt* (New York: Harper, 1956) pp. 542–5.

20 To some extent, this mirrored the views of many within the Bush Administration and Blair Cabinet about the decision to go to war in the first place. While the neo-conservatives within the Bush Administration were willing (reluctantly) to tolerate Security Council debate and involvement in the decision-making process (they were happy for Iraq to be 'brought to court' as it were), they also were very prepared to take political action to eliminate the regime outside the parameters of even this very thin version of legality.

21 E.g. J. Clayton, 'Warlords take piracy to new extremes', *The Times*, 14 October 2005; International Maritime Organisation, *Reports of Piracy and Armed Robbery against Ships*, MSC.4/Circ. 75 (2005). See, too, the recent agreement between South-East Asian states to establish a regime for combating piracy: Regional Cooperation Agreement on Combating Piracy and Armed Robbery against Ships in Asia (28 April 2005). There are 300 incidents of piracy reported each year ranging from stealing food to the hijacking of ships and cargo (David Osler, 'Maritime Mugging', *Observer Magazine*, 13 November 2005, p. 7). Compare these figures with those of Marcus Rediker, whose study of eighteenth-century piracy in the Atlantic suggests around 250 attacks a year during the *golden* age of piracy (Rediker, 2004: 34–5).

22 Simpson, 2004, passim. For a discussion of the pirate state see Shawcross, 'Opening Speeches of Prosecutors', Trial of the Major War Criminals before the International Military Tribunal, Nuremberg, November 14th, 1945 to October 1st, 1947 (1947) at 57–8.

23 *Guardian Weekly*, 8–14 April 2004, p. 1.

24 The United States, in turn, has been characterized as a 'torture state'. 'The CIA Archipelago' at http://www.opendemocracy.net/conflict-terrorism/CIA_3107.jsp.

25 When Gilbert and Sullivan arrived at D'Oyly Carte with their new opera, *The Pirates of Penzance*, the actors were in the middle of a season of *H.M.S. Pinafore*. They transformed themselves from sailors in the Royal Navy to pirates by tying handkerchiefs around their heads.

26 See, too, Shawcross, Opening Speeches of Prosecutors at 57–8 (discussing the idea of the pirate state). Conspiracy charges have been laid, also, against contemporary software 'pirates'. See http://www.usdoj.gov/criminal/cybercrime/pirates.htm.

27 Individuals, too, underwent these transformations: Sextus Pompeius, a Roman legend, begins as a brigand in Spain, then is cast as a pirate before being appointed commander of the Roman naval forces, a position he uses to engage in more acts of plunder until the challenge from another Roman force obliges him to return again to piracy (Ormerod, 1921: 13).

28 Petition of James Wilson and others quoted in William R. Casto, 'The Origins of Federal Admiralty Jurisdiction', *American Journal of Legal History* 37 (1993): 124. Supreme Court Justice William Paterson spoke of privateers at the same time in language familiar to recent judicial pronouncements on war criminals and torturers: 'Activated by a predatory spirit . . . How often do privateers perpetrate outrages that shock the moral sense and disgrace the human character?' (Unpublished Opinion of William Paterson, quoted in Casto (1993: 125).

29 Pirates became 'enemies of mankind' because they attacked the interests of the ruling classes (recent protests against the occupation of Iraq and the privatization of Iraqi industry and natural resources have featured an organization called 'Corporate Pirates' who, dressed as pirates, have demonstrated against the 'plunder' of Iraq by large corporations). On the 'pillage' of Iraq see B. Whitaker, 'Spoils of War', *The Guardian*, 13 October 2003).

30 The language is from Rawls, 1999. See, too, John Kerry's comment that, 'In dealing with states that are outright criminal, the United States may, at times, need to take unilateral action to protect its citizens, its interests, its integrity' (J. Kerry, *The New War: The Web of Crime that Threatens America's Security* (1997) p. 182, cited in A. Cockburn, 'Surrendering Quietly', *New Left Review* 29 (2004): 5 at 17).

31 On the 'lack' of international law, see Karen Greenberg and Joshua Dratel, *The Torture Papers* (New York: Cambridge University Press, 2005). On the image of Guantanamo Bay as a legal black hole, see Johan (Lord) Steyn, 'Guantanamo Bay: The Legal Black Hole', *International and Comparative Law Quarterly* 53 (January 2004): 1–15; on extraordinary renditions, see Ian Black, 'Tortuous Distinctions', *The Guardian*, 16 December 2005.

32 For a discussion of this idea in relation to barbarians or outlaws see Simpson (2004a).

Select Bibliography

Acheson, D. 1963. 'Remarks' *Proceedings of the American Society of International Law*, 57th Annual Meeting: 14.

af Jochnick, C. and R. Normand 1994. 'The Legitimation of Violence: A Critical Analysis of the Gulf War', *Harvard International Law Journal* 35: 387.

Akhavan, P. 1993. 'Punishing War Crimes in the Former Yugoslavia: A Critical Juncture for the New World Order', *Human Rights Quarterly* 15: 262–89.

Akhavan, P. 2001. 'Beyond Impunity: Can International Criminal Justice Prevent Future Atrocities?', *American Journal of International Law* 95: 7–31.

Allott, P. 2002. *The Health of Nations: Society and Law Beyond the State*. Cambridge: Cambridge University Press.

Alvarez, J. 1999. 'Crimes of States/Crimes of Hate: Lessons from Rwanda', *Yale Journal of International Law* 24: 365.

Alvarez, J. E. 2004. 'Trying Hussein: Between Hubris and Hegemony', *Journal of International Criminal Justice* 2: 319.

Amis, M. 1991. *Time's Arrow*. London: Jonathan Cape Ltd.

Amis, M. 2000. *Experience*. New York: Hyperion.

Amis, M. 2002. *Koba the Dread: Laughter and the Twenty Million*. London: Jonathan Cape Ltd.

Anonymous 1996. 'Human Rights in Peace Negotiations', *Human Rights Quarterly* 18 (2): 249–58.

Arbour, L. 2002. *War Crimes and the Culture of Peace*. Toronto: University of Toronto Press.

Archibugi, D. 2002. 'Demos and Cosmopolis', *New Left Review* 13 (Jan/Feb).

Arendt, H. 1969. 'Reflections on Violence', *New York Review of Books*, February.

Arendt, H. 1970. *On Violence*. New York: Harcourt, Brace and World.

Arendt, H. 1994. *Eichmann in Jerusalem: A Report on the Banality of Evil*. Harmondsworth: Penguin.

Bacher, D. 2003. 'Bush's Illegal War', *Counterpunch* (30 May) at http://www.counterpunch.org/bacher05302003.html.

Bacque, J. 1999. *Other Losses*. Toronto: Stoddart Publishing Company Ltd.

Ball, H. 1999. *Prosecuting War Crimes and Genocide: The Twentieth-Century Experience*. Lawrence: University Press of Kansas.

Bass, G. J. 2000. *Stay the Hand of Vengeance: The Politics of War Crimes Tribunals*. Princeton and Oxford: Princeton University Press.

Bassiouni, M. Cherif (ed.) 1986. *International Criminal Law, Volume 1: Crimes.* New York: Transnational Publishers.

Bassiouni, M. Cherif 1987. *A Draft International Criminal Code and Draft Statute for an International Criminal Tribunal.* Boston: Martinus Nijhoff.

Bassiouni, M. Cherif 1997. 'From Versailles to Rwanda in Seventy-Five Years: The Need to Establish a Permanent International Criminal Court', *Harvard Human Rights Journal* 10: 11.

Bauman, Z. 1989. *Modernity and the Holocaust.* Cambridge: Polity.

Beckett, A. 2002. *Pinochet in Piccadilly.* London: Faber and Faber.

Bederman, D. 2002. 'Collective Security, Demilitarization and "Pariah" States', *European Journal of International Law* 13 (1): 121.

Beigbeder, Y. 1999. *Judging War Criminals: The Politics of International Justice.* New York: St Martin's Press.

Belgion, M. 1949. *Victor's Justice.* Illinois: Regnery.

Benes, R. 1993. 'Iraqi Crimes and International Law: The Imperative to Punish', *Denver Journal of International Law* 21: 335.

Benvenuti, P. 2001. 'The ICTY's Prosecutor and the Review of the NATO Bombing Campaign against the Federal Republic of Yugoslavia', *European Journal of International Law* 12 (3): 503–35.

Beschloss, M. 2002. *The Conquerors.* New York: Simon & Schuster.

Bhuta, N. 2005. 'Between Liberal Legal Didactics and Political Manichaeism: The Politics and Law of the Iraqi Special Tribunal', *Melbourne Journal of International Law* 6 (2): 245–72.

Binder, G. 1989. 'Representing Nazism: Advocacy and Identity at the Trial of Klaus Barbie', *Yale Law Journal* 98: 1321.

Blass, T. 2004. *The Man Who Shocked the World: The Life and Legacy of Stanley Milgram.* New York: Basic Books.

Bloxham, D. 2001. *Genocide on Trial, War Crimes Trials and the Formation of Holocaust History and Memory.* Oxford: Oxford University Press.

Boraine, Alex. 2000. *A Country Unmasked: Inside South Africa's Truth and Reconciliation Commission.* Oxford and New York: Oxford University Press.

Borger, J. 2002. 'Straw threat to bypass UN over attack on Iraq', *The Guardian* 19 October at http://www.guardian.co.uk/Iraq/Story/0,2763,815190,00.html.

Bothe, M. 2001. 'The Protection of the Civilian Population and NATO Bombing on Yugoslavia: Comments on a Report to the Prosecutor of the ICTY', *European Journal of International Law* 12 (3): 531–6.

Bowcott, O. 2001. '"I will defeat the West's puppets" vows Milosevic', *The Guardian*, 30 July, at http://www.guardian.co.uk/international/story/0,3604,529462,00.html.

Braithwaite, J. and P. Drahos 2000. *Global Business Regulation.* Cambridge: Cambridge University Press.

Brierly, J. 1928. *Law of Nations.* Cambridge: Cambridge University Press.

Browning, C. R. 1992. *Ordinary Men: Reserve Police Battalion 101 and the Final Solution in Poland*. New York: HarperCollins.

Brownlie, I. 1998. *Principles of Public International Law*, 5th edition. Oxford: Oxford University Press.

Brunnée, J. and S. J. Toope 2004. 'The Use of Force: International Law After Iraq', *International and Comparative Law Quarterly* 53: 785–806.

Bull, M. 2004. 'States don't really mind their citizens dying (provided they don't all do it at once): they just don't like anyone else to kill them', *London Review of Books* 26 (24).

Burns, J. 2005. 'Firings cause turmoil in Saddam's tribunal', *International Herald Tribune*, 21 July at http://www.iht.com/articles/2005/07/20/news/saddam.php.

Byers, M. 2004. 'The Ultimate Justice Show', *London Review of Books* 26 (1).

Carmichael, J. 1976. *Stalin's Masterpiece: The Show Trials and Purges of the Thirties – The Consolidation of the Bolshevik Dictatorship*. New York: St. Martin's Press.

Cass, D. 2005. *The Constitution of the World Trade Organisation*. Oxford: Oxford University Press.

Cassese, A. 2003a. *International Criminal Law*. Oxford: Oxford University Press.

Cassese, A. 2003b. 'International Criminal Law' in M. Evans (ed.) *International Law*. Oxford: Oxford University Press.

Casto, W. R. 1993. 'The Origins of Federal Admiralty Jurisdiction', *American Journal of Legal History* 37: 124.

Cesarini, D. 2004. *Eichmann: His Life and Crimes*. London: Heinemann.

Chomsky, N. 1989. *Necessary Illusions: Thought Control in Democratic Societies*. London: Pluto Press.

Cilga, A. 1940. *The Russian Enigma*. London: Routledge and Sons.

Clark, I. 2005. *Legitimacy in the International Order*. Oxford: Oxford University Press.

Clay, L. 1950. *Decision in Germany*. New York: Doubleday & Co.

Cohen, S. 2000. *States of Denial: Knowing About Atrocities and Suffering*. Cambridge: Polity.

Collins, T. 2005. 'They'll destroy the qualities that made our Forces great', *Daily Telegraph*, 21 July.

Constantinople, G. R. 1986. 'Towards a New Definition of Piracy', *Virginia Journal of International Law* 26: 723.

Cotic, M. 1987. *The Prague Trial*. New York: Herzl Press.

Craven, M. et al. 2004. 'We are Teachers of International Law', *Leiden Journal of International Law* 17: 363–74.

Cryer, R. 2001. 'The Boundaries of Liability in International Criminal Law', *Journal of Conflict and Security Law* 6 (1): 3–31.

Cryer, R. 2005. *Prosecuting International Crimes*. Cambridge: Cambridge University Press.

Dallaire, R. 2005. *Shake Hands with the Devil*. New York: Carroll & Graf.

D'Amato, A. 1984/85. 'Is International Law Really "Law"?', *Northwestern University Law Review* 75.

Danner, A. and J. Martinez 2006. 'Guilty Associations: Joint Criminal Enterprise, Command Responsibility and the Development of International Criminal Law', Stanford Law School, Public Law and Legal Theory Working Papers Series, no. 87.

Darwish, A. 2003. 'Halabja: whom does the truth hurt?', *OpenDemocracy*, 17 March at http://www.opendemocracy.net/media/feature_articles.jsp.

Dink, H. 2005. 'The water finds its crack', *OpenDemocracy*, 13 December at http://www.opendemocracy.net/democracy-turkey/europe_turkey_armenia_3118.jsp.

Dinstein, Y. and M. Tabory 1996. *War Crimes in International Law* (eds) The Hague, Boston: M. Nijhoff Publishers.

Diski, J. 2004. 'Doing What We're Told', *London Review of Books* 26 (22).

Dixon, R. 2002. 'Rape as a Crime in International Humanitarian Law: Where to from Here?', *European Journal of International Law* 13 (3): 697–720.

Douglas, L. 1996. 'The Memory of Judgement: The Law, Holocaust and Denial', *History and Memory* 7: 100–20.

Douglas, L. 2001. *The Memory of Judgment: Making Law and History in the Trials of the Holocaust*. New Haven: Yale University Press.

Douzinas, C. 2000. *The End of Human Rights*. Oxford: Hart Publishing.

Ellman, M. 2001. 'The Soviet 1937 Provincial Show Trials: Carnival or Terror?', *Europe-Asia Studies* 53 (8): 1221–33.

Evening Standard 2006. 'Pirates attack cross-channel ferry', 6 March.

Farer, T. 2000. 'Restraining the Barbarians: Can International Law Help?', *Human Rights Quarterly* 22: 90–117.

Fein, H. 1993. *Genocide: A Sociological Perspective*. London: Sage.

Felman, S. 2001. 'Theaters of Justice: Arendt in Jerusalem, the Eichmann Trial, and the Redefinition of Legal Meaning in the Wake of the Holocaust', *Critical Inquiry* 27 (Winter): 201–38.

Ferencz, B. 1980. *An International Criminal Court, Volume I*. New York: Oceana.

Finkielkraut, A. 1992. *Remembering in Vain: The Klaus Barbie Trial and Crimes Against Humanity*, trans. Roxanne Lapidus with Sima Godfrey; introduction by Alice Y. Kaplan. New York: Columbia.

Fletcher, G. 2000. 'The Storrs Lectures: Liberals and Romantics at War: The Problem of Collective Guilt', *Yale Law Journal* 111: 1501–73.

Foucault, M. 2004. *Society Must Be Defended*, trans. David Macey. London: Penguin.

Franck, T. 1990. *The Power of Legitimacy Among Nations*. New York: Oxford University Press.

Franck, T. 1995. *Fairness in International Law and Institutions*. New York: Oxford University Press; Oxford: Clarendon Press.

Franck, T. 2006. 'The Power of Legitimacy and the Legitimacy of Power', *American Journal of International Law* 100 (1): 88–106.

Frum, D. and R. Perle 2003. *An End to Evil*. New York: Random House.

Gaparayi, I. 2004. 'The Milošević Trial at the Half Way Stage: Judgement on the Motion for Acquittal', *Leiden Journal of International Law* 17 (4): 737–66.

Garber, M. and R. L. Walkowitz 1995. *Secret Agents: The Rosenberg Case, McCarthyism & Fifties America*. New York and London: Routledge.

Gardam, J. 1994. 'The Law of Armed Conflict: A Gendered Regime?' In D. Dallmeyer (ed.) *Reconceiving Reality: Women and International Law*, Washington, DC: 171–202 American Society of International Law Studies in Transnational Legal Policy, no. 25.

Gilbert, G. M. 1995. *Nuremberg Diary*. New York: Da Capo Press.

Gittings, J. 2001. 'Last hope of justice for the Cambodian killing fields', *The Guardian*, Friday 3 August: 18.

Glasius, M. 2005. *The International Criminal Court: A Global Civil Society Achievement*. London: Routledge.

Glass, Charles 2003. 'The New Piracy', *London Review of Books*, 18 December: 3–7.

Glennon, M. 2001. *The Limits of the Law, Prerogatives of Power*. New York and Basingstoke: Palgrave.

Goldhagen, D. 1996. *Hitler's Willing Executioners*. New York: Knopf.

Goldstone, R. 2000. *For Humanity. Reflections of a War Crimes Investigator*. New Haven: Yale University Press.

Gonzales, A. 2005. 'Memorandum for the President', 25 January, in Karen Greenberg and Joshua Dratel, *The Torture Papers*. Cambridge: Cambridge University Press, p. 118.

Gooding, G. 1987. 'Fighting Terrorism in the 1980s', *Yale Journal of International Law* 12: 158.

Gosse, P. 1928. *The History of Piracy*. London: Longmans.

Granta 1982. 'Eichmann Interrogated' in *A Literature of Politics. Granta* 6.

Gray, J. 2006. 'The Mirage of Empire', *New York Review of Books*, 12 January: 4–8.

Grayling, A. C. 2006. *Among the Dead Cities*. London: Bloomsbury.

Green, L. C. 1961. 'The Santa Maria: Rebels or Pirates', *British Yearbook of International Law* 37: 496.

Greenwood, C. 2003. 'Trying Saddam', *The Guardian*, 17 December at http://www.guardian.co.uk/analysis/story/0,3604,1108532,00.html.

Gubar, S. 2003. *Poetry after Auschwitz: Remembering What One Never Knew*. Bloomington: Indiana University Press.

Guttenplan, D. D. 2001. *The Holocaust on Trial. History, Justice and the David Irving Libel Trial*. Cambridge: Granta.

Haan, V. 2005. 'The Development of the Concept of Joint Criminal Enterprise at the International Criminal Tribunal for the Former Yugoslavia', *International Criminal Law Review* 5: 167–201.

Halberstam, M. 1988. 'Terrorism on the High Seas: The Achille Lauro, Piracy and the IMO Convention on Maritime Safety', *American Journal of International Law* 82: 269.

Hankey, The Right Hon. Lord 1950. *Politics, Trials and Errors*. Chicago: Henry Regnery Company.

Hart, H. L. A. 1961. *The Concept of Law*. Oxford: Clarendon.

Hausner, G. 1966. *Justice in Jerusalem*. New York: Harper & Row.

Hayden, P. 2004. 'Cosmopolitanism and the Need for Transnational Criminal Justice: The Case of the International Criminal Court', *Theoria* 104.

Hayner, P. 2001. *Unspeakable Truths: Confronting State Terror and Atrocity*. New York and London: Routledge.

Hazard, J. N. 1968. 'Why Try Again to Define Aggression?', *American Journal of International Law* 62 (3) (July): 701–10.

Herman, E. S. and N. Chomsky 1995. *Manufacturing Consent*. Vintage Press: New York.

Higgins, R. 1995. *Problems and Process: International Law and How We Use It*. Oxford: Clarendon Press.

Hilberg, R. 2002. *The Politics of Memory*. Chicago: Ivan Dee.

Hiro, D. 2003. *The Essential Middle East*. New York: Carroll and Graf.

Hirsh, D. 2003. *Law Against Genocide: Cosmopolitan Trials*. London: Glasshouse Press.

Hitchins, C. 2001. *The Trial of Henry Kissinger*. London: Verso.

Hodos, G. 1987. *Show Trials*. New York: Praeger.

Horne, C. (ed.) 1923. *Source Records of the Great War, Vol. III*. National Alumni.

Hoyle, Lord 14 July 2005. Col. 1223, Hansard at http://www.publications.parliament.uk.

Jones, J. and S. Powles 2003. *International Criminal Practice*. Oxford: Oxford University Press.

Jones, J. R. W. D. 2004. 'The Gamekeeper-Turned-Poacher's Tale', *Journal of International Criminal Justice* 2: 486.

Judah, T. 2005. '"War crimes" storm over former PM', *The Observer*, 30 October.

Judt, T. 2005. *Postwar*. London: William Heinemann.

Kadri, S. 2005. *The Trial*. London: HarperCollins.

Kadri, S. 2006. 'The wrong way to combat terrorism', *OpenDemocracy*, 3 May at http://www.opendemocracy.net/conflict-terrorism/wrong_way_3501.jsp.

Kaldor, M. 1999. *New Wars*. Cambridge: Polity.

Kaplan, R. 1994. 'The Coming Anarchy', *Atlantic Monthly* (February).

Kaplan, R. 2002. *Warrior Politics: Why Leadership Demands a Pagan Ethos*. New York and Toronto: Random House.

Kelsen, H. 1957. *Collective Security under International Law*. Washington, DC: US Government Printing Office.

Kelsen, H. 1973. *Peace Through Law*. New York: Garland.

Kennan, G. 1951. *American Diplomacy 1900–1950*: Chicago.

Kirchheimer, O. 1961. *Political Justice*. Princeton: Princeton University Press.

Kissinger, H. 1994. *Diplomacy*. New York: Simon & Schuster.

Kitichaisaree, K. 2001. *International Criminal Law*. Oxford: Oxford University Press.

Klinghoffer, A. J. and J. A. Klinghoffer 2002. *International Citizens' Tribunals*. New York and Basingstoke: Palgrave.

Knop, K. 2000. 'Here and There: International Law in Domestic Courts', *New York University Journal of Law and Politics* 32: 501.

Koestler, A. 1946. *Darkness at Noon*. London: Penguin.

Koh, H. 2001. 'Transnational Law', in G. Simpson, *The Nature of International Law*. Aldershot: Ashgate.

Kontorovich, E. 2004. 'The Piracy Analogy: Modern Universal Jurisdiction's Hollow Foundation', *Harvard Journal of International Law* 45 (1): 183–237.

Kopelman, E. 1991. 'Ideology and International Law: The Dissent of the Indian Justice at the Tokyo War Crimes Trial', *New York University Journal of Law and Politics* 23 (2): 373.

Koskenniemi, M. 1991. 'The Future of Statehood', *Harvard International Law Journal* 32 (2): 397.

Koskenniemi, M. 1999. 'Letter to the Editors of the Symposium', *American Journal of International Law* 93: 351.

Koskenniemi, M. 2001. 'The Future of Statehood', in G. Simpson, *The Nature of International Law*. Aldershot: Ashgate.

Koskenniemi, M. 2002. 'Between Impunity and Show Trials', *Max Planck UNYB* 6: 1–36.

Kratochwil, F. 1984. 'Thrasymmachos Revisited: On the Relevance of Norms and the Study of International Law for International Relations', *Journal of International Affairs* 37: 343.

Lacquer, T. 2004. 'Four pfennige per track km', *London Review of Books* 26 (21) (4 November).

Leigh, M. 1996. 'Yugoslavia Tribunal: Use Of Unnamed Witnesses Against Accused', *American Journal of International Law* 40: 235.

Leites, N. and E. Bernaut 1954. *Rituals of Liquidation*. Glencoe, Ill.: Free Press.

Levi, P. 1966. *The Truce*. London: Four Square Books.

Levinson, S. 1973. 'Responsibility for Crimes of War', *Philosophy and Public Affairs* 2: 244–73.

Lipstadt, D. 1993. *Denying the Holocaust: The Growing Assault on Truth and Memory*. London: Penguin.

Luban, D. 1987. 'The Legacies of Nuremberg', *Social Research* 54 (4) (Winter): 779–829.

McCarthy, R. 2003. 'They must be brought to court', *The Guardian*, 20 June at http://www.globalpolicy.org/security/issues/iraq/attack/crisis/2003/0620justice.htm.

McCormack, T. and G. Simpson 1997 *The Law of War Crimes*. The Hague and Boston: Kluwer Law International.

Macmillan, M. 2001. *Peacemakers*. London: John Murray.

Maga, T. 2001. *Judgment at Tokyo: The Japanese War Crimes Trials*. Lexington: University of Kentucky Press.

Mandelbaum, M. 2005. *The Case for Goliath: How America Acts as the World's Government in the 21st Century*. New York: Public Affairs.

Maogoto, J. 2004. *War Crimes and Realpolitik: From World War I into the 21st Century* (International Studies and Comparative Politics Series). Colorado: Lynne Rienner Publishers.

Marrus, M. 1997. *The Nuremberg War Crimes Trials 1945–1946: A Documentary History*. Bedford: St Martin's.

Maugham, Viscount 1951. *UNO and War Crimes* (with a postscript by Lord Hankey). London: J. Murray.

Mégret, F. 2001. 'Three Dangers for the International Criminal Court: A Critical Look at a Consensual Project', *Finnish Yearbook of International Law XII*.

Mégret, F. 2002. 'The Politics of International Criminal Justice', *European Journal of International Law* 13 (5): 1261.

Mégret, F. 2003. 'Epilogue to an Endless Debate: ICC "third-party" jurisdiction and the Looming Revolution of International Law', *European Journal of International Law* 11: 247.

Merleau-Ponty, M. 1969. *Humanism and Terror: An Essay on the Communist Problem*, trans. J. O'Neill. Boston: Beacon Press.

Meron, T. 1999. *War Crimes Law Comes of Age*. Oxford: Oxford University Press.

Minear, R. 1971. *Victor's Justice*. Princeton, NJ: Princeton University Press.

Minow, M. L. 1998. *Between Vengeance and Forgiveness: Facing History After Genocide and Mass Violence*. Boston: Beacon Press.

Mitchell, D. 1976. *Pirates*. London: Longman.

Morgan, E. 1988. 'Retributory Theater', *American University Journal of International Law and Policy* 3 (1): 1.

Morgan, T. 1990. *An Uncertain Hour: The French, the Germans, the Jews, the Barbie Trial, and the City of Lyon, 1940–1945*. London: Bodley Head.

Mullins, C. 1921. *The Leipzig Trials: An Account of the War Criminals' Trials and a Study of German Mentality*. London: H. F. & G. Witherby.

Murray, D. 2004. 'Hutton – the wrong inquiry', *OpenDemocracy*, 29 January at http://www.opendemocracy.net/media-journalismwar/article_1699.jsp.

Mutua, M. 1997. 'Never Again: Questioning the Yugoslav and Rwanda Tribunals', *Temple International and Comparative Law Review* 11 (Spring): 167.

Neave, A. 1978. *Nuremberg*. London: Hodder and Stoughton.

O'Brien, J. 1993. 'The International Tribunal for Violations of Humanitarian Law in the Former Yugoslavia', *American Journal of International Law* 87: 639.

O'Neill, S. 2005. 'Ship's crew at mercy of pirates on deadly seas', *The Times*, Monday 7 November.

Oppenheim, L. 1955. *International Law*, 8th edn. Cambridge: Cambridge University Press.

Ormerod, H. A. 1921. *Piracy in the Ancient World*. Liverpool: Liverpool University Press.

Orwell, G. 1970. 'As I Please', *Tribune*, 1943–49. London: Penguin.

Orwell, G. 1996. *Animal Farm*. London: Penguin.

Osiel, M. 1997. *Mass Atrocity, Collective Memory and the Law*. New Jersey: Transaction Publishers.

Osiel, M. 2000. 'Why Prosecute? Critics of Mass Atrocity', *Human Rights Quarterly* 22: 118–47.

Osiel, M. 2005. 'The Banality of Good, Aligning Incentives Against Mass Atrocity', *Columbia Law Review* 105: 1751.

Overy, R. 2002. *Interrogations: The Nazi Elite in Allied Hands*. London: Penguin.

Overy, R. 2003. 'The Nuremberg Trials' in P. Sands (ed.) *From Nuremberg to The Hague*. Cambridge: Cambridge University Press.

Pal, R. 1953. *IMTFE Dissentient Judgement of Justice Pal*. Calcutta: Sanyal & Co.

Pal, R. 1955. *Crimes in International Relations*. Calcutta: University of Calcutta Press.

Pellet, A. 1999. 'Can a State Commit a Crime? Definitely, Yes!', *European Journal of International Law* 10: 425.

Pelletiere, S. C. 1992. *The Iran-Iraq War: Chaos in a Vacuum*. New York: Praeger.

Persico, J. 1995. *Nuremberg: Infamy on Trial*. New York: Penguin.

Poliakov, L. 1956. *Harvest of Hate: The Nazi Programme of Destruction of Jews in Europe*.

Power, S. 2002. *A Problem from Hell: America and the Age of Genocide*. New York: Basic Books.

Prevost, M. 1992. 'Race and War Crimes: The 1945 War Crimes Trial of General Tomoyuki Yamashita', *Human Rights Quarterly* 14: 303.

Pritchard, J. 1998. *The Tokyo Major War Crimes Trials*. Ceredigion and New York: Edwin Mellen Press.

Rabkin, J. 2006. 'Global Criminal Justice', *Cornell International Law Journal* 38 (3): 753–77.

Randall, K. 1988. 'Universal Jurisdiction under International Law', *Texas Law Review* 66: 785.

Rangelov, I. 2004. 'International Law and Local Ideology in Serbia', *Peace Review* 16 (3) (Special Issue on Law and War): 331–9.

Ratner, S. 1998. 'The Schizophrenia of International Criminal Law', *Texas International Law Review* 33 (2): 237.

Rawls, J. 1999. *The Law of Peoples*. Cambridge, Mass.: Harvard University Press.

Rayfield, D. 2005. *Stalin and his Hangmen*. London: Penguin.

Rediker, M. 1987. *Between the Devil and the Deep Blue Sea*. Cambridge: Cambridge University Press.

Rediker, M. 2004. *Villains of All Nations: Atlantic Pirates in the Golden Age*. Boston: Beacon Press.

Reid, K. 1994. LLB Dissertation, University of Melbourne.

Reisman, M. 2001. 'In Defence of Public Order', *American Journal of International Law* 95 (4): 833.

Reus-Smit, C. 2004. 'The Politics of International Law' in C. Reus-Smit, *The Politics of International Law*. Cambridge: Cambridge University Press.

Rich, R. 1993. 'Recognition of States: The Collapse of Yugoslavia and the Soviet Union', *European Journal of International Law* 4 (1).

Robertson, G. 1999. *Crimes Against Humanity: The Struggle for Global Justice*. New York: The New Press.

Robertson, G. 2005. 'Ending Impunity: How International Criminal Law Can Put Tyrants on Trial', *Cornell International Law Journal* 38 (3): 649–70.

Robertson, G. and C. Devereux 2006. 'The Tyrannicide Brief: An Extract' is at http://www.opendemocracy.net/globalization-institutions_government/extract_2980.jsp.

Roche, D. 2003. *Accountability in Restorative Justice*. Oxford: Oxford University Press.

Roche, D. 2005. 'Truth Commission Amnesties and the International Criminal Court', *British Journal of Criminology* 45: 565–81.

Roht-Arriaza, N. (ed.) 1995. *Impunity and Human Rights in International Law and Practice*. New York: Oxford University Press.

Röling, B. 1993. *The Tokyo Trial and Beyond*. Cambridge: Polity.

Röling, B. 1999. 'Separate Judgement' in J. Pritchard (ed.) *Tokyo War Crimes Trials*, vol. 109. Ceredigion and New York: Edwin Mellen Press.

Romano, C. P. R., André Nollkaemper and Jann K. Kleffner 2004. *Internationalized Criminal Courts: Sierra Leone, East Timor, Kosovo, and Cambodia*. Oxford: Oxford University Press.

Rosenman, S. I. 1956. *Working with Roosevelt*. New York: Harper.

Rubin, A. 1988. *The Law of Piracy*. Newport: Naval War College Press.

Rubin, A. 1994. 'An International Criminal Tribunal for Former Yugoslavia', *Pace International Law Review* 6 (7): 7–17.

Rumsfeld, D. 2004. Hamburg Speech, *Guardian Weekly*, 19–25 February.

Sands, P. (ed.) 2003. *From Nuremberg to The Hague*. Cambridge: Cambridge University Press.

Sands, P. 2005. *Lawless World*. London: Allen Lane.

Scharf, Michael P. 1997. *Balkan Justice: The Story Behind the First International War Crimes Trial Since Nuremberg*. Durham: Carolina Academic Press.

Schmitt, C. 1996. *The Concept of the Political*, trans. George Schwab. Chicago: University of Chicago Press.

Schmitt, C. 2003. *The Nomos of the Earth, in the International Law of the Jus Publicum Europeaeum*. New York: Telos Press.

Schwarzenberger, G. 1943. *International Law and Totalitarian Lawlessness*. London: Jonathan Cape.

Schwarzenberger, G. 1950. 'The Problem of an International Criminal Law', *Current Legal Problems* 3: 263.

Schwarzenberger, G. 1962. 'The Eichmann Judgement: An Essay in Censorial Jurisprudence', *Current Legal Problems* 15: 248–65.

Scott, C. 2001. *Torture as Tort: Comparative Perspectives on the Development of Transnational Human Rights Litigation*. Oxford: Hart.

Sereny, G. 1996. *Speer: His Battle with Truth*. London: Picador.

Sheftel, Y. 1994. *The Demjanjuk Affair*. London: Gollancz.

Shklar, J. 1964. *Legalism*. Boston: Harvard University Press.

Silving, H. 1961. 'In Re Eichmann: A Dilemma of Law and Morality', *American Journal of International Law* 55: 307–58.

Simons, M. 2001. 'Belgian Jury Convicts 4 of 1994 War Crimes in Rwanda', *New York Times*, 9 June.

Simpson, G. 1997. 'War Crimes: A Critical Introduction' in T. McCormack and G. Simpson, *The Law of War Crimes*. The Hague and Boston: Kluwer Law International.

Simpson, G. 1999. 'Didactic and Dissident Histories in War Crimes Trials', *Albany Law Review* 60: 801.

Simpson, G. 2000. 'The Situation on the International Legal Theory Front', *European Journal of International Law* 11 (2): 439–64.

Simpson, G. 2004a. *Great Powers and Outlaw States: Unequal Sovereigns in the International Legal Order*. Cambridge: Cambridge University Press.

Simpson, G. 2004b. *War Crimes Law, Volume 2: Dissenting Judgements*. Aldershot: Ashgate.

Simpson, G. 2005. 'Punishment and Memory: War Crimes Trials in History', *International Journal of Law in Context* 1 (1): 101–13.

Singh, R. and A. MacDonald 2002. 'Legality of Use of Force Against Iraq' at http://www.lcnp.org/global/IraqOpinion10.9.02.pdf.

Slaughter, A. M. 2004. *The New World Order*. Princeton: Princeton University Press.

Smis, S. and K. Van der Borght 1999. 'Belgium: Act Concerning the Punishment of Grave Breaches of International Humanitarian Law', *International Legal Materials* 38: 918, 919.

Snare, A. (ed.) 1995. 'Beware of punishment', *Scandinavian Studies in Criminology* 14.

Steiner, G. 1961. *The Death of Tragedy*. London: Faber.

Stone, J. 1958. *Aggression and World Order: A Critique of United Nations Theories of Aggression*. London: Stevens.

Stone, J. 1961. *The Eichmann Trial and the Rule of Law*. International Commission of Jurists, Australian Section.

Taylor, T. 1970. *Nuremberg and Vietnam: An American Tragedy*. Chicago: Quadrangle Books.

Taylor, T. 1992. *Anatomy of the Nuremberg Trials*. New York: Knopf.

Teitel, R. 2000. *Transitional Justice*. New York: Oxford University Press.

Teitel, R. 2002. 'Humanity's Law: Rule of Law for the New Global Politics,' *Cornell International Law Journal* 35: 335.

Tesón F. 1992. 'The Kantian Theory of International Law', *Columbia Law Review* 92 (1): 53.

Thucydides 1996. *The Landmark Thucydides*, ed. Robert B. Stassler. New York and London: Free Press.

Tisdall, S. 2005. 'A chance for justice, but will it be seized?', *The Guardian*, 19 October.

Todorov, T. 2003. *Hope and Memory: Lessons from the Twentieth Century*, trans. David Bellos. Princeton: Princeton University Press.

Tweedie, N. 2005. 'Uproar over war crimes trials', *Daily Telegraph*, 21 July, at http://www.telegraph.co.uk/news/main.jhtml?xml=/news/2005/07/21/narmy21.xml.

Vaksberg, A. 1990. *The Prosecutor and the Prey*. London: Weidenfeld and Nicolson.

Wai, R. 2003. 'Countering, Branding, Dealing: Using Social Rights in and around the International Trade Regime', *European Journal of International Law* 14 (1): 35–85.

Walzer, M. 1994. *Thick and Thin: Moral Argument at Home and Abroad*. Notre Dame: University of Notre Dame Press.

Ward, E. and M. Hieman 2005. 'Iraqi-run tribunal is major progress towards rule of law system', *Christian Science Monitor*, 19 July at http://www.csmonitor.com/2005/0719/p09s02-coop.html.

Watson, J. S. 1999. *Theory and Reality in the International Protection of Human Rights*. New York: Transnational Publishers.

Wheeler, N. 2000. *Saving Strangers*. Oxford: Oxford University Press.

Willis, J. 1982. *Prologue to Nuremberg: The Politics and Diplomacy of Punishing War Criminals of the First World War*. Westport and London: Greenwood Press.

Wilson, R. 1984. *The Confessions of Klaus Barbie*. Vancouver: Arsenal Pulp Press.

Wilson, S. 2005. *The Man in the Grey Flannel Suit*. London: Penguin.

Woetzel, R. 1960. *The Nuremberg Trials in International Law*. London: Stevens and Son.

Wright, Q. 1925. 'The Outlawry of War', *American Journal of International Law*. 19: 76.

Young-Bruehl, E. 1981. *Hannah Arendt: For the Love of the World*. New Haven: Yale University Press.

Zimmern, A. 1936. *The League of Nations*. London: Macmillan.

Žižek, S. 2004. *Iraq: The Borrowed Kettle*. London: Verso.

Case law

English and Scots case law

Athens Maritime Enterprises Corp. v. Hellenic Mutual War Risks Assn. Ltd. (1983) QB 647.

Cameron v. HM Advocate (1971) SC 50.

Chandler v. DPP [1964] (AC) 763.

CND v. Prime Minister and others [2002] EWHC 2777 (Admin) at http://www. hmcourts-service.gov.uk/judgmentsfiles/j1458/cnd_v_prime_minister. htm.

In Re Piracy Jure Gentium [1934] (AC) 586.

R v. Bartle and the Commissioner of Police for the Metropolis and Other Ex Parte Pinochet (Second Appeal hearing from a Divisional Court of the Queen's Bench Division) 2 All ER 97, [1999] 2 WLR 827 at http://www.parliament. the-stationery-office.co.uk.

R v. Jones [2006] UKHL 16 at http://www.publications.parliament.uk/pa/ld200506/ldjudgmt/jd060329/jones-1.htm.

R v. Sawoniuk [2000] 2 Cr App R 220 at http://www.icrc.org/ihl-nat. nsf/46707c419d6bdfa24125673e00508145.

R (Al-Skeini) v. Secretary of State for Defence, 21 December 2005, [2005] EWCA Civ 1609 at http://www.hmcourts-service.gov.uk/judgmentsfiles/j3670/al_skeini_v_state_1205.htm.

Republic of Bolivia v. Indemnity Mutual Marine Assurance Co. (1909) 1 KB 785.

International case law

Democratic Republic of Congo v. Belgium (Case Concerning the Arrest Warrant of 11 April 2000); Request for Provisional Measures, 8 December 2000, at http://www.icj-cij.org/icjwww/idocket/iCOBE/iCOBEframe.htm.

In Re Yamashita 327 U.S. 1 (1946).

Prosecutor v. Akayesu, ICTR-96-4-T (1998) at http://www.un.org/ictr.

Prosecutor v. Delalic, IT-96-21 (Trial Chamber Judgment) at http://www.un. org/icty/celebici/trialc2/judgement/index.htm.

Prosecutor v. Furundzija, IT-95-17 (Trial Chamber Judgment), 10 December 1998, at http://www.un.org/icty/furundzija/trialc2/judgement/index.htm.

Prosecutor v. Krstic, IT-98-33 ('Srebrenica-Drina Corps') (Appeals Chamber) 19 April 2004, at http://www.un.org/icty/krstic/Appeal/judgement/index. htm.

Prosecutor v. Milosevic, IT-02-54 (Decision on Preliminary Motions) (Trial Chamber), 8 November 2001, at http://www.un.org/icty/milosevic/trialc/decision-e/1110873516829.htm.

Prosecutor v. Milosevic IT-02-54 (Interlocutory Appeal Hearing on Joinder of Issues), 18 April 2002, at http://www.un.org/icty/milosevic/appeal/decision-e/020418.htm.

Prosecutor v. Tadic IT-94-1-T (Appeals Chamber) (Decision on the Defence Motion for Interlocutory Appeal on Jurisdiction) 2 October 1995, at http://www.un.org/icty/tadic/appeal/decision-e/51002.htm.

Prosecutor v. Tadic, IT-94-1-T (Appeals Chamber) (Judgment), 15 July 1999, at http://www.un.org/icty/tadic/appeal/judgement/index.htm.

Prosecutor v. Milosevic, IT-02–54 (Decision on Motion for Acquittal) (16 June 2004) para. 285, at http://www.un.org/icty/milosevic/trialc/judgement/index.htm.

Prosecutor v. Milosevic, IT-02-54 (Trial Transcripts) at http://www.un.org/icty/transe54/020212IT.htm (12 February 2002) http://www.un.org/icty/transe54/020214IT.htm (14 February 2002) and http://www.un.org/icty/transe54/020130IT.htm (30 January 2002).

Prosecutor v. Oric, IT-03-68 (Amended) (Indictment) at http://www.un.org/icty/indictment/english/ori-3ai050630e.htm.

The S.S. 'Lotus' (France v. Turkey), P.C.I.J., Ser. A., No. 9 (1927).

United States v. von Weizsacker et al. (Judgment), 11–13 April 1949, 319.

Other cases

Attorney-General of the Government of Israel v. Eichmann, 36 ILR (1961) 5.

'Barbie' Trial (*Fédération National des Déportées et Internés Résistants et Patriots and Others v. Barbie*), 78 ILR 124 (French Cour de Cassation 1985); 100 ILR 330 (French Cour de Cassation 1988).

Demjanjuk v. Petrovsky, 603 F. Supp. 1468, aff'd 776 F. 2d 571 (6th Cir. 1985). *In the Matter of Extradition of John Demjanjuk,* 776 F. 2d 571 (6th Cir. 1985) at 582–3, cert. denied, 457 U.S. 1016 (1986).

Doe v. Bush 323 F.3d 133; 2003 U.S. App. LEXIS 4477 at http://www.ca1.uscourts.gov/pdf.opinions/03-1266-01A.pdf.

Texas v. Johnson, 491 US 397, 422 (1989).

The Touvier Trial, 10 ILR 338 (French Cour de Cassation 1992).

United States v. Ambrose Light, 25 Fed. 408, 412–13 (S.D.N.Y. 1885).

United States v. Brig Malek Adhel, 43 U.S. (2 How.) 210, 232 (1844).

United States of America v. Alstötter et al. ('The Justice Case') 3 T.W.C. 1 (1948), 6 L.R.T.W.C. 1 (1948), 14 Ann. Dig. 278 (1948).

Official reports, statutes, treaties

Charter of the IMT Nuremberg (1945), reprinted in *UN Treaty Series,* vol. 82, p. 279, at http://www.yale.edu/lawweb/avalon/imt/imt.htm.

Commission on the Responsibilities of the Authors of the War on the Enforcement of Penalties (1920), *American Journal of International Law* 14(1): 95–154.

Council of Europe, Convention on the Prevention of Terrorism (2005).

Geneva Conventions (1949) *and Protocols* (1977) at http://www.icrc.org/ihl.nsf/WebCONVFULL?OpenView.

Global Policy Forum at http://www.globalpolicy.org/intljustice/icc/index.htm.

Goldsmith, Peter (Lord) 2006. 'British Attorney General's (Secret) Advice to Blair on Legality of War' (7 March) at http://www.globalpolicy.org/security/issues/iraq/document/2003/0307advice.htm.

ICC Finalised Draft Text of the Elements of Crimes at http://www.un.org/law/icc/asp/1stsession/report/english/part_ii_b_e.pdf.

ICC Prep Com Nine, Working Group Paper on History of Aggression at http://www.un.org/law/icc/prepcomm/report/prepreportdocs.htm.

ILC Articles (2001) at http://www.lcil.cam.ac.uk/projects/state_responsibility_document_collection.php#1.

ILC Draft Articles on State Responsibility (1996) at http://www.lcil.cam.ac.uk/Media/ILCSR/#Draft%20Arts%201.

ILC Draft Code of Crimes (1996) at http://untreaty.un.org/ilc/texts/instruments/english/draft%20articles/7_4_1996.pdf.

ILC Draft Code of Offences Against the Peace and Security of Mankind (1954) at http://www.un.org/law/ilc/.

ILC Draft Statute for an International Criminal Court (1994) at http://untreaty.un.org/ilc/texts/instruments/english/draft%20articles/7_4_1994.pdf.

IMT Judgment: The Accused Organisations (1946) at http://www.yale.edu/lawweb/avalon/imt/proc/judorg.htm.

International Criminal Court Act 2001 (UK) at http://www.fco.gov.uk. Iraq Special Tribunal at http://www.iraq-ist.org/.

Jackson Report (1949) United States Representative to the International Conference on Military Trials, London, 1945. Washington, DC: Department of State Division of Publications: 433.

JCS 1067 Directive to Commander-in-Chief of United States Forces of Occupation (April 1945) at http://usa.usembassy.de/etexts/ga3-450426.pdf.

London Conference on Military Trials, 'Minutes' (19 July 1945) at http://www.yale.edu/lawweb/avalon/imt/jackson/jack37.htm.

Nuremberg Principles, UNGAOR, 5th Session, Supp. No. 12, *UN Doc. A/1316* (1950).

Potsdam Protocol (1 August 1945) at http://www.yale.edu/lawweb/avalon/decade/decade17.htm.

Report of the Secretary-General on Khmer Rouge Trials (2004) at http://www.globalpolicy.org/intljustice/tribunals/cambodia/2004/1012sgreport.pdf.

Report of the Secretary-General's High Level Panel (2004) at http://www.un.org/secureworld/report.pdf.

Rome Statute for an International Criminal Court, adopted 17 July 1998, at http://www.un.org/law/icc/statute/romefra.htm
(See also, http://www.access.gpo.gov/congress/senate/senate11sh105.html.)

Statute of the International Tribunal for the Former Yugoslavia, adopted 25 May 1993 (ICTY) rep. 32 ILM (1993) 1203 at http://www.un.org/icty/index.html.

Statute of the International Tribunal for Rwanda, adopted 1994 (ICTR) rep. 33 ILM (1994) 1600 at http://www.ictr.org.

Statute of the Special Court for Sierra Leone at http://www.sc-sl.org/ documents.html.

United Nations Convention on the Law of the Sea (1982) 1833 U.N.T.S. 3, Articles 100–7.

United Nations Convention on the High Seas (1958) 450 U.N.T.S. 11, Article 15.

UN G.A. Resolution 57/228 'Agreement between UN and Cambodian Government', (entered into force 2005) at http://daccessdds.un.org/doc/UNDOC/ GEN/N03/358/90/PDF/N0335890.pdf?OpenElement.

United States National Security Strategy (2002) at http://www. whitehouse.gov/nsc/nss/2002.

Versailles Peace Treaty Part VII at http://www.yale.edu/lawweb/avalon/imt/ partvii.htm.

World Summit Report (2005) at http://www.un.org/summit2005/documents. html.

Index